CW00348270

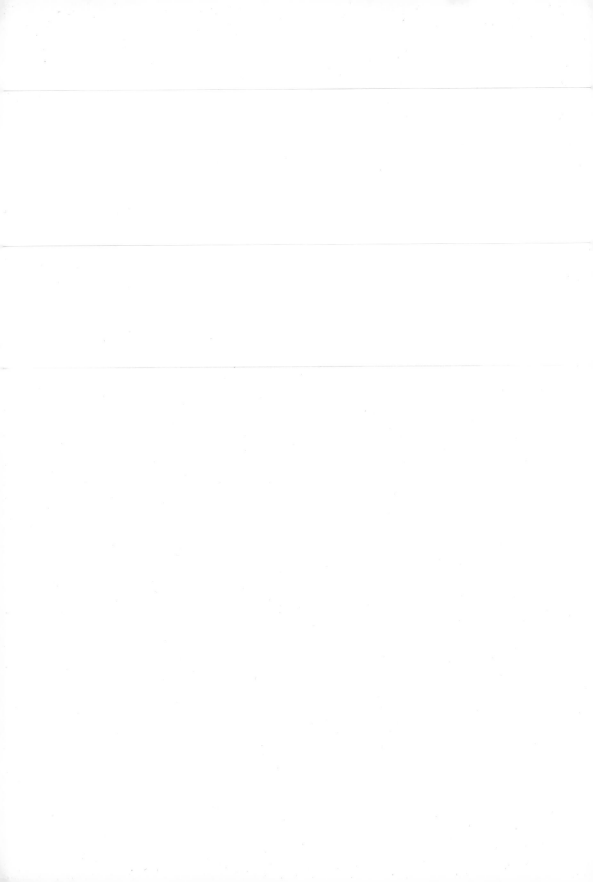

LABRADOR RETRIEVERS

Anthony W. Jury

The Crowood Press

First published in 1996 by
The Crowood Press Ltd
Ramsbury, Marlborough
Wiltshire SN8 2HR

This impression 1999

© Anthony W. Jury 1996

All rights reserved. No part of this publication may be reproduced or transmitted in any form or by any means, electronic or mechanical, including photocopying, recording, or any information storage and retrieval system, without permission in writing from the publishers.

British Library Cataloguing-in-Publication Data
A catalogue record for this book is available from the British Library.

ISBN 1 85223 956 5

Acknowledgements
I should like to acknowledge the tremendous help that I have received from a wide variety of sources while writing this book. From the beginning, I am indebted to Gwen Broadley, Harold Clayton, Louise Wilson-Jones, Anne Wynyard, Daphne Walter and Sarah Richardson. With regret, I record a posthumous tribute to Mary Roslin Williams, who was a personal inspiration and fun to talk to at the same time. I must also pay a posthumous tribute to Keith Hart, who was a great raconteur. Both are sorely missed.

My gratitude is due to Rachael Montgomerie-Charrington, George Caddy, Didi Hepworth, Richard Edwards, Lynne Minchella, Anne Roslin-Williams, Sheila Yoxall, Glenda Crook and Anne Taylor; also to Janice Pritchard and Jim Keizer MRCVS for their help.

I owe a special debt of gratitude to Lady Jacqueline Barlow of St John's, Newfoundland for the historical background, to Lisa Harris of the National Gallery in London and Gundula Boerner of the Staatliche Museen, Kassel, Germany, and to Jan Morris for her special assistance.

I extend grateful thanks to some old and new friends overseas: Jane Borders, Reverend Parsons and Mary Wiest; Pat Dunstan, Denece Hutcheson, Sylvia Power, Lena and Henrick Johansen, Helena and Anna-Liisa Kaitila, Eeva Rautala, Gunille E.K., Marc Gad, Christina Gabriel, Rod Copestake, and Dr Reid MRCVS.

I am also indebted to Simon Blythe (Breeding Manager of The Guide Dogs for the Blind Association), Jill Mowlam (Dogs for the Disabled), Miss P. Allison (PAT Dogs), the Warwickshire Constabulary, and RAF Newton for their help.

For photographs, I thank Anne Roslin-Williams, David Bull, David Dalton, Thomas Fall, John Hartley, and Marc Henri. I thank my editor, Elizabeth Mallard-Shaw, and finally, my gratitude is due in no small part to my wife, Chris, for her interest and forebearance, but who started it all in the first place.

Photographs by: S. Bean, p179; David Bull, pp66, 132, 134 (top), 137, 140, 155; Dorothy Carter (USA), pp95, 118; Sven Daler (Sweden), p165; David Dalton, pp4, 44, 71, 182; A. De Raad (Holland), p131; Thomas Fall, pp18, 20, 21, 24, 30, 32, 163; B. Greenwood, p81; John Hartley, p124 (bottom); Carol Ann Johnson, p169; Harris Morgan, p99; George Outram, p114; Anne Roslin Williams, pp26, 25, 108, 115, 130, 158, 164; Russell Fine Art, p126; Sally Ann Thompson, p23.

Line-drawings by Annette Findlay.

Photograph page 4: Hugo

Typeset by D&N Publishing, Ramsbury, Wiltshire.

Printed and bound in Great Britain by Redwood Books, Trowbridge.

Contents

Introduction

Although we have had Labradors at home for more than twenty-five years, and have been associated with them for a great deal longer, I do not claim to understand their ways completely. On the contrary, part of their appeal to me is that one never stops learning about them. However, to all those considering life with a Labrador – whether with a rumbustious puppy in the family home, or with a promising wide-eyed youngster at his trainer's heel or with an up-and-coming show dog who thinks he is God's gift to the opposite sex – to all of you I offer this record of my experiences. I wish sincerely that you may not make the same mistakes that I have made, but rather that you will share in the great joy that it is to own a Labrador, and that you and your dog achieve the success due to you.

To those who have the advantage of many years of experience in breeding and training, or who have scaled the heights of field-trialling honours, or who have achieved eminence in the show ring, I humbly beg your indulgence.

I have stewarded at field trials and seen some excellent, elegant Labradors retrieving under the expert eye of an experienced handler. In complete contrast, I have competed in working tests and tangled in impenetrable undergrowth where both dog and handler have been totally confused, and miserably lost. I have handled a dog in the show ring at Crufts (and won!). But, as always, it was the dog who was the winner. Ignoring the hint of self-congratulation implicit in these statements, the point I would make is, as exciting and stimulating as these experiences were to me in their different ways, my delight at our combined success was totally insignificant compared to the sheer pleasure and fulfilment expressed in the eyes of my Labrador. Because I am but an onlooker in his eyes, a custodian of the prize, namely, 'He who shall be obeyed'. What was, and still is, patently obvious to me is that he is succeeding at a job that he was designed for and he was earning my acclaim, and my love; these are the real rewards, no more and no less than that.

1

A History of the Breed

A breed is a group of animals that has been bred from selections made by man, and which therefore possesses a uniform appearance that is inheritable and distinguishes it from other groups of animals within the same species. Breed, variety and race are terms used to describe the diversity of the dog within that species.

Apart from the obvious physical characteristics, some uniquely desired attributes may be said to be 'bred in': for example, gentleness, obedience, willingness to learn, tenacity, resourcefulness, and so on. These features are among those which comprise a dog's 'intellect' and can be strengthened by successive breeding. Thus, eventually they overcome a dog's baser instincts to a greater or lesser extent, but they do not suppress them. Hence, we must bear in mind that an otherwise obedient animal could (and will) instinctively revert to very aggressive behaviour if caught unawares or put in a life-threatening situation.

Ch. Keysun Teko of Blondella, born 1974, by Ch. Sandylands Mark ex Keysun June Rose.

The Gundog

To a certain extent the development of the hunting and sporting dog has proceeded in parallel with the increasing sophistication in the design of weapons for hunting. The first breech-loading gun was invented in about 1836. From well before this time, however, different types of spaniel had been bred according to the needs of the hunter. Mainly they were used for flushing wild game like Woodcock, giving great excitement to the chase. And at this time began the heyday of the retriever. Not only was this dog a vehicle for returning the quarry to his hunter, who was able to stay under cover and comparatively dry, but he was also indispensable for retrieving wounded birds from both land and water. In the Middle Ages the sporting noblemen and their ladies made much of the excellence of their dogs in the hunting field and in the home. In 1486, Dame Juliana Berners, the Prioress of Sopwell Nunnery, wrote about 'Huntynge' in her *Boke of St Albans*. Conveniently, she made a list of some of the dogs that were around at this time, which I will quote: `Tryndel taylles, Pryck-eryd Curries, Ladyes Popees, Butcher's hounds, Spanyels, Terriers, Bastards and Dunghyll Dogges'. These were possibly the forerunners of Sheepdogs, Greyhounds, Poodles, 'Newfoundlands' and Cocker Spaniels respectively, not to mention a selection of fragrant crossbreeds.

In the 1550s, Dr John Caius the refounder of Gonville Hall, Cambridge (which was to become Gonville and Caius College), and who was also a sportsman, compiled a similar list to which he added 'Bird-dogs', a fact that challenges the current belief that bird-dogs are American, which brings me to the retrievers of today.

Over several hundred years, four basic kinds of retriever have been developed. By breeding selectively, some planned and some purely by chance, each type was evolved to carry out a particular job. And within these varieties, further selection by height, weight and coat characteristics, plus some introduced 'foreign' (i.e. non-gundog) blood, the features which we associate with the modern gundog breeds were established. This is a priceless legacy. And it has been placed in our trust.

There are now five recognized breeds of retriever, in addition to those which are considered to be multi-purpose, which are called 'Hunt, Point and Retrieve' breeds and I must not forget to mention the Irish Water Spaniel and the Nova Scotia Duck-Tolling Retriever. These specialized breeds, the last two included, are out of the scope of this book, but I would advise the interested reader to study their unique roles and compare them with that of the Labrador.

Sh.Ch. Sandylands Midnight Magic, born January 1971, by Ch. Sandylands Mark ex Sh.Ch. Sandylands Katrinka of Keithray.

The retrievers are: the Chesapeake Bay Retriever, the Curly-Coated Retriever, the Flat-Coated Retriever, the Golden Retriever and the Labrador Retriever. Of these, the Labrador Retriever is arguably the most popular, if not the most populous, breed of dog in the world.

Allowing for several hundred years of selective breeding, like to like, as the saying goes, it is safe to say that each of the respective retriever types should now be breeding true in temperament, type, coat colour, and so on, producing the 'pure' breeds that we recognize today.

Labrador, North America

The country of Labrador, together with Newfoundland, are both provinces of Canada. Labrador lies on a peninsula in eastern North America between the Hudson Bay and the Gulf of St Lawrence. Popularly thought to have been discovered by the explorer Giovanni 'John' Cabot who landed in Newfoundland, Labrador owes its name, literally 'the land of labourers', to a later adventurer called Cortereal who landed there in about the year 1500. Many other explorers visited Newfoundland and the shores of Labrador. As trade with the various parts of the world increased, the sailors of Europe crossed and recrossed the North Atlantic; and, as was common practice, they carried many a useful dog with them.

That the Labrador Retriever is a water dog *par excellence* goes without saying. Anyone who has taken him along the river bank will understand that his affinity with water is quite uncanny. It is his second home, and it is not beyond the bounds of imagination to suppose that his ability to carry a considerable weight in his mouth while swimming strongly at the same time, made him a very useful carrier for a sailor's throwing line.

In the days of sailing vessels, with their poor manoeuvrability and bad sightlines, the safe landing of a valuable cargo depended on using the best anchorage and often necessitated beaching a ship until the tide was right. General Hutchinson recounts how a large 'Newfoundland' was regularly carried by a ship from the Mediterranean, and who on reaching port would jump ashore to return eventually and then 'bark, until the bight of a rope was hove to him' so that he could be hauled up by the sailors who, needless to say, were much attached to him.

In the past, several authors have suggested that the Labrador Retriever originated in Labrador (a popular misconception), or Canada or even Greenland! I am very fortunate to have corresponded with Lady Jacqueline Barlow who lives in St John's, Newfoundland, and

Lady Barlow with
Sandringham Chive.

who has had Labradors since 1929. Presently she owns several Labradors, including Sandringham Chive who was bred by Her Majesty Queen Elizabeth II. Lady Barlow insists that the Labrador Retriever was so named by the 3rd Earl of Malmesbury, whose estate was near Bournemouth. Further, I would like to quote Lady Barlow's version of how this came about. This is what she says:

A resident of Labrador born and bred (except for schooling in England) said to me on the phone not so long ago, 'Anyone who thinks these dogs (Labradors) came from Labrador is nuts; they don't have the coat to stand up to eight months' Arctic weather, only a Husky has that!' Not something I had actually thought about as I knew, and grew up (in England) knowing where Labradors came from, i.e. the island of Newfoundland itself.

Before the Second World War, breeders and owners of all Labradors knew where their dogs came from originally, but since then and the vast increase of Labradors today, the true origins often seem to have been lost in name.

In 1822, the 2nd Earl of Malmesbury first saw a black water dog retrieving sticks for some boys in Poole Harbour. The dog had come back with the Newfoundland fishing fleet. As his estate was swampy in places, he thought what a good thing it would be to have a dog that retrieved so well in water. Lord Malmesbury bought the dog, and finding he was every bit as good as he appeared, arranged for several more of these water dogs to be brought back the next time the fleet returned. He called them 'Little Newfoundlanders'.

It was the 3rd Earl, a lonely widower who seriously began breeding these dogs and, finding the name too wordy, called them Labradors. Labrador, the mainland part of Newfoundland, was also well known to those who lived in Dorset's fishing ports, as being where the cod were plentiful in summer.

Lord Malmesbury gave some of these dogs to his friends, and according to Col. Claud Scott, a son of Lord George Scott, who managed his brother the Duke of Buccleuch's dogs, the first Buccleuch Labradors were from the Malmesbury Kennels. The Buccleuchs to this day have dogs descended from those original dogs imported by the Malmesburys. Sadly the Malmesbury dogs all died out during the First World War when their Gamekeeper, Beech, was called up. The present and 6th Lord Malmesbury said the last dog literally pined to death. The 6th Lord Malmesbury is my authority for all of this. He is one of the most marvellous dog men I have ever met. Naturally, the Malmesbury family still have Labradors to which they are devoted.

Once the water dogs of Labrador became popular, a regular trade developed between there and Poole Harbour, and a Col. Peter Hawker, who had trading ventures between Newfoundland and Poole, arranged for many of them to be brought over as he himself was a notable sportsman. I talked to his granddaughter, who lives in Harbour Grace, Newfoundland.

The dogs were called various things at first: the St John's dog (after the port of embarkation), the Lesser (meaning smaller) Newfoundland, but in Newfoundland itself they were just 'Water Dogs'. The last dogs to be shipped were one or two in the 1930s, notably to the Duke of Buccleuch. The Sheep Act of 1927 virtually wiped them out in Newfoundland, and once the Rabies Quarantine Law was established in England, it put an end to the importation of 'Water Dogs' from Newfoundland. Nowadays, only in the remote isolated outposts of Newfoundland are there one or two water dogs. I was lucky to find two dogs in Grand Bruit on the south coast in 1968. The only bitch had been put down for chasing chickens, so they were the last of them.

However, I have, after a thirty-year search, found the connection of our yellow Labradors. Two old histories of Newfoundland mentioned the Yellow Dogs of Petty Harbour. Petty Harbour is a fishing village about twenty miles south of St John's and was well known throughout the rest of the island for its very dark yellow water dogs. Apparently, the water dogs in the rest of the island were black, and the identical dog in Petty Harbour was a very, very dark yellow. The last of these was remembered about forty to fifty years ago.

Richard Wolters, the American author of many books on Labradors went to Grand Bruit and photographed the black dogs and they can be found in his book, *The Labrador Retriever – The History, The People*. Another accurate and well-researched English author was the late Mary Roslin Williams.

I am greatly indebted to Lady Barlow for such valuable first-hand information.

I am also indebted to the late, much loved and admired, Mary Roslin Williams, whose book *The Dual-Purpose Labrador* is considered a modern classic. She owned the famous Mansergh kennel of black Labradors. In her book, she alludes to the early history of the retriever, naming Pyreneans, mastiffs and Esquimo dogs as some of their possible ancient antecedents! But she insists that by the time 'Labradors' were being imported into Britain they were breeding 'fairly pure' and self-black, save for a little white on the chest, and the recessive yellow colours were well established.

Early Retrievers

It is interesting to consider how the Labrador Retriever may have arisen before he found a home in Newfoundland.

In the book *The Dual-Purpose Labrador* is a picture of a Portuguese dog, the 'Cane di Castro Laboreiro' copied from a plate in an Italian book, *Le Razzi Canine* (Dog Breeds) by Florenzo Fiorini. Obviously a breed of ancient origin, he takes his title either from a village in Portugal of the same name (Castro Laboreiro) or from its literal meaning which is a 'labourer's' or 'worker's' dog. Mrs Roslin Williams supposed that the dog in the picture, with its uncanny likeness to the Labrador (having a correct coat, kind expression and otter tail), might have found its way to Newfoundland with Portuguese sailors, and therefore given a name that was then corrupted into the well-known name of the locality.

'Satyr Mourning Over a Nymph', a painting by Piero di Cosimo, 1495, depicts a beautiful Nymph or Water Maiden and four retriever-like dogs. The fourth dog – a bitch I think – has distinctly Labrador-like characteristics: an apparent stop, a good muzzle, and an absolutely soulful expression. Only her tail is a little feathery.

I discovered a further reference to retrievers in Italy in Jan Morris' book, *A Venetian Bestiary*, in which is reproduced Titian's sixteenth-century portrait of an Italian nobleman posed with his beloved dog at his feet. The dog is described elsewhere as a 'solid, plain-featured gun-dog' and the man as a 'gaudy aristocrat'. To me the noble dog bears a very good resemblance to a Labrador and it is the earliest possible likeness

Di Cosimo's Faithful 'Retriever' c. 1495. (Rep. by permission of The National Gallery, London.)

Titian's Portrait of a Nobleman with his 'Retriever' c. 1500. (Rep. by permission of the Staatliche Museum, Kassel.)

that I have ever come across. As Mary Roslin Williams surmised regarding the Portuguese working dog, it may be that such a dog as that shown in the picture, highly prized by his wealthy owner, could also have found his way on a voyage of exploration to the burgeoning New World. The marshy flood plains of the Tagus, the Rhône, and the Po are not so unlike the fens, or even the coastline of the Poole estuary for that matter.

To pursue further a possible Mediterranean origin for the Labrador, I turned to Brian Vesey-Fitzgerald's book, *About Dogs*, which is quite specific:

> The name Labrador, by the way has nothing to do with Labrador, Canada. It is Spanish – roughly, it means 'workman' – and the breed originated in Spain from a Mastiff-Sheepdog cross. The great artist Velasquez (1599-1660) painted many of them and in almost all the pictures there is a man with a gun.

The question of whether a Castro Laboreiro, di Cosimo's dog, a retriever as painted by Titian or Velasquez' workman's dog could be the ancestors of the Labrador Retriever cannot be answered unequivocally. It is a question that only you and your imagination can answer.

14

The Modern Retriever

During a period of about sixty years, commencing about the middle of the nineteenth century, the popularity of the Labrador in England increased enormously. Sportsmen appreciated his speed and versatility and pedigree dog fanciers of both sexes loved his handsome appearance and affectionate temperament. Such was the demand for them that kennels which had previously bred pointers and setters soon owned more Labradors than any other breed.

Consistency

By breeding Labradors consistently with a similar stamp to others of the same type and colour, the quality of the Labradors produced became more fixed and true. Little was known of colour inheritance and still less about hereditary problems. Fortunately, much of the actual breeding was carried out by keepers and stockmen who were not fools and backed up their intuition with much common sense and practical knowledge. Breeding programmes were often initiated by the employers, some of whom were wealthy landowners in their own right, others were gentlemen of private means and military backgrounds. The Hon. Arthur Holland-Hibbert, later 3rd Viscount Knutsford, The Duke of Buccleuch and, of course, Lorna, Countess Howe rank highly among these.

Litters were whelped in sometimes Spartan conditions with a minimum of veterinary assistance and often relied on only rough comforts and the persistence and nature of the bitch to survive. Rearing was done using simple foods compared with that available nowadays. The puppies were then closely scrutinized and assessed under the eagle eye of the benefactors. Those that did not meet with approval were not bred from again.

Litters were also subjected to another, sometimes sterner test. Canine diseases were widespread at this time and only puppies with a strong constitution lived to maturity. These then spent their lives in the field for much of the year or on the show bench during the show season. The best and most successful were used for breeding or stud work. Hence, from the late nineteenth century onwards, the quality of the Labrador in all its aspects improved under the twin forces of human guidance and natural selection.

This state of affairs was achieved very gradually and probably reached a zenith between the two World Wars. The reasons were two-fold: first, the breeding of pedigree dogs was in the hands of a relatively small and powerful group of people. Possibly the number of really influential kennels did not reach three figures. Second, to the majority of people, transport over long distances was impractical and only the most dedicated could contemplate using a stud-dog living more than fifty miles away. There were good facilities for sending bitches by rail but this was not to everyone's taste and pocket.

As a result of the above, Labradors achieved a consistency in both appearance and capability. The progeny produced by outstanding stud-dogs took on the characteristics of their kennel-mates, e.g. tending to have lovely conformation, balance, strength without lumber or clumsiness (to paraphrase another breed's description); and they developed good proportions: length of neck to depth of chest, say, or length of back to depth of quarters. Strong stud-dogs were able to 'rule the roost' in their own part of the world. These dogs' individual qualities put a stamp on the Labradors bred in different parts of the United Kingdom. Later on, a similar pattern emerged in different countries of the world due to the export of certain pre-potent sires. For a period of years it was possible to deduce the area of influence of a stud-dog by reference to the geographical distribution of his progeny.

When breeding to certain lines, many of the owners of important kennels held fast and strong to their beliefs. They only bred with the dogs that they approved of and refused to be swayed by fashionable or commercial reasons. One result of this was that retrieving ability was not sacrificed at the expense of handsomeness, and speed was not sought at a cost of lack of substance. And so at a time when the show world was smaller and more tightly knit, a dual champion with both field and show ability was an achievable aim. But in the early 1900s the advent of specialization was apparent and some thought standards were slipping. Something had to be done about it.

In 1916 the Labrador Retriever Club was formed to protect the purity of the breed and to organize field trials for Labradors. The first Chairman was Lord Knutsford. Foremost in the minds of the members was to establish a definition or standard description by which the Labrador could be recognized. Previously it was possible to register a mixed-bred retriever with the Kennel Club merely by stating the description preferred by the owner or breeder, and this led to inconsistency and some confusion among the showing fraternity. So a description was agreed by the club and published in 1916. This was the first specific Labrador Retriever Standard, and henceforth breeders aspired to produce dogs that met the requirements outlined within it.

The Founding Fathers

During the period leading up to and just after the Second World War, a wide variety of Labrador kennels were established in England. Many were owned by outstanding stockmen, breeders totally devoted to Labradors, and the animals that they produced showed not only that variety but the great depth in quality that the breed achieved at this time. Space does not permit an in-depth study of breed lines here, so reference to more specific books is necessary in order to understand fully the Labrador's development. However, the following aims to provide a brief introduction to some of the kennels whose influence has helped to form the breed as we know it today.

Most of the early kennels contained solely black dogs and bitches, and it was not until the foundation of the Yellow Labrador Club in 1924 (an early name suggested for the Club was the 'Golden Labrador Club', but this was disallowed by the Kennel Club) that yellow Labradors increased in popularity. In those days, chocolates were unheard of in the show ring and according to Mrs Gwen Broadley, if there were any they were hushed up! The first yellow dog to be registered at the Kennel Club was Ben of Hyde (sometimes referred to as Hyde Ben) owned by Major C. Radclyffe. Ben was registered in 1899.

In those days it was possible, albeit a great achievement, to have a dog with the ability to become a field trial champion and at the same time, the outstanding looks and personality to become a show champion. The late Lorna, Countess Howe of the Banchory kennel owned the first dual champion Labrador in the breed, Banchory Bolo (born in 1915). She recalls how she obtained the dog who achieved such prominence, and to whom she was extremely devoted. Dual Ch. Banchory Bolo was related to Malmesbury Tramp through his male line; his sire was Scandal of Glynn; Scandal's sire was Peter of Faskally (1908); Peter's sire was Munden Sixty (1897), owned by Lord Knutsford; and the sire of Sixty was The Duke of Buccleuch's Avon (1888) whose sire was Malmesbury Tramp (1878). It is likely that every black Labrador can be traced back to either Avon or the 11th Earl of Howe's Nell (born about 1856). Later on, in the 1930s, Lady Howe obtained another black dog, Ch. Ingleston Ben, bred by a Scottish gentleman called Dobie. He proved to have both trial and show abilities but, above all, he sired some excellent dogs and bitches. His progeny included a dual champion, eight champions and a dozen field-trial winners. Ben was truly a 'foundation stone' of the Labrador breed.

The Banchory strain formed a base for the Sandringham Labradors

Dual Champion Banchory Bolo, born 1915,
by Scandal of Glynn ex Caerhowell Nettle.

of the late King George VI. Sandringham Stream, sired by Ch. Banchory Trueman, was shown at Crufts in 1939. More recently, Sandringham dogs bred by Her Majesty Queen Elizabeth II have competed and won well at field trials. These include F.T.Ch. Sandringham Ranger, contemporary F.T. Champions Sandringham Slipper and Sherry, and perhaps the best known of them all, F.T.Ch. Sandringham Sydney, out of Sherry, by Ch. Creedypark Digger.

Gwen Broadley's Labradors were soundly established in that for several years Mrs Broadley had been associated with Countess Howe and the Banchory strain. She mated Ch. Jerry of Sandylands to Juno of Sandylands (a great-great-granddaughter of Peter of Faskally, who was himself of Malmesbury descent) to produce Ch. June of Sandylands (1936). Thus began a strong line of black Labradors. However, it was not until after the Second World War that Mrs Broadley obtained Ch. Sandylands Tweed of Blaircourt (a son of Ch. Ruler of Blaircourt), from Mr and Mrs Cairns. As a result, two of the most prepotent Labrador sires were to emerge on the scene. One was the black Ch. Sandylands Mark (a grandson of Tweed) and the other was the yellow Ch. Sandylands Tandy, who was produced from a mating of Sandylands Tan (a yellow son of Tweed, and later an Australian champion) to Sandylands Shadow (a black bitch of Diant and Blaircourt lineage). Also produced by this combination were a succession of Sandylands champions: Int. Ch. Tanna and Champions Tarnia, Tarna, Tanita, Tarmac, Timber and Truth. Subsequently these dogs and bitches were to form the foundations of, and set the stamp on, many of the present-day top kennels (*see* Appendix).

The Sandylands Kennel, presently owned in partnership with Mr Garner Anthony of Australia, has been in the forefront of Labradors for many years with over seventy champions having gained their titles. In the dogs, Champions Tweed, Tandy and Mark have been mentioned already and their influence has had a phenomenal effect on subsequent kennels. Tandy sired several champions, as did Mark, who proved to be a most influential sire from the mid-1960s onward and whose progeny included Sh.Ch. Sandylands Midnight Magic, an important brood-bitch. Abroad, Int. Ch. Sandylands Midas was influential in the USA, as was S.A. Ch. Sandylands Masterpiece of Breckondale in South Africa. Other excellent Sandylands stud-dogs included Sandylands Charlston and Sh.Ch. Sandylands Clarence of Rossbank, while of the many excellent brood-bitches Sh.Ch. Sandylands Longley Come Rain (1974), a granddaughter of Tandy, proved to be especially important.

Influential Black Kennels

The late Mary Roslin William's Ch. Midnight of Mansergh (1954) and a winner of open stake awards, had the most typical of Labrador out-lines with a most handsome neck and head. He can be traced back to Banchory lines in his maternal pedigree. Her kennel was one of the few to concentrate entirely on the careful breeding of all-black dual-purpose lines. Ch. Groucho of Mansergh (1969) was a great grandson of Midnight. Ch. Mansergh Ships-Belle (1976), carried the lines of Ch. Sandylands Tandy through Ch. Follytower Merrybrook Black Stormer. In a nutshell, her pedigree shows how different dogs and bitches of the same type were bred by Mrs Roslin Williams to produce the lovely brood-bitch, Mansergh Blackthorn Winter, the dam of Mansergh Spring Songstress (1968). When looking at the photographs of dogs and bitches from the Mansergh kennel, these show a type of Labrador that has been maintained solidly over more than forty years of breed-ing; an outstanding achievement (see Appendix).

Mr and Mrs Grant Cairns owned one of the outstanding kennels in Scotland. Ch. Ruler of Blaircourt (1956) won Res. Best in Show at Crufts in 1959, a marvellous achievement. As the sire of Ch. Sandylands Tweed of Blaircourt, his breeding was central to the development of the afore-mentioned Sandylands strain, which went on to prove itself such a solid backbone for Labradors not only nationally, but worldwide.

From Mr M. Gilliat's kennel, Holton Baron (1951) was a very well admired and successful black Labrador male. Together with the bitch Ch. Holton Joyful (1939), he did well both in trials and in the show ring. Baron was twice best black Labrador at Crufts and also won four Certificates of Merit at field trials. Baron was a grandson of Ch. Sandy-lands Ben, himself a grandson of Mrs Broadley's foundation pair, Ch. Jerry of Sandylands and Juno of Sandylands. The Holton kennel is

Ch. Sandylands Mark, born 1965, by Ch. Reanacre Mallardhurn
Thunder ex Ch. Sandylands Truth. Top winning stud-dog, all breeds,
and sire of twenty-nine British Champions.

presently maintained by Mr Gilliat's daughter, Mrs D. Walter, and a recent addition to the line is Holton Holly, a direct descendant of Baron and Joyful.

The foundation bitch of Mr and Mrs Wilkinson's Keithray kennel was Ch. Hollybank Beauty (1959). She gained six CCs and when mated to Ch. Sandylands Tweed of Blaircourt produced three English champions, Sh.Ch. Hollybeaut (who sired Int. Ch. Kinky of Keithray and Sh.Ch. Sandylands Katrinka of Keithray), Hollybunch (sire of Sh.Ch. Poolstead President) Ballyduff Hollybranch of Keithray, and the American champion Hollyberry of Keithray. An outstanding run of success for the strain was the three times winning of Best in Show at the Labrador Retriever Club by three generations of bitches: Ch. Hollybrook Beauty in 1961, Hollybeaut in 1965, and Katrinka in 1966.

The lines of Holton and Tweed are found in the breeding of Mr H. Saunders's Ch. Liddly Buddleia (1966). She was a lovely black bitch and typical of the Liddly kennel which was one of the true founders of the breed. Thirty years previously, to take one example, Ch. Liddly Geranium was born; he was a great-great-grandson of Dual Ch.

20

Banchory Bolo. It is to the great credit of the Liddly kennel that over a period of thirty years dogs and bitches of such lovely type should have been bred consistently.

Early Labradors owned by Mr and Mrs H. Taylor of the Whatstandwell kennel were Ch. Honey of Whatstandwell, and F.T.Ch. Hiwood Brand, a son of Dual Ch. Staindrop Saighdear. A lovely black bitch of the Post-war era was Ch. Ballyduff Whatstandwell Rowena (1948), Best of Breed at Crufts in 1952, bred by Mr and Mrs Taylor, and later owned by Mrs Bridget Docking of the Ballyduff Labradors. A photograph of her shows her to be a truly lovely Labrador, absolutely typical of the breed. Her sire was the influential Ch. Whatstandwell Ballyduff Robin, who also sired Ch. Whatstandwell Venus.

The late Mrs Bridget Docking's Ballyduff kennel was founded in 1929 and contained some important black dogs: F.T.Ch. Ballyduff Jassie, winner of Open Stake at the Labrador Retriever Club, Ch. Ballyduff Hollybranch of Keithray (a son of Tweed), and Eng. and Am. Ch. Ballyduff Seaman (a Tweed grandson), who sired Ch. Ballyduff Marina out of Electron of Ardmargha. When mated to Ch. Sandylands Mark Marina produced another influential dog, Ch. Ballyduff Marketeer, who

Ch. Holton Baron, born 1951, by Sh.Ch. Sandylands Bob ex Holton Whimbrel.

21

sired Ch. Squire of Ballyduff (1974). The Ballyduff strain now prospers under the guidance of Mrs Docking's daughter, Mrs S. Cuthbert.

Influential Yellow Kennels

The Zelstone Kennel was founded by Mrs Audrey Radclyffe (Chairman of the Labrador Retriever Club from 1956 to 1993), who obtained her first Labrador, a descendant of Ben of Hyde, in 1926. Her early field-trialling, Zelstone Sandy, won a certificate of Merit, and she began breeding yellow dual-purpose Labradors in 1929. Ch. Zelstone Leap Year Lass (1952) was a granddaughter of Dual Ch. Staindrop Saighdear, and the dam of F.T. Ch. Zelstone Moss (by Dual Ch. Knaith Banjo). Not only could Lass win in strong company (she was Best in Show at the Yellow Labrador Club Open show in 1956) but she regularly competed and won in field trials.

In 1925, the Yellow Labrador Club was formally established and the first secretary was Major Wormald. Major and Mrs Wormald owned the famous kennel of yellow Labradors of which Dual Ch. Knaith Banjo (1946) was a superb representative. During his career, Banjo was Best of Breed three times and won over forty field trial awards. Mrs Broadley (Sandylands) recalls the early days of showing Labradors, about 1923, when the entries were almost exclusively black dogs, and the drama that arose when a yellow dog entered the ring at Crufts. Mrs Wormald was the exhibitor. The steward told her politely that she was in the wrong ring, 'Golden Retrievers', he said, 'are further down the hall'. Mrs Wormald was not a woman to be trifled with: 'This is a Labrador and I'm staying put', she said. Mrs Wormald was the Hon Secretary of the Yellow Labrador Club from 1953 to 1977.

From the late Edgar Winter's Staindrop kennel came a very famous yellow stud-dog of the 1950s, Dual Ch. Staindrop Saighdear. This handsome dog was a great character and had the honour of being the first yellow dual champion. It is of interest that, although he was yellow in colour, he was a great-grandson of Banchory Bolo on both his paternal and his maternal lines.

Fred Wrigley's Kinley kennels produced Kinley Charm, who was described by Countess Howe as 'a very attractive yellow bitch, typical in every way with lovely hazel eyes, correct otter tail and the thick, weather-resisting coat that goes so often with this colour'. Charm was a granddaughter of Dual Ch. Staindrop Saighdear, and she bred the outstanding Ch. Kinley Melody who was as much at home in the show ring – winning four CCs – as she was in the trial field.

Ch. Braeduke Joyful, born 1959, with son Int. Nord. Ch. Braeduke Silsdale Music Man and dam Diant Joy of Braeduke.

The Landyke kennel was founded by J.P. Hart, JP, and is now owned by his son Keith, a well-respected judge of the breed. Ch. Landyke Velour, a much-admired yellow bitch, carried the well-known lines of Ch. Liddly Jonquil, Janet of Sandylands and Ch. Badgery Richard. In later years the Landyke breeding was much influenced by Poppleton blood, and particularly that of Ch. Poppleton Lieutenant.

Mrs Outhwaite's Poppleton kennel had a great influence on the breeding of yellow Labradors. Lieutenant's grandfather, Ch. Poppleton Golden Flight was another of this kennel's influential dogs. He sired one of the most outstanding post-war yellow Labradors at stud, Ch. Diant Swandyke Cream Cracker, who was the only dog in a litter bred by Mr Tillson. Cracker went on to sire Ch. Diant Juliet, an outstanding bitch of great character and of lovely Labrador type and substance, owned by Mrs Louise Wilson Jones of the Diant Kennel.

Mrs Anne Wynyard's Braeduke kennel obtained Diant Joy of Braeduke from which she bred Ch. Braeduke Joyful (1959). Joy's sire was Ch. Poppleton Lieutenant and her dam was Ch. Diant Juliet. Joyful was a very handsome dog winning Certificates of Merit at Open and All-aged stakes. He sired Int. & Nor. Ch. Braeduke Silsdale Music Man and several field trial winners.

Post-War Kennels

Mrs Kinsella founded the Brentchase kennel in March 1946. Her first Labrador was Brentchase Anna Lady who, when mated to a yellow son of Ch. Ballyduff Orangeman, produced Brentchase Heidemarie.

Heide's daughter Polly Flinders had a litter by Ch. Cornlands Peter So Gay (a grandson of Ch. Diant Swandyke Cream Cracker), which included Ch. Brentchase Pompadour and Sh.Ch. Brentchase Pistachio (1959). The kennel has continued with a succession of lovely bitches, which includes Brentchase Hanna (sired by Ch. Sandylands Tandy), Brentchase Regina and Brentchase Wild Mink.

The Brentchase line provided the foundation for some of Mr Boothroyd's Roydwood kennel, in that Brentchase Kilkee (a great-granddaughter of Ch. Cornlands Peter So Gay and Brentchase Polly Flinders) was put to Ch. Roydwood Reveller (later to become an Italian champion) and produced the good-looking yellow Sh.Ch. Roydwood Right on Time.

In the early 1950s, Mrs Rae started the Cornlands kennel. This resulted in a lovely line of dogs including Ch. Cornlands Peter So Gay (1953) and Ch. Cornlands My Fair Lady (1965), one of the loveliest bitches that I can remember personally. The Cornlands line also has Diant and Poppleton dogs predominant in the background, while Cornlands Lady Lavender (1971) was mated to Ch. Squire of Ballyduff producing Ch. Cornlands Blonde Lady who won Best of Breed at Crufts in 1982. Sandylands, Timspring and Lawnwoods blood has also been used to produce some handsome yellow dogs.

Mrs 'Cis' Williams's Nokeener dogs were used fairly extensively for their looks and working ability. Nokeener Novelcracker sired Ch. Landyke Lancer, the sire of Nokeener Novelty out of a Diant bitch called Chloe. A Novelty grandson, Nokeener New Novel was bred to the famous Ch. Candlemas Rookwood Silver Moonlight to produce

Ch. Cornlands My Fair Lady, born 1965, by Ch. Cornlands Kimvalley Crofter ex Cornlands Lady Be Good.

Birdrock Nokeener New Moon owned by Mrs Rogan. Sh.Ch. Nokeener Taffy was the grandfather of Ch. Nokeener Black Spark (1974), who Mrs Roslin Williams purchased to complement her Mansergh lines, which he carried going back through Am. Ch. Mansergh Moose to Sandylands Tarmac.

Another well-established line is Mrs Hepworth's Poolstead kennel which was based on two strong lines: two yellows, Ch. Poolstead Kinley Willow (a Novice Stake winner) and Braeduke Julia of Poolstead (by Ch. Landyke Stormer out of Diant Joy of Braeduke). A significant dog used at stud in the 1970s was Sh.Ch. Poolstead Problem, who was sired by a Mark son, Eng. & Aust. Ch. Sandylands My Lad out of a Kinley Willow daughter, Poolstead Pussy Willow (*see* Appendix).

At the Ardmargha kennel, Mr and Mrs Clayton's Monarch of Admargha (1964) was a yellow dog by Sh.Ch. Sandylands Sam (Holton Baron and Diant Juliet Lines) out of the black bitch Hollybarn Ebony of Ardmargha (Sandylands Tweed and Holton lines). He gained several field trial awards. Later, two champions, Kimbo and Kilree of Ardmargha were bred. Both were grandchildren of Tandy and carried his style and overall looks. By breeding Ch. Sandylands Mark to a yellow bitch, Hope of Ardmargha (a daughter from a Tandy to Kilree

Monarch of Ardmargha, born 1964, by Sh.Ch. Sandylands Sam ex Hollybarn Ebony of Ardmargha.

mating), Sh.Ch. Ardmargha Mad Hatter (1975) was produced. Mad Hatter won Reserve Best in Show at the West of England Ladies Kennel Society Championship show (all breeds) in 1978, and proved to be an important stud-dog when used on stock with a strong Sandylands background. Amongst others, he sired Sh.Ch. Croftspa Hazelnut of Foxrush, who holds the record for the most number of Challenge Certificates won by a Labrador bitch (see Appendix).

Mrs Woolley's Follytower kennel had as its foundation bitch Follytower Silsdale Old Chelsea (sired by Ch. Braeduke Joyful) who became a full Champion. By breeding Chelsea to Hollybranch of Keithray, Follytower Old Black Magic was obtained and she in turn was mated to Ch. Sandylands Tandy. The resulting litter contained, possibly, one of the 'few' outstanding post-war dogs, Ch. Follytower Merrybrook Black Stormer. Stormer produced many offspring, including the very beautiful Sh.Ch. Bradking Black Charm.

Mrs Slatterthwaite's Lawnwoods kennel of Labradors was largely based on the mating of Sc.Ch. Braeduke Silsdale Music Man to

Ch. Mansergh Ships-Belle, born 1976, by Sh.Ch. Sandylands Storm-Along ex Ch. Mansergh Ooh-La-La. (Pedigree, see Appendix.)

26

Spinnyhill Lilac of Lawnwood, whom she obtained from Mr P. Morgan's Spinnyhill kennel. Lilac was mated to Rockabee Tobin (a Tandy son bred by the partnership of Miss Thorpe and Miss Walker) to get Ch. Lawnwoods Fame and Fortune. A later introduction to the kennel, Ch. Poolstead Personality of Lawnwood, was mated to Fame and Fortune resulting in Lawnwoods Tapestry, who in 1973 produced Lawnwoods Fandango (by Ch. Follytower Merrybrook Black Stormer), who went on to sire Ch. Lawnwoods Midnight Folly and Eng. & Am. Ch. Lawnwoods Hot Chocolate, one of the best examples of a chocolate Labrador that I can remember (*see* Appendix).

Chocolate Labradors

In 1859, John Henry Walsh (who, under the pseudonym Stonehenge, wrote a number of excellent books, the best-known of which is probably *The Dog in Health and Disease*), refers to the Labrador as being 'always black', but at the same time he draws attention to the 'esquimaux dog, a native of North America and the adjacent islands'. This dog, although broadly Spitz in type, was said to be '22 to 23 inches high with a low, strong body, long hair with an undercoat of thick wool, and colour almost always a dark dun (grey brown)'.

Around the turn of the twentieth century, Rawden Lee refers to 'straight-coated brown retrievers, produced from black parents'. He notes how he fancied the pale chocolate-brown ones shown at the Kennel Club Show of June 1889 in a class for 'Retrievers, any colour than black'.

Mary Roslin Williams suggested some time ago that 'livers', as she originally termed them, could have emerged following inadvertent outcrossings with Pointers or Flat-coated Retrievers, because there is evidence that such dogs form a common background with the Chesapeake Bay Retriever. She also suggested that the great weight and substance of some chocolates might be the result of inclusions of Rottweiler blood, which would account for the very strong-boned, barrel-chested dogs sometimes seen. Poorer examples might have less desirable characteristics also, such as a 'bully' head (Bull breeds being behind the Rottweiler) with a round eye, and the colour of tan rather than a liver colour.

Mrs Roslin Williams agreed that, since then, all conscientious breeders had tried to accentuate the good points (as had been done when earlier Flat-coat blood had been introduced, producing the over-dark eye and feathering, which had taken a long time to breed out). Regarding the

Flat-coat cross, she enjoyed the comment made to her at the ringside at Crufts some time ago by a very knowledgeable dog person. 'Since when did we need to trim the breeches and feathering off Labradors for the ring?'

Chocolate Kennels

The first chocolate-coloured Labrador mentioned by Countess Howe was Nawton Pruna, who was run in field trials before the First World War. Mr J.G. Severn (Tibshelf) mated a yellow dog (Midas of Metesford) to a chocolate bitch (Sea Otter of Metesford) and produced a 'nice specimen' called Chocolate Soldier, about the year 1938. However, later he said that he regretted introducing 'outside blood' as it had resulted in a vicious and nervous strain.

Post-war, the attractively-coloured chocolate Labrador has gained an increasing number of followers and their quality is steadily improving. The number of British chocolate Labradors registered in 1992 was 2,200, about 9 per cent of the total number of Labradors registered at the Kennel Club. The following kennels, which I shall mention in rough chronological order, illustrate the development of the chocolate Labrador.

The first ever chocolate Labrador champion was Mrs Y. Pauling's Ch. Cookridge Tango, whose sire, Ch. Sandylands Tweed of Blaircourt, and dam, Cookridge Gay Princess, were both black. Prior to this mating, a Tibshelf dog, Coco, had been mated to Ch. Cookridge Otter about mid-1950. The resulting litter included three chocolate bitches, two of which subsequently bred champions themselves: Ch. Cookridge Cormorant and Nor. Ch. Ramah Chocolate Chip. A second litter by Otter, this time out of a black called Newly Lass, produced Cookridge Gay Princess, the dam of Tango.

A strong influence on the breeding of chocolates – although not chocolate himself – was Ch. Follytower Merrybrook Black Stormer, who sired no less than three chocolate champions: Sh.Ch. Follytower Merry-go-round, Eng. & Am. Ch. Lawnwoods Hot Chocolate and Sh.Ch. Morningtown Stormtrooper. Other successful progeny included Marbra Leprechaun, Morningtown Stormette, and Bradking Bonny's Prince of Jeronga, who later became a South African champion.

Several other kennels, whilst certainly not exclusively breeding chocolates, have produced some excellent winning dogs, including Sh. Ch. Bradking Bridget of Davricard, Can. Ch. Boothgates Krazy Kaper, Sh.Ch. Boothgates Kountry Kurio, Boothgates Headliner, Charway Sally Brown, Copper Kettle of Balrion, Oakhouse Mocha, and Sh.Ch. Lougin Lamara, a daughter of Headliner.

2

The Breed Standards

The Labrador Retriever Club's 1916 Standard formed a sound foundation for determining the points of the Labrador and it is a tribute to the early compilers that it has changed only in detail during the eighty years of its continuance. It is interesting to compare the description, drawn up by the Labrador Retriever Club and published in 1916, with that drawn up by John Henry Walsh (Stonehenge) some fifty years earlier (in 1859):

> Skull, wide, with a slight furrow down the middle, moderately long with a brow only just rising from the straight line. Jaws, long enough to carry a hare. Wide nasal organ with open nostrils. Ears, small. Eyes, of medium size, intelligent and soft. Neck, as long as can be got. Chest, tends to be barrel-like but better narrow and deep. Deep back ribs. Bent stifles seldom met in this breed. Legs, straight, strong in bone. Feet, large. Tail, bushy without a feather, but should not be curled over the back. Coat, short, wavy, glossy and close, admitting wet with difficulty owing to oiliness, but no undercoat. Colour, rich jet black without rustiness, no white, but best-bred puppies often have white toe or star. Symmetry of importance. Of good disposition and temper.

The Labrador Club Standard appeared in abbreviated form in the magazine *The Field* in the August 1916 issue:

> The general appearance of the labrador should be strongly built, short-coupled and very active. Compared with the Wavy- or Flat-coated Retriever, he should be wider in head, chest and ribs, and wider and stronger over the loins and hindquarters. Coat: close, short, dense and free from feather. Skull: wide with slight 'stop', brow slightly pronounced. Head: clean, free from fleshy cheeks. Jaws: long, powerful, free from snipiness (i.e. weakness). Nose: wide, nostrils well developed. Ears: not large. eyes: medium size, should express intelligence and good temper, brown, yellow or black.

Ch. Zelstone Leap Year Lass, born 1952, by Braedrop Bruce ex F.T.Ch. Zelstone Darter.

The author added, 'That the Standard has been drawn up with great care cannot be doubted, but we are quite prepared to hear of certain points being criticized.'

It was not until the formation of the Yellow Labrador Club in 1924 that the question of coat colour was considered important enough to be included in the Standard description. Up to then, to paraphrase Henry Ford: You could have a Labrador of any colour – so long at it was black! In a detailed description set out in the 1925 Annual Report of the Yellow Labrador Club, the coat is described as:

> ...short, thick without wave, practically double; undercoat thick and woolly, overcoat smooth. Colour may vary from fox-red to cream, a whole colour and not of a flaked appearance... [the eye should be] dark brown [and the neck] stocky, may be inclined to be throaty.

Today, 'flaked' would be termed 'flecked', 'snowflaked' or 'spotted'.

A. Croxton-Smith, writing in the 1940s (although his work relates to descriptions of dogs which existed in the previous decade and earlier), quotes the 1916 Standard almost word for word except that the skull is described as 'broad', the ribs 'well sprung', the stifles 'well-turned', the hindquarters 'well developed', and the toes 'well arched' with the pads 'well developed'. He adds, 'The colour is usually black, but of later years yellows have come into prominence.' However, his description of the tail is distinctive; '...thick towards the base and tapering at the tip, of medium length, free from feathering, clothed with short thick coat giving a rounded appearance which is described as the otter tail.'

The Standard for the breed set out in 1950, quoted by Countess Howe in her book *The Popular Labrador Retriever* (*see* Bib.), shows little by way of variation on the above except that 'broad' rather than 'wide' is used to define the skull, chest, loins and hindquarters. However, at this time significant additions were made, including a desired size:

> Movement neither too wide nor too close in front and behind. Hocks slightly bent and the dog must not be cow-hocked (hocks not parallel) nor move too wide nor too close behind. The eyes, either 'brown or hazel' (NB. hazel is defined in the dictionary as 'greenish brown'). Teeth, lower teeth just behind but touching the upper. Shoulders, well-placed. Feet should be round. The tail should not curl over the back. The coat, short, dense, without wave, with a weather-resisting undercoat and a fairly hard feeling to the hand. Colour, black, chocolate or yellow – which may vary from fox-red to cream – free from white markings. Spot on chest allowed. Coat should be whole colour not flecked. Desired height: dogs 22–22½in; bitches 21½–22in.

The reason I have made this rather laborious journey into the past is to emphasize the vast debt which we as modern dog breeders owe to the early Labrador enthusiasts. The portrayal given by Stonehenge is of a distinctive kind of dog, but one that obviously varied quite a lot in height, weight and substance. He also carried several 'foreign' characteristics more related to other breeds of retrievers plus some others, for example a bushy, curly tail, straight stifles and no undercoat! However, even from this beginning a good kind temperament was paramount.

By the second decade of the twentieth century, under the guidance of the Labrador Retriever Club, a true Labrador 'type' had been established. This proved to be a sound foundation because any future modifications would be relatively minor. For example, a yellow or a jet-black eye were not compatible with a good-tempered, intelligent expression, and feathering was more appropriate to Flat-coated or Golden Retrievers. The requirement for a scissor bite was once thought to be a prerequisite for a whelping bitch, in that it enabled her to cut the umbilical cord, but most Labrador mothers use their back teeth for this operation. I tend to the view that a 'correct bite' is commensurate with typically correct proportions of the skull and jaw. Not only does it give a neat and tidy appearance but it means that for retrieving a soft or slippery object a scissor bite is a more efficient tool if the teeth are regular and overlap correctly, which in turn makes work easier and less tiring for the dog, providing he does not bite too hard!.

The different coat colours, black, chocolate or yellow (with its variations) were included in the 'type description' because it was recognized that these were cosmetic differences and did not affect the overall conformation or working ability of the dog. Later still, some changes were made more for consistency.

Surprisingly, some peculiar terms have been retained in the Standard – snipey, for example, even though it is a word not often used now – whereas other colourful expressions, such as 'Jaws long enough to carry a hare' have been discarded. Specific 'faults' which enabled the layman to understand what was clearly not acceptable are no longer listed, presumably in an effort to limit 'faulting' in judging. This is commendable because one should encourage 'positive' judging, but this is not really of much help to the non-exhibiting breeder who would like to improve his stock.

The Breed Standard that follows here is the current one. Essentially it is the same as the 1950 version, but the Labrador is a living, breathing animal and is still evolving. Since its creation, the Standard has been amended, revised, simplified and standardized in order that it may be more readily understood when translated into other languages. The Labrador is now bred, worked and exhibited all over the world. He is a marvellous ambassador.

In an attempt to improve the judging of potential sires, a note was

Ch. Squire of Ballyduff, born 1974, by Ch. Ballyduff Marketeer ex Sparkle of Tuddenham.

added to all the Standards requiring males to have testicles descended into the scrotum. The necessity for stud-dogs to be fully entire (possess two descended testicles) in order to reproduce is still the subject of debate.

Certain parts of the Standard (shown in italics) have not changed in essence in over 130 years. I think that this is a tribute to all custodians of the pure-bred Labrador, both past and present. I hope that it may remain so.

Breed Standard of Great Britain

(Reproduced by kind permission of the Kennel Club.)

General Appearance
Strongly built, short-coupled, very active; broad in skull; broad and deep through chest and ribs; broad and strong over loins and hindquarters.

Characteristics
Good tempered, very agile. Excellent nose, soft mouth; keen love of water. Adaptable, devoted companion.

Temperament
Intelligent, keen and biddable, with a strong will to please. Kindly nature, with no trace of aggression or undue shyness.

Head and Skull
Skull broad with defined stop; clean cut without fleshy cheeks. *Jaws of medium length,* powerful not snipey. *Nose wide, nostrils well-developed.*

Eyes
Medium size, expressing intelligence and good temper; brown or hazel.

Ears
Not large or heavy, hanging close to the head and set rather far back.

Mouth
Jaws and teeth strong with a perfect, regular and complete scissor bite, i.e. upper teeth closely overlapping lower teeth and set square to the jaws.

Neck
Clean, strong, powerful, set into well-placed shoulders.

Forequarters
Shoulders long and sloping. Forelegs well-boned and straight from elbow to ground when viewed from either front or side.

Body
Chest of good width and depth, with well sprung *barrel ribs.* Level topline. *Loins wide,* short-coupled and strong.

Hindquarters
Well-developed not sloping to tail; *well turned stifle.* Hocks well let down, cow hocks highly undesirable.

Feet
Round, compact; well-arched toes and *well-developed pads.*

Tail
Distinctive feature, very thick towards base, gradually tapering towards tip, medium length, *free from feathering, but clothed thickly all round with short, thick, dense coat,* thus giving 'rounded' appearance described as 'otter' tail. *May be carried gaily, but should not curl over the back.*

Gait/Movement
Free, covering adequate ground; straight and true in front and rear.

Coat
Distinctive feature, *short dense* without wave or feathering, giving fairly hard feel to the touch; *weather resistant undercoat.*

Colour
Wholly black, yellow or liver/chocolate. Yellows range from light cream to red fox. Small white spot on chest permissible.

Size
Ideal height at withers: dogs 56–57cm (22–22½in); bitches 54–56cm (21–21½in).

Faults
Any departure from the foregoing points should be considered a fault and the seriousness with which the fault should be regarded should be in exact proportion to its degree.

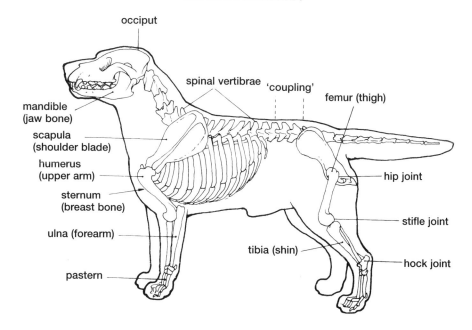

Bone structure of the Labrador.

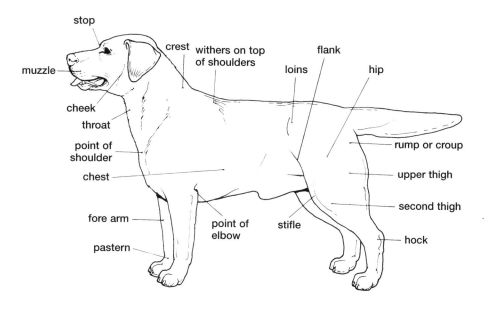

Parts of the Labrador.

Note Male animals should have two apparently normal testicles fully descended into the scrotum.

The British Standard is accepted by many countries in the world. These include Australia, New Zealand and South Africa. In the main, the European and Scandinavian countries that are members of the Fedèra-tion Cynologique Internationale (FCI) and the Nordic Kennel Union (NKU) – for example, Denmark, Finland, France, Germany, Holland, Iceland, Ireland, Italy, Norway, Spain, Sweden and Switzerland – also accept the Kennel Club Standard.

The official American Kennel Club (AKC) Standard for the Labrador Retriever in the United States was drawn up in 1957. However, the Standard was revised comprehensively in 1994, primarily by the parent breed club, The Labrador Retriever Club Inc., which has authority over the Breed Standard.

The American Breed Standard

(Reproduced by kind permission of the American Kennel Club.)

General Appearance
The Labrador Retriever is a strongly built, medium sized, short-coupled dog possessing a sound, athletic, well-balanced conformation that allows it to function as a retrieving gun dog; the substance and soundness to hunt waterfowl or upland game for long hours under difficult conditions; the character and quality to win in the show ring; and the temperament to be a family companion. Physical features and mental characteristics should denote a dog bred to perform as an efficient retriever of game with a stable temperament suitable for a variety of pursuits beyond the hunting environment.

The most distinguishing characteristics of the Labrador Retriever are its short, dense weather-resistant coat; an 'otter' tail; a clean-cut head with a broad back-skull and moderate stop; powerful jaws; and its 'kind' friendly eyes, expressing character, intelligence and good temperament.

Above all, a Labrador Retriever must be well balanced, enabling it to move in the show ring or work in the field with little or no effort. The typical Labrador possesses style and quality without over refinement, and substance without lumber or cloddiness. The Labrador is bred primarily as a working gun dog; structure and soundness are of great importance.

Am. Ch. Beechcroft Clover of OHenry WC. (Owner: Mrs Wiest.)

Size, Proportion and Substance

Size: The height at the withers for a dog is 22½ to 24½ inches; for a bitch 21½ to 23½ inches. Any variance greater than ½ inch above or below these heights is a disqualification. Approximate weight of dogs and bitches in working condition: dogs 65 to 80 pounds; bitches 55 to 70 pounds. The minimum height ranges in the paragraph above shall not apply to dogs or bitches under 12 months of age.

Proportion: Short-coupled; length from the point of the shoulder to the point of the rump is equal to or slightly longer than the distance from the withers to the ground. Distance from the elbow to the ground should be equal to one half of the height at the withers. The brisket should extend to the elbows, but not perceptibly deeper. The body must be of sufficient length to permit a straight free and efficient stride; but the dog should never appear low and long or tall and leggy in outline.

Substance: Substance and bone proportionate to the overall dog. Light, 'weedy' individuals are definitely incorrect; equally objectionable are cloddy lumbering specimens. Labrador Retrievers shall be shown in working condition, well-muscled and without excess fat.

Head

Skull: The skull should be wide; well developed without exaggeration. The skull and foreface should be on parallel planes and of approximately equal length. There should be a moderate stop – the brows slightly pronounced so that the skull is not absolutely in a straight line with the nose. The brow ridges aid in defining the stop. The head should be clean cut and free from fleshy cheeks; the bony structure of the skull chiselled beneath the eye with no prominence in the cheek.

The skull may show some median line. The occipital bone is not conspicuous in mature dogs. Lips should not be squared off or pendulous, but fall away in a curve towards the throat. A wedge-shaped head, or a head long and narrow in muzzle and back-skull is incorrect as are massive cheeky heads. The jaws are powerful and free from snipiness – the muzzle neither long and narrow nor short and stubby.

Nose: The nose should be wide and the nostrils well developed. The nose should be black on black or yellow dogs, and brown on chocolates. Nose colour fading to a lighter shade is not a fault. A thoroughly pink nose or one lacking in any pigment is a disqualification.

Teeth: The teeth should be strong and regular with a scissors bite; the lower teeth just behind, but touching the inner side of the upper incisors. A level bite is acceptable, but not desirable. Undershot or overshot or misaligned teeth are serious faults.

Ears: The ears should hang moderately close to the head, set rather far back, and somewhat low on the skull; slightly above eye level. Ears should not be large and heavy, but in proportion with the skull and reach to the inside of the eye when pulled forward.

Eyes: Kind, friendly eyes imparting good temperament, intelligence and alertness are a hallmark of the breed. They should be of medium size, set well apart, and neither protruding nor deep set. Eye colour should be brown in black and yellow Labradors, and brown or hazel in chocolates. Black or yellow eyes give a harsh expression and are undesirable. Small eyes set close together or round, prominent eyes are not typical of the breed. Eye rims are black in black and yellow Labradors, and brown in chocolates. Eye rims without pigmentation are a disqualification.

Neck, Topline and Body
Neck: The neck should be of proper length to allow the dog to retrieve game easily. It should be muscular and free from throatiness. The neck should rise strongly from the shoulders with a moderate arch. A short, thick or ewe neck is not desirable.

Topline: The back is strong and the topline is level from the withers to the croup when standing or moving. However, the loin should show evidence of flexibility for athletic endeavour.

Body: The Labrador should be short-coupled with good spring of the ribs tapering to a moderately wide chest. The Labrador should not be narrow chested, giving the appearance of hollowness between the front legs, nor should it have a wide-spreading, bulldog-like front. Correct chest conformation will result in tapering between the front legs that allows unrestricted limb movement. Chest breadth that is either too wide or too narrow for efficient movement and stamina is incorrect. Slab-sided individuals are not typical of the breed; equally objectionable are rotund or barrel-chested specimens. The underline is almost straight with little or no tuck-up in mature animals. Loins should be short, wide and strong; extending to well-developed, powerful hindquarters. When viewed from the side, the Labrador Retriever shows a well-developed, but not exaggerated forechest.

Tail

The tail is a distinguishing feature of the breed. It should be very thick at the base, gradually tapering towards the tip, of medium length, and extending no longer than the hock. The tail should be free from feathering and clothed thickly all round with the Labrador's short dense coat, thus having the peculiar rounded appearance that has been described as the 'otter' tail. The tail should follow the topline in repose or when in motion. It may be carried gaily, but should not curl over the back. Extremely short tails or long thin tails are serious faults. The tail completes the balance of the Labrador by giving it a flowing line from the top of the head to the tip of the tail. Docking or otherwise altering the length or natural carriage of the tail is a disqualification.

Forequarters

Forequarters should be muscular, well co-ordinated and balanced with the hindquarters.

Shoulders: The shoulders are well laid back, long and sloping: forming an angle with the upper arm of approximately 90 degrees that permits the dog to move his forelegs in an easy manner with a strong forward reach. Ideally, the length of the shoulder blade should equal the length of the upper arm. Straight shoulder blades, short upper arms or heavily muscled or loaded shoulders, all restricting free movement, are incorrect.

Front Legs: When viewed from the front, the legs should be straight with good strong bone. Too much bone is as undesirable as too little bone, and short-legged, heavy-boned individuals are not typical of the breed. Viewed from the side, the elbows should be perpendicular to the ground and well under the body. The elbows should be close to the ribs without looseness. Tied-in elbows or 'being out at the elbows' interfere with free movement and are serious faults. Pasterns should be strong and short and should slope slightly from the perpendicular line of the leg. Dewclaws may be removed. Splayed feet, hare feet, knuckling over, or feet turning in or out are serious faults.

Hindquarters

The Labrador's hindquarters are broad, muscular and well-developed from the hip to the hock with well-turned stifles and short strong hocks. Viewed from the rear, the hind legs are straight and parallel. Viewed from the side, the angulation of the rear legs is in balance with the front. The hind legs are strongly boned, muscled with moderate angulation at the stifle, and with powerful, clearly defined thighs. The stifle is strong and there is no slippage of the patellae while in motion or when standing. The hock joints are strong, well let down and do not slip or hyper-extend while in motion or when standing. Angulation of both stifle and hock joint is such as to achieve the optimal balance of drive and traction. When standing, the rear toes are only slightly behind the point of the rump. Over-angulation produces a sloping topline not typical of the breed. Feet are strong and compact, with well arched toes and well developed pads. Cow hocks, spread hocks, sickle hocks and over-angulation are serious structural defects and are to be faulted.

Coat

The coat is a distinctive feature of the Labrador Retriever. It should be short, straight and very dense, giving a fairly hard feel to the hand. The Labrador should have a soft weather-resistant undercoat that provides protection from water, cold and all types of ground cover. A slight wave down the back is permissible. Woolly coats, soft silky coats and sparse slick coats are not typical of the breed and should be severely penalized.

Color

The Labrador Retriever coat colors are black, yellow and chocolate. Any other color or combination of colors is a disqualification. A small white spot on the chest is permissible, but not desirable. White hairs from aging or scarring are not to be misinterpreted as brindling.

Black: Blacks are all black. A black with brindle markings or black with tan markings is a disqualification.

Yellow: Yellows may range in color from fox-red to light cream, with variations of shading on the ears, back and underparts of the dog.

Chocolate: Chocolates can vary in shade from light to dark chocolate. Chocolate with brindle or tan markings is a disqualification.

Movement

Movement of the Labrador Retriever should be free and effortless. When watching a dog move towards oneself, there should be no sign of elbows out. Rather the elbows should be held neatly to the body with the legs not too close together. Moving straight forward without pacing or weaving, the legs should form straight lines, with all the parts moving in the same plane. Upon viewing the dog from the rear, one should have the impression that the hind legs move as nearly as possible in a parallel line with the front legs. The hocks should do their full share of the work, flexing well, giving the appearance of power and strength. When viewed from the side, the shoulders should move freely and effortlessly, and the foreleg should reach forward close to the ground with extension. A short, choppy movement or high knee action indicates a straight shoulder; paddling indicates long, weak pasterns; and a short, stilted rear gait indicates a straight rear assembly and all are serious faults. Movement faults interfering with performance including weaving, sidewinding, crossing over, high knee action, paddling, and short, choppy movement should be severely penalized.

Temperament
True Labrador Retriever temperament is as much a hallmark of the breed as the 'otter' tail. The ideal disposition is one of a kindly, outgoing, tractable nature, eager to please and non-aggressive towards man or animal. The Labrador has much that appeals to people: his gentle ways, intelligence and adaptability make him an ideal dog. Aggressiveness towards humans or other animals, or evidence of shyness in an adult should be severely penalized.

Disqualifications
1. Any deviation from the height prescribed in the Standard.
2. A thoroughly pink nose or one lacking any pigment.
3. Eye rims without pigment.
4. Docking or otherwise altering the length or natural carriage of the tail.
5. Any color or combination of colors other than black, yellow or chocolate as described in the Standard.

The American Breed Standard is to be complimented on its detailed and exhaustive explanations which are an aid to the understanding of the conformation of the Labrador. For the serious breeder it is instructive to compare the current British and American Standards with previous ones, beginning with Stonehenge's 1879 description, which I have outlined in this chapter. Some, albeit not all, of the sense of what Stonehenge *et al* were attempting to quantify may still be discerned in the current Standards. In my view, perhaps the very early breed writers were not so very far off the mark, after all.

3

Selecting Your Puppy

A fully grown Labrador is a big, heavy, clumsy, hairy beast, who has bouts of high energy alternating with periods of deep torpor. He is quite intelligent, but he is sometimes too cute to show it. When he is adult, he will take a great deal of exercise if you are inclined to it, or none at all if it is high summer. Generally, he likes to bathe in any kind of water-hole available, after which, if he is not to be allowed indoors, he will need to be towelled down.

He can be taught to sit and make retrieves and he can take part in shows and competitions. He may teach himself to bury his trophies, such as his owner's patent leather shoe in the deepest of holes. He may very well learn to open the kitchen door. Over the years our Labradors have been known to bring presents to guests who may be visiting at the time. They may not have appreciated the opened tin of creosote or decomposing Blackbird, but it was a very well-meant gesture.

He likes to eat well, usually twice daily, although he may steal or beg for elevenses if not corrected. He will require constant, although not excessive, care if he is to remain healthy and he will need occasional veterinary attention and this can be costly.

He will also need a great deal of love and affection and time.

The purchase of any puppy must not be undertaken lightly. Aside from the time and commitment that it will require from you, there is also the financial cost. The expense will not end with the initial purchase: even if the dog is never ill, he will still require trips to the vet for vaccinations and check-ups; then there is feeding, which for a puppy will require the buying of a certain amount of raw meat, along with quite probably a vitamin supplement; then there are toys, bedding, a strong lead or two, and a collar (also a spare!). Apart from these regular costs, there are kennel or dog sitter's fees when you go away on holiday. So it can be seen that even if your dog remains very healthy and you do not intend to incur the costs involved in showing, breeding or some other activity the basic cost of caring properly for a fully grown Labrador cannot be dismissed.

However, if having considered all aspects of Labrador ownership, you decide that you are willing and able to accept the commitment and responsibilities involved, the following guidelines will help you to make a wise purchase.

Purchase

Since the purchase of a Labrador puppy is likely to change your lifestyle for the next twelve years, it is essential to make your purchase from a reputable breeder, and thus avoid most potential problems. Try not to be influenced by advertisements in the local newspaper which state such imponderables as 'From good working parents' or 'Bred from a line of show champions', and so on. It is better to write or telephone the Labrador correspondents who write informed columns in the canine press such as *Dog World* or *Our Dogs*. Alternatively, contact the Kennel Club for names of the Labrador Breed Societies, whose secretary will know details of the breeders and kennels in your area. Talk to as many breeders and Labrador owners as you can. If you can get details of a dog show in your area, ask a few questions round the ringside, but be prepared to be patient: if they are competing, owners will not be able to concentrate on you. Be courteous and you will eventually get all the information.

Having identified a reputable breeder whose style appeals to you, let the breeder know that you are interested in buying a puppy. If a puppy is not immediately available, it is worth waiting. If you have done your homework and have sound reasons for purchasing from a particular breeder, it is better to wait than to go elsewhere and settle for your second best.

Potential Problems

Make certain that the puppy's parents have both been checked, and are free from the most common problems known to affect Labradors. These are: hip dysplasia (HD) which may lead to arthritis of the hips in later life; and progressive retinal atrophy (PRA) which can result in blindness. In the UK, the Kennel Club in conjunction with the British Veterinary Association issues certificates for dogs that are free from these conditions. (Incidentally, PRA certificates are renewable annually.) You are entitled to ask to see these certificates when you book to see a litter of puppies, even if the sire is not owned by the breeders. They should be in possession of copies of all the paternal documents.

All sincere breeders will willingly discuss these matters and show you the relevant information.

Osteochondrosis (OCD), which can affect the elbow joint and cause limping, has been more prevalent in Labradors in recent years. Most of the serious owners check their adult dogs routinely before considering them for breeding. These X-rays may be available for you to see.

Epilepsy (sometimes known as 'fitting') can occur in nearly all dog breeds, but nowadays is not commonly found in Labradors. However, fits do arise and conscientious breeders are not blind to the fact. Epilepsy can be of the inherited kind or it can be caused by a variety of other means, such as injury, tumour or illness during puppyhood. The condition can usually be stabilized by drugs, but these must be given for the rest of the dog's life. Again, a reputable breeder will discuss the condition openly.

It is inadvisable to buy two puppies from different kennels before they have had their inoculations. A change of environment means a change of

Hwicci's Herstmonceaux at Tibblestone, born, 1989, by Sh.Ch. Tibblestone the Chorister ex Barrimar Hunipot of Hwicci.

'microbes' and infection can lie dormant until a suitable recipient appears. Personally, I would not purchase two puppies from the same litter unless I had the means to kennel them separately outside. Littermates, whether of the same or different sex are notoriously competitive and as they grow bigger their 'games' become rougher. Serious injury can result if you are not aware of where they are and what they are doing.

Timing

It is essential to consider the correct time to obtain a puppy in the light of your commitments and those of the family. If you are not at home during some of the day or if you are going to plan the initial part of the puppy's home life during the school holidays, you *must* make arrangements for the puppy to be supervised by a knowledgeable person. At the tender age of eight weeks, he must never be left alone for more than an hour at the most. Not only will he pine and become miserable when he awakes – ensuing boredom will lead him to search for solace in chewing, first his toys for a while, then he will progress to furniture and household appliances.

Do not plan holidays for some months after the purchase as the puppy should not be put in kennels or in someone else's care before he is at least six months old; do not plan to take him on long journeys; and do not plan him as a surprise present for someone, who will not be properly prepared for his care, or even be that committed to Labrador ownership. You must discuss your potential puppy ownership with your spouse or partner and all the family some months in advance. Such responsibilities should be shared by all the beneficiaries.

It is not advisable to combine a pregnancy with puppy rearing as these occupations tend to be mutually exclusive. That is to say, the tasks of feeding, house-training and socializing a new puppy are not always compatible with the demands of a teething infant. In short, it is much better to wait until children are approaching school age before embarking on puppy ownership. It will not stop you learning about dogs and ownership, meanwhile. And, you can always borrow a Labrador for a short time if you make a friend of a suitable owner who lives nearby. Responsible dog walkers always make welcome friends.

Temperament

Try to obtain a Labrador with a true, kind temperament. You must see and meet the mother of the litter, and also any brothers and sisters she may have. The dam's nature and outlook is an excellent guide to that of her offspring in later life. If she is exceptionally shy or, in contrast, over-excitable or even aggressive, my advice is not to buy the puppy. I must add a proviso here, which is that some bitches can be very maternal and initially will resent the intrusion of humans into their 'maternity ward'. This is a perfectly natural reaction and must be respected. Eventually, provided that you are quiet and undemanding (and that includes any children who might be with you), curiosity will get the better of her and she will come and fuss you of her own accord. No adverse opinion of the bitch should be formed from such initial wariness.

Age

Never buy a puppy aged less than seven and a half weeks. The brood bitch is by far the better equipped to provide the correct care and upbringing of a small puppy. The stewardship of young animals requires much patience, so why not wait a few days longer. The chances are that you could fail to integrate the puppy into your home and that would spell disaster for both parties.

Sex

Be clear in your mind whether you want a dog or a bitch. As a very general rule, dogs tend to be very affectionate, but can be domineering and territorial when they are approaching maturity (from age about eleven months) if not corrected firmly but kindly. And not many dogs become famous stud-dogs! On the other hand, bitches are more independent, sometimes a little 'sneaky', and they will come into 'season', usually at six monthly intervals. This usually lasts for about three weeks, and consists of intermittent spots of blood from the vulva which can be quite messy. However, the spots are quite water-soluble and can be easily removed with a damp cloth before they are dry. During this time she will be *extremely* attractive – and attracted to – the opposite sex. A period of purdah is necessary to avoid unofficial liaisons! However, bitches can be extremely loyal. Obviously, if you want to start off in the breed with a little showing and, eventually, progress to breeding, you will need a bitch with a good background. Don't be fobbed off with a dog at this stage if breeding is your eventual aim. It is better to buy an older bitch, say between eight and ten months old, if you can get one. But you may have to pay considerably more for her as she will have had her inoculations and may even have had a few modest show wins.

Colour

Generally the difference between Labradors of different colours is purely aesthetic, provided that they have been carefully and sensibly bred. It is a matter of personal preference; traditionally, some sportsmen preferred blacks because they are supposed to be excellent swimmers! They are, usually, but so are the yellows and the chocolates. Sometimes, sportsmen chose yellows because they could be seen more clearly against dark tree roots and foliage, yet blacks show up better against a moorland sky.

Pet or Show

You must decide whether you want a typical Labrador as a family pet or a potential show dog. A carefully reared Labrador puppy, with affectionate, decent-looking, soundly constructed and fit parents, both holding 'clear' hip and eye certificates, should be the 'norm' for all purchasers of Labradors. Animals do not come with guarantees. Breeders, in general, try to do their best for their stock, some may require a short agreement noting that you understand the pitfalls of ownership!

You must be absolutely clear and explain your intentions to the breeders; that you are seriously interested in showing, if the puppy is good enough, for example, or that you will train it to the gun, or that you intend to breed from her in the future. A good breeder will try to provide you with a suitable puppy, but there are no guarantees, so the best you can expect is to buy a soundly reared and bred youngster, do your best for him or her, learn as much as you possibly can about the sphere in which you are interested, and hope! It was a wise man who said, 'You will try to teach your first dog, but end up just loving it. Your second dog will teach you, but you will fail to learn. By the time you are on your third dog, you'll be ready for success.'

Choosing Your Puppy

If you are fortunate enough to be given the choice from more than one puppy in a litter, what should you look for? For my part, I would stand each puppy on a mat on the kitchen table so that its feet do not slip, and look each one in the eye, in turn. The eyes should be clear and bright with dark pigment around the rims. No discharge should be visible in the eye corners, neither should there be any discharge from the nose.

A litter of twelve Tibblestones, five weeks old.
(Rep. by permission of the Gloucestershire Echo.*)*

Hold the puppy's head with your left hand under his chin and very gently widen the eye upwards with your right thumb. Look at the iris, at six weeks old or thereabouts, it should be brown in colour, which as a general rule indicates that the eye will become a nice hazel or dark brown colour as the puppy matures. A fawn, yellow or light grey colour indicates that the mature eye will probably be light, which is undesirable.

The youngster should have a nice, outgoing nature and be happy and waggy. Very gently raise his lips and look at his milk teeth. The top row, even at this age, should lie over the bottom row without an appreciable gap between them. His head should be rounded and the muzzle should not be 'snubby'. His ears should appear 'smallish' rather than large.

Feel the point of his shoulders; they should lie approximately just behind the plane of his elbows. His chest should be nice and round and there should be a space about two fingers wide between his front legs. He should look sturdy and 'square'. His pelt should feel thick and soft and fit him rather loosely, like a good quality sweater. His tail should be good and thick at the root, not thin or weak-looking, and never 'curly'. Finally, his feet should be nice and round and compact, not flat or claw-like.

When he is put on the floor he should run around confidently and brightly. Beware of the runt who heads for the darkest corner of the room.

Usually, one little puppy will look at you directly. Is this the one you have had your eye on? If it is, that's the one. Take a moment to consider; ask yourself the following questions (I make no apologies for the repetition):

Has the mother got a nice temperament (i.e. does she behave like a Labrador?); is she the right type (i.e. does she look like a Labrador?); and transportation (does she – and the puppy– move soundly like a Labrador should?). Use the three Ts – Temperament, Type and Transportation (*see* Chapter 9) – for reference.

When you have made your choice in your mind, ask to see the 'next best' (in your estimation) and compare them nose to nose on the table. Use this 'final view' to satisfy yourself that you have made the right choice and leave it at that. Do not change your mind. And do not allow yourself to be persuaded to alter your view on the way home. I think it is essential to pay a deposit of between one half or a third of the purchase price then and there. Then arrange a suitable time to collect your puppy.

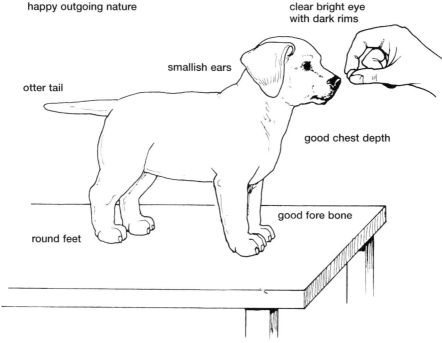

Looking at a puppy for show potential.

49

Documents

When you go to collect your puppy, it is usual to pay the balance of the purchase price. In return you will receive a Kennel Club Registration Certificate, which shows his registered name, his date of birth and also the names of his sire and dam and the status of both parents' hips and eyes. Make sure that the portion on the reverse of the document relating to 'Transfer of ownership' has been signed and dated by the breeder. You will also receive a four- or five-generation pedigree signed by the breeder. This should be on an original form, written or typed out. A photocopy is *not* acceptable.

A vaccination certificate may also be provided, indicating that he has started his series of inoculations, and a list of simple instructions outlining his feeding routine and when he was wormed for the first time (usually at three weeks old) are also necessary. In addition, most Labrador breeders will provide you with a 'survival pack' containing two or three days' supply of the food that he has been used to. This helps to bridge the gap as he adjusts to his new home life.

You should also receive a receipt, and the majority of serious Labrador breeders also arrange an insurance policy covering the life and veterinary care for the first vital few weeks of the puppy's new ownership. Costs may vary and can be for one month, six months or even twelve months. Sometimes the cost of this is added to the purchase price. I think insurance is an essential safeguard, not only for the breeder but for the new owner.

Occasionally, if you are buying a bitch puppy you may be offered 'breeding terms'. Traditionally, this means that you promise to breed from your puppy in due course and offer one or more of the resulting offspring, or the agreed value in cash, to the breeders of your bitch. For my part, breeding terms are best left until you gain more experience of dogs. In any event, written evidence of the terms should be properly drawn up. The Kennel Club publishes guidelines for this arrangement.

The Homeward Journey

You must give a little thought to the puppy's welfare on the journey home. Labrador puppies are strong, agile and *fast* and you could be caught unawares. He is highly unlikely to sleep quietly behind the back seat of the car when all the action is behind the steering wheel. This is a whole new world! There are such things as seat belts for dogs, but they do not fit puppies and I would not advise them anyway. Nor do I recommend that you entrust the new puppy to the loving arms of a small child. In my experience this doubles the problem.

Arrange to collect the puppy before lunch time and take a sensible helper with you. Place a plastic sheet under the dog's blanket and have a roll of of absorbent kitchen paper to hand. A loose bowl of water is unlikely to be needed.

If it is likely that you will need to make an overnight stop on the journey home, book the hotel room in advance and check whether dogs, however small, are allowed in the rooms. If they are, you will need to obtain a travelling cage for the puppy and line the base with newspaper. The best type have a sealed base and solid sides. A fleecy rug is not necessary and could prove dangerously indigestible to the puppy's tummy if he chews it.

If you have arranged to collect your puppy on a lovely summer's day, now is the time to absorb one very important rule: Never leave a dog unattended in a car. DOGS CAN DIE IN HOT CARS. A car can heat up very quickly, even with the windows ajar, and a puppy in a cage would have no chance of survival. So plan very carefully every journey that you make with him on board, so that it is never necessary to leave him in a car.

Summary

1. Buy from a recommended breeder.
2. Know what costs you will incur.
3. Check status of parents' hips and eyes.
4. Meet the puppy's mother (and father, if possible) and check for the three Ts.
5. Don't buy until he is about eight weeks old.
6. Dog or bitch? – Make up your mind before you buy.
7. Plan his arrival in your home with care. Ring your vet when you have collected him and register your puppy with the surgery.
8. Decide what you want of him – company, breeding or competition.
9. Make sure you obtain all the correct documents before you go. Ask when he was wormed and whether he has been vaccinated.
10. Never leave a dog in a car on a warm day. It can be fatal.

4

Puppy Care and Management

Housing

The best place for a new Labrador puppy to sleep in is a cool, not cold, utility room or outhouse with a connecting door. Before you install him, check that there are no dangling electrical leads or rubber water pipes for him to play with. Check also that the plug sockets are out of reach or suitably covered. Also remove any tins of paint, creosote, slug pellets, packets of soap powder or toilet rolls from floor level and store them above waist height. Auto spares, children's plastic toys and rubber boots will also keep a puppy occupied, at considerable expense.

I would not advise kennelling a new puppy outside immediately. He is much more likely to take to an outside kennel at four or five months old when he has settled to his new surroundings and smells. However, it is a good idea to prepare a little outside exercise run for him by fencing off a small part of the garden near to the house. A 'baby gate' will also prove useful; the best ones have an integral sliding gate which will allow you to come and go without effort. A puppy pen is an excellent safe area where he can play outside, for short periods in dry weather, whilst he is very small.

A good sound bed can be made from a tea chest (check inside it for sharp nails) or a strong cardboard carton, one that is not held together by metal staples. Line it with an old blanket folded to fit. Another good type of bed is provided by an airline travel box (not an open cage) which gives him a lovely home to call his own.

Be prepared for him to cry from time to time for the first few nights in his new home. But do not scold him or threaten him. Naturally, he is missing the proximity of his mother and his brothers and sisters. You could try giving him something to cuddle up to such as an old-fashioned stone (crock) water bottle, but not the rubber kind! Fill it with boiling water and let it warm up to blood heat. Test its temperature

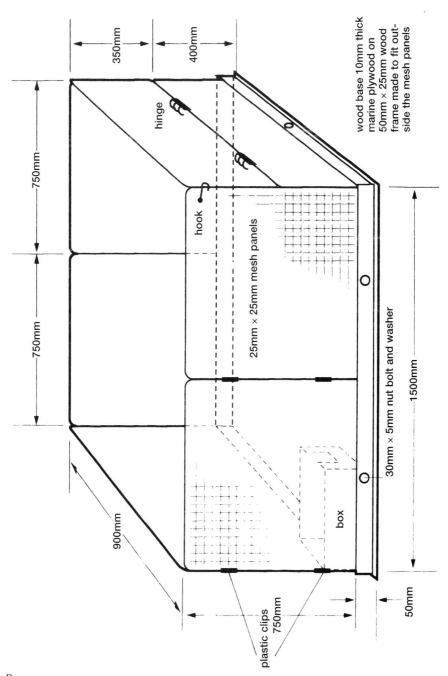

350mm

400mm

wood base 10mm thick
marine plywood on
50mm × 25mm wood
frame made to fit out-
side the mesh panels

hinge

750mm

hook

750mm

25mm × 25mm mesh panels

1500mm

30mm × 5mm nut bolt and washer

900mm

box

50mm

plastic clips
750mm

Puppy run.

with your elbow, then empty the water out and wrap it in an old blanket and put it in his bed.

If he persists in howling, go to him once or twice on the first few nights and give him five minutes of affection and reassurance. Then put him down and leave him to get on with it for the rest of the night if need be. If you relent and let him share your bedroom, bear in mind that it will be difficult to prevent his doing so in the future when he is a large adult. And he is unlikely to grow a thick coat if he is allowed to sleep in a centrally heated room.

Safety

Before you let your puppy have the run of the garden, you must check all fences and gates. Examine them carefully for holes through which a puppy could escape, maybe on to the road. Don't bodge up the holes with a piece of tin, make a good job of it.

You will have checked that there are no chemicals in the garage or utility room when you prepared the puppy's bedroom. Now look in the garden shed, the greenhouse and the wood store and stables if you have them. Before you collect your puppy you *must* stop using slug-bait, sodium chlorate, paraquat or rat poisons in the garden or in any outhouses.

Do take extra care when you reverse the car out of the garage. Are you sure you know where your puppy is? The chances are, if he is not in his run or in the house, he is trying to come with you. Do not take it on trust that someone else has shut him up safely.

Swimming pools are potential death traps to all puppies because there is no way, once he has fallen in, that he can climb out. If the pool has a *secure* cover, put it on before you collect him, otherwise it is essential to fence off all the swimming area and make it out of bounds to dogs. I know from a personal acquaintance that the consequences of such a disaster are terrible, almost beyond recall.

In the house, especially in those rooms where he is likely to go, put *all* houseplants out of his reach; some are poisonous to dogs (and small children). Now is the time to fix any loose locks on kitchen cupboards, fridge door, and so on. Some very expensive saucepans have lovely heat-proof handles, which somehow appeal to a dog's taste. Whilst on the subject of plastic, remember that a puppy will love to eat children's toys (especially when they have jam on them!) but plastics do not show up on X-rays.

Feeding

At eight weeks of age a typical Labrador puppy will need four meals each day. Buy him a stainless steel dish of his very own. One about seven inches (18cm) in diameter is a good size. Personally, I prefer to feed a diet based on balanced proportions of meat and biscuit or a biscuit-type product such as a proprietary puppy mixer meal made by one of the large pet food manufacturers. There are many kinds of 'all-in-one' or complete pet foods which claim to be excellent for rearing puppies, even from the age of three or four weeks old. I have never found them to be completely successful because they are not always appetising enough to every puppy in the litter, hence someone usually appears to lag behind in gaining sufficient weight. However, many breeders swear by their favourite kind of food and achieve the most excellent results which cannot be denied. If your puppy has been fed in this way, I would counsel you to continue following closely the instructions supplied by the manufacturer. At the same time, enquire from the breeder whether any modifications or simplifications have been made to the instructions and proceed along the lines suggested. By no means try to make any swift changes to an established feeding routine or diet which has probably been devised over a long period: at the least it will cause a tummy upset and diarrhoea.

As your puppy grows, keep your eyes open and your mind alert to any minor warning signs: a frequent refusal of his food, for example, or a very pronounced increase in his thirst, or depraved appetite, that is the eating of faeces (coprophagia), sometimes known as 'yaffling'. Another sign that all may not be well is extreme looseness (fluidity) of faeces, with or without traces of blood. All these conditions may be the result of incorrect or unbalanced diet and you should contact your vet for his advice.

A Typical Diet

This diet is one that I have used for many years. It is based on meat and biscuit with occasional vitamin supplements. If you have already commenced with a proprietary all-in-one puppy food, which contains all the necessary vitamins and trace elements, use the example below to make comparisons with the relative amounts which you are feeding so that you keep up with the increasing quantities which he will need as he grows on. You must follow the manufacturer's instructions. Do not give added vitamin and mineral supplements to an all-in-one food.

Up to Twelve Weeks Old
8.00 a.m. Give him one wheat cake cereal (Weetabix) and a teacupful (⅓pt/200ml) of warm milk which you can sweeten with glucose, if you like.
Noon One teacupful of fine wholemeal digestive puppy meal or similar, plus about a teacupful of beef mince or ox cheek cut up very finely and a teaspoonful of cooked vegetables. Soak the meal in hot water or gravy for ten minutes and pour off the residue. Cut up his meat into small pieces, add it to the meal and let it cool before you put it down for him.
4.00 p.m. This is his milk feed. Give him about a cupful of warmed rice pudding or a proprietary puppy milk thickened with baby cereal, which may be sweetened as above. Sugar is to be avoided. You can add one mashed hard-boiled egg to this feed occasionally.
8.00 p.m. This meal is a repeat of the noon meal, to which you should add a little (no more than a level teaspoonful) of a general vitamin supplement. Follow the recommendations for dosage on the tin and avoid the temptation to add a little more for luck. (As with garden fertilizer, overdosing can do much more harm than good.)

As he grows up you can give him two or three dog biscuits occasionally. These are best given as a reward for good behaviour. Do not feed him after 8 p.m. because this will not enable him to be clean during the night. Remember he will not want to blot his copy book. Give him a strong rubber bone to chew on after this time.

You must remember to increase the amount of food gradually as he grows. As Labrador breeders ourselves, it is sometimes heartbreaking to see the results of our endeavours return with their proud owners for a chat and a cup of tea. One was very proud to point out that the dog still needed only one tin of 'Happychap' a day to keep his coat glossy. There was certainly plenty of coat, but there wasn't much Labrador! The moral is, feed him plenty but watch closely what is produced in the way of faeces. If stools are firm, such that they may be shovelled into a waste bucket easily, your feeding is well-balanced; if not the chances are you are feeding him a little too much!

From Twelve Weeks Old
8.00 a.m. Increase to two Weetabix in one and a half cups (15fl.oz/440ml) of warm milk.
12.30 p.m. One and a half cups of mincemeat or ox cheek or half a tin of tinned meat, all cut up small and one and a half cups of soaked biscuit prepared as before.

6.00 p.m. Repeat as for 12.30 p.m. Make sure he has a bowl of water to drink. If you think he needs a little more water, colour it with a little milk.
9.30 p.m. A handful of dog biscuits.

At six months old, he should be having three good meals per day (as above) plus a snack at 9.30 p.m. The quantities should be increased to include at least 1lb (500g) of meat in total (for example, ox cheek or minced tripe) plus the other essential vitamins and minerals. (Remember that recommended supplement doses must not be exceeded.) Minced tripe may be obtained in frozen form from good pet shops. Always defrost it overnight. Proprietary vacuum-packed meat can also be obtained from a good pet shop. These are not deep-frozen, but must be stored in a cool place. When opened, treat them as you would fresh meat.

If he is not a good eater for any reason, a few meals of minced tripe plus gravy-soaked biscuits nearly always do the trick. Or an egg custard. And, always have a bowl of clean water available.

At nine months of age, cut out the milk meal above, but still have plenty of water available. Give him his first meat meal at about 9.00 a.m. rather than at 12.30 p.m. You will probably find that he now needs a larger dish (one about 10in/25cm diameter will serve him well).

For supper he should be having a good heaped cup of biscuit meal (soaked as per directions) plus a few cooked vegetables and *at least* 1lb (500g) of meat as above each day. Don't forget to add a vitamin supplement (dose as instructions) if you are feeding tripe.

Sometimes puppies can get a little tummy rash as they are growing up. This may be accompanied by a slight lack of pigmentation of the eyes and mouth. This could be because his diet is too rich. Labradors, although they can be very energetic dogs, do not burn up food energy at a great rate unless they are very active during the shooting season. Consequently, they do not need a high-protein diet when they have finished growing. Sometimes, reducing the protein content of his food by say, feeding minced tripe or white chicken-based meat will do the trick. Alternatively, replacing the adult-size biscuit meal with small-bite mixer can be effective.

Many complete foods contain flakes of maize which have been known to cause a little rash or 'overheating of the blood' as it is called. In the extreme, changing the diet to a rice-based cereal food can remedy this.

A Labrador puppy should grow into an affectionate, rounded, strong and active friend. I would suggest that you build up his intake with increasing amounts of good meat or tripe until the age of eighteen months and then give him gradually less thereafter.

Ch. Gallybob Caraway, born 1981, by Sh.Ch. Stajantors Honest John ex Arrowshaft Squires Daughter of Gallybob.

Points to Remember
- Never feed a dog poultry bones, potatoes, white bread, sweets or cake.
- Give treats especially manufactured for dogs instead of sweets or tit-bits.
- Always have a bowl of clean water available.

Teething

Your puppy will begin to lose his milk teeth when he is about four months old. These are pushed out naturally by the adult teeth growing beneath them and it is unlikely that you will ever see one. You will, however, notice a few sore gums and his tendency to chew his toys with a wet mouth. Sometimes his ears will take on a particular 'set', giving him a quizzical expression. It looks rather comical but is no fun for the dog! Respect his sore mouth and watch that he does not neglect his food. He should soon have his old appetite back. By the time he is six months old he will have forty-two permanent teeth: In the upper jaw, these will comprise six incisors, two canines, eight premolars and four molars; in the lower jaw, there will be six incisors, four canines, eight premolars, and six molars. Four of these molars, known as the carnassial teeth and located behind the premolars of each jaw, are noticeably larger than the others. They have more than one root and are deeply embedded in the jaw, which makes extraction (when necessary) difficult. Human dentition has no precise equivalent of the carnassials.

58

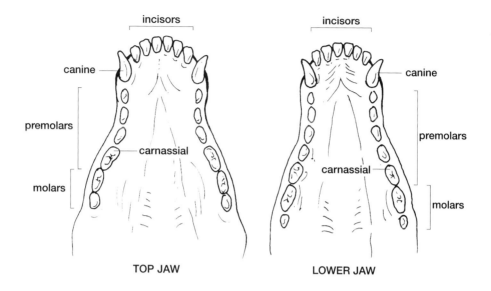

Dentition of the adult dog.

The incisors should be set closely together in order to nip and bite like scissors: the upper teeth should closely overlap the lower incisors and be set squarely in the jaw. This is most important both for consuming gristle and sinewy kinds of food and, for bitches, to enable them to remove their new-born puppies from the birth membrane without harming them. The canine teeth are used to tear and shred bulky pieces of food, especially the meat portion of his ration. The premolars and molars are used to grind hard food and cereals, while the extra strong carnassial molars are used to crack and crush bones. A diagram of the teeth can be seen in Chapter 9.

Vaccinations

All dogs must have a series of injections to protect them from the five most common canine infectious diseases. These are: distemper, hepatitis, leptospirosis, parvovirus and kennel cough. Consult your vet as to the best time to give the injections and follow his advice. Usually the

first shot is administered at about eight weeks old followed by a second at twelve weeks. A booster injection will then follow on twelve months later. Keep your puppy on your own ground until two weeks after the last injection. Do not take him for walks in the park, or to see friends or relatives until he has had his last jab at twelve weeks. It pays to take extra care up to six months old. If you are in touch with the 'doggy fraternity' through training classes or similar, you will learn when to avoid local outbreaks of kennel cough, for example.

Parasites

Worming

Your Labrador puppy will have been wormed several times since birth. The breeder's instructions will contain details of the worming medicine. Worming is done typically at three weeks, five weeks and seven weeks old, but you should contact your vet as all have their own methods which you must adhere to. Worm again for roundworms under his supervision, but not during the period when he is having his injections. He should then be wormed for tapeworms annually. Again, be instructed by your vet. All puppies contain worms which they will have inherited from their mother. Always wash your hands, and those of your children, after handling your dog and preparing his food, especially when you have small children in the family. Pregnant women should take extra care. Basic cleanliness is very simple.

Fleas

It is just possible that, in the process of grooming a new puppy you will encounter a flea! I will go further than that. It is highly likely that in the process of grooming your puppy you will encounter a flea! Especially if you have other pets such as cats in the house or you have been to dog training classes. Apart from the obvious irritation to your dog and possibly yourself, fleas can cause skin problems as some dogs are allergic to their bites. Contact your vet immediately and use a modern treatment which is easily administered directly to the surface of the skin. It will also be necessary to spray his bed and blanket with a different preparation in order to rid the dog's environment of flea eggs and larvae. Again, your vet will advise you.

Parasites and their treatment are discussed further in Chapter 12.

Discipline and Early Training

All Labradors are capable of being trained. They have a great deal of 'dog sense', a large amount of inherited obedience (the will to please) and an inherent retrieving ability. The shortest time spent, even as little as five minutes every other day, will do immense good for his ego, because it tells him you care. And this matters very much to him. You must try to develop his abilities to your mutual advantage. You are the leader of his 'pack' and he needs the reassurance of this if he is not to feel insecure at first in his new home. Later, as he matures, he will naturally explore the possibilities of being master in his own house, if you have not trained him otherwise. This can make for great difficulties because you then have to try to put him in his place without him being able to understand why. It is far better to establish the hierarchy of your pack from the beginning. An obedient dog is a happy dog and a much closer friend of his master's.

There are three sound 'Don'ts' which may be applied to the training of a very new puppy, and for which I am indebted to Lady Barlow:

- Don't wait until it is too late for him to be clean – put him out early and often.
- Don't ever allow him to be free on his own for any reason.
- Don't ever use a choke training lead on a young puppy, use a collar and lead.

I would add another 'Don't' which is for your benefit:

- Don't *ever* hit your dog. No matter how strongly you feel at the time. Simply, he will not understand you.

He will respond to the tone of your voice and the nearer you can imitate the growl his mother made when he was naughty, the more he will respond. If you feel he is becoming more and more unruly, first ask yourself, 'Am I setting *him* a fixed routine, i.e. feed, out, sleep, out, play, feed, out, sleep, out, play, and so on? Is he getting enough food? Is he getting enough sleep?' If you are sure that you are not at fault, you must improve your technique in your 'brood-bitch' role.

When he misbehaves in a minor way – stealing from the vegetable rack, for instance – pick him up firmly by the scruff of the neck with one hand, but making sure you support his rump with the other. Give his scruff a little shake (as the bitch would have done), and growl, 'Bed!' at him as you place him in his bed. Whilst he is still submitting, repeat the growl, 'Bed!' (which sounds like 'Bad!') and leave him.

61

Should he persist in stealing, or worse, you must reinforce your 'growl' with the aid of a rolled-up newspaper. This is the ultimate weapon, but I must repeat: don't ever be tempted to hit him with it, he will not understand. Strike your hand with the newspaper and use the sharp whack to reinforce your growl of 'Bed!' or 'Bad!' He will soon learn to relate the sight of a rolled newspaper with 'She (or he) who must be obeyed'!

House Training

When your Labrador puppy lived in kennel surroundings with the rest of the litter, he probably trained himself to perform on sawdust or newspaper. Check with the breeder which material he was used to using. If you are in doubt, spread a few newspapers near the back door; do not use single sheets as they are not absorbent enough. Usually he will oblige on these and you can experiment over the first few days by moving them through the door and finally outside, until he 'gets the message'.

Always feed him in the same place and at the same times and he will develop a routine. Keep him out of the food preparation area until you can trust him unsupervised. After every meal or after he has been asleep and awakens, put him in his little run outside straight away. Stay with him and praise him when he performs. Give him a lot of encouragement. In this way, he will quickly learn to be clean in the house. Should he have an accident, do not be cross with him; just say, 'No', firmly, and take him outside. He will not necessarily perform again but he will soon link the action to the location.

Whoops!

A puppy's faeces should be firm, with the shape and consistency of a small sausage which, in general terms, indicates that the diet and quantities of food are correct. A loose formation means that he is having too much food at one time. Reduce the amounts given to correct the balance. If a complete food is used, soak it well beforehand in boiling water, feed it cool, but halve the amount given at one time until he produces the right kind of consistency.

Restrain yourself and the other members of the household from disturbing him when he is asleep. Let sleeping puppies lie. He may look extremely cuddly, but avoid surprising him when he is dreaming.

Do not ruin your Labrador's temperament in the early stages by trying to house-train him too sternly. Let him make the odd mistake and show him where you would like him to perform. Study his mannerisms when he awakes and after he has been fed and put him in his outside run so that he knows where it is acceptable to relieve himself. And make sure you praise the successes highly and the mistakes too. In the event of a 'serious' mistake when he is older, take him firmly by the scruff and growl 'No!', as his mother would have done. He will take this very seriously indeed.

The same form of correction should be applied to chewing. In the early stages it is very natural that he should want to chew to allow his baby teeth to be removed naturally and his new teeth to be firmly established. Give him plenty of chewable toys, leather off-cuts or hide 'chews'. As a rule, I do not recommend plastic for Labradors to play with.

Grooming

Your Labrador will love a daily grooming with a good quality hairbrush. The best kind has tufts of bristle set in a pliable rubber backing. Do not use a wire 'slicker' brush, the sort that has a flat hard-backed handle, as this will tear out his undercoat. Hold him gently by his collar and gently brush him starting with his neck and chest. always brush him in the direction his coat grows. Try to teach him to stand still while he is being groomed and don't allow him to steal the brush! When you have completed his back, rump and tail, finish him off with a dry chamois leather, smoothing him all over. This has the action of buffing up the natural oils in his coat stimulated by the brushing. You will be surprised at the 'bloom' you can get on him and he will feel very proud of himself.

It is important to get your puppy accustomed to grooming and handling at an early age. It will pay dividends later on when he has to visit the vet or be examined in the show ring.

63

Lead-training

There are several schools of thought regarding the correct lead for a puppy. Personally, I prefer a good leather collar about ¾ inch (20mm) wide. This should be fastened fairly tight, that is, so that two adult fingers may still be inserted between the puppy's neck and the collar. A good-quality leather lead with a stout dog-clip is the other necessity. However, expensive leather collars and leads are considered a gourmet treat by all Labradors! Guard them with care and hang them well out of reach.

Training or check-chains are useful for the more active youngster. But, a word of warning here, they must be used with very great care. If you put a puppy on a check-chain without careful supervision you could literally choke him. Also, there is a tendency to jerk a check-chain too viciously if a youngster misbehaves, which could dislocate the neck bones, trap a nerve or, unthinkably, result in a broken neck. Check-chains may be used with care on an older dog, say at twelve months old. In any case, it is essential that a check-chain is correctly fitted if it is not to prove dangerous even in light hands (*see* Chapter 6).

When your puppy begins to go for short walks on a lead, that is when he is about four months old, begin to teach him six simple commands, one at a time as follows:

1. 'HEEL.' As you set off, give the command and at the same time give a tug on the lead and make him walk quietly on your left hand side. Do this for about three weeks until he has got the hang of it. Do not proceed to No. 2 until you are in command.

2. 'SIT.' On this command, push his bottom gently but firmly to the ground while holding the lead in your right hand. Repeat the procedure a few times on each walk at an appropriate place, such as the kerb.

3. 'LEAVE.' This command should be accompanied by a sharp tug on the lead. If you are confident, he will (he must) learn to ignore other dogs.

4. 'HERE.' This is the very beginning of his retrieving training. Start by letting him walk to the extent of a lead about 8ft (2.5m) long. Then gently draw him to you and give him a tit-bit. Repeat the exercise at greater distances. An extender lead, which works on a spring-returned reel, allowing a puppy a range of up to about 11yds (10m), is useful. Later, when he is six or seven months old, you can incorporate it into retriever training, enabling you to coax him back to you for a reward.

Make sure he is obedient before you let him off the lead in a public place. If you have any doubts, keep him on the lead.

When you are both confident that you have mastered the above:

5. 'DOWN.' This is necessary when you want him to rest in one place until you need him. Put him at the Sit and let him settle. Then, take his front paws and gently ease him down to the lying position with the command 'Down'. He will resist you at first, but do not force him. If it is not working, do not get into a wrestling match. Wait until he is about to drop of his own free will and give the command 'Down' as he does so. When he is down (even if he was going to lie by himself) your praise will encourage him to link the action with the command.

6. 'STAY.' This command allows you to leave your dog after he has obeyed either 'Sit' or 'Down' and still has your attention. This is a difficult act for a dog at first because instinctively he will want to follow you. In order to understand what you want him to do, he will interpret the tone of your voice. If you adopt a different tenor to your voice (even a little hint of reprimand in it) it will jolt him slightly, even to the extent of making him think that you do not want him near to you (which is true, for the moment). Therefore, on the command 'Stay' you must use a sharp tone of voice and slowly move away from him, repeating the command to encourage him to remain either at the Sit or Down, whichever position he has adopted earlier. This requires a fair degree of practice and you must be patient. Give him a day at least between sessions for learning commands 5 and 6 so that he does not become stale.

There are many excellent training schools for puppies once they are over about five months old. Obviously, training for competition such as, obedience, agility, ring-craft (for shows), or gundog field trials is specialized and you will need to check out the appropriate classes held in your area. Contact your local canine society or the Kennel Club. There are also some excellent videos which may help you get started.

Exercising a Youngster

About a week after the last injection your puppy will be ready for a few short walks each day. Try to keep to the same walk times each day. He

Thrumsdorn Braydon, born 1987, by Ch. Carpenny Chevalier ex Thrumsdorn Seraphina.

will also need to go out last thing, before he goes to bed. This will help him to establish a routine and encourage his house-training.

If you are not prepared to take him out at least two or three times a day, you should not have a dog! However, a Labrador does not need a *vast* amount of exercise, especially when he is young and growing. He must not be over-exercised, particularly before his joints have formed and while his muscles are immature. He does not need to be walked for three or four miles per day and neither do you, and certainly not before he is eighteen months old. I do not give prolonged exercise to youngsters under eight or nine months old. A walk around a small paddock, or a few minutes of free running allows them to let off steam. Under six months old no puppies should leave the garden or dog-run on their own. This will reduce the likelihood of their injuring themselves, straining muscles or, worse, getting into trouble.

An extending lead allows a puppy range of up to about 11 yards (10m) while enabling you to keep him under control. It must be clipped to a well-fitted collar to give absolute security. When he is older and ready for more strenuous exercise, a thick rope slip-lead is ideal (and it doesn't hurt your fingers, should he catch you unawares!).

If you have horses or ponies, do not be tempted to exercise a youngster behind them, although when he is mature and fit, and probably over eighteen months old, a trained obedient Labrador is perfectly capable of following his mounted handler for an hour over common land. Personally, I do not approve of riding with loose Labradors near a busy road at any time. While most (but not all) drivers slow down for horses, you cannot count on their doing so, and even less on their seeing the dog at all because he is too near to the ground.

During exercise, it is a great temptation to throw whatever is nearest to hand for your Labrador to 'retrieve'. You should try to resist throwing sticks, stones or other rubbish, in spite of the dog's willingness and seemingly boundless energy. Sticks may be of the dry brittle kind and Labradors, especially young ones are invariably clumsy. As a result he could sustain a terrible injury if he falls on to the stick in his mouth. Stones should never be used as playthings: they might be swallowed and are likely to chip the teeth. Furthermore, such bad habits are almost impossible to cure if you decide to progress to more advanced training. For playtime, use an old tennis ball, a 6in (15cm) rubber ring or a cloth dummy. All of these can be borrowed, or bought from a reputable pet-goods retailer.

Labradors love water and enjoy a swim with a purpose. However, the water should not be too deep, and fast-flowing currents, locks, weirs and mill-races should be avoided at all costs. (It is surprising how many dogs are encouraged to swim in harbours and marinas.) It is common sense to avoid stretches polluted with oil and those backwaters where small boats and motor cruisers are often being manoeuvred by inexperienced holidaymakers.

If you have a Labrador that obviously enjoys swimming – which is quite likely since water is his second 'natural' environment – remember that not all Labradors may be used to the shock of entering cold water, especially in early summer when the days may be hot and sunny yet the water courses (and, of course, the sea) may be still very cold. An early swim in cold river water, or even a prolonged plunge in a domestic paddling pool, which is not followed by a complete drying-out, might lead to his catching a chill or kennel cough, if his resistance is low; or it could result in a type of cramp, which will give him a stiff shoulder or stifle joint, or even a stiff tail. This last condition is painful as it makes the tail droop from just behind the root, almost as though it has been broken. It is a sorry sight and frequently prevents him from competing in the next test or show. The safest remedy is confinement and rest for a couple of days, plus a little extra tender loving care, although if the condition persists you must call the vet.

5

Adult Care and Management

If you keep your dog or dogs indoors, much of the information contained in the sections on housing, safety and exercise in Chapter 4 will apply equally to the management of adolescent and adult Labradors. However, if you intend to kennel your dogs outside – perhaps because you have too many to accommodate easily indoors! – there are a number of other factors that will have to be taken into account if you are to ensure the general good health and happiness of your dogs.

Labradors are good-sized hardy dogs who thrive on an outdoor lifestyle. They are well suited to living in kennels but I think it is asking too much to expect a single dog, with the intelligence and family instincts of a Labrador, to enjoy being kennelled alone. Two dogs, or a dog and bitch will share a kennel happily, even if they are separated by a partition wall.

Outdoor Kennelling

The minimum size of kennel compartment for one dog should be about 4ft wide and 6ft deep (1.2 × 1.8m). Two dogs together need a compartment at least 5 × 7ft (1.5 × 2.1m). However, if you decide to buy a new kennel or have one made, it is false economy to cater for two single dogs under one roof. The chances are that you will keep a second (or third!) Labrador eventually. In the meantime, the spare section will make an excellent tack room for storing bulk food and equipment. Personally, I prefer the wooden 'corridor' type of kennel with separate dog runs leading from each compartment.

The overall length of the kennel shown in the diagram is 16ft (4.8m) and the width (including a corridor of decent size) is 8ft 6in (2.55m). Each exercise run is just over 5ft (1.5m) wide and 7ft (2.1m) deep, with 6ft (1.8m) high walls. There is a reasonable amount of room in each compartment for a 'double bed' made of heavyweight plastic material plus space for the occasional 'accident' when the dogs are shut up, say in very bad weather.

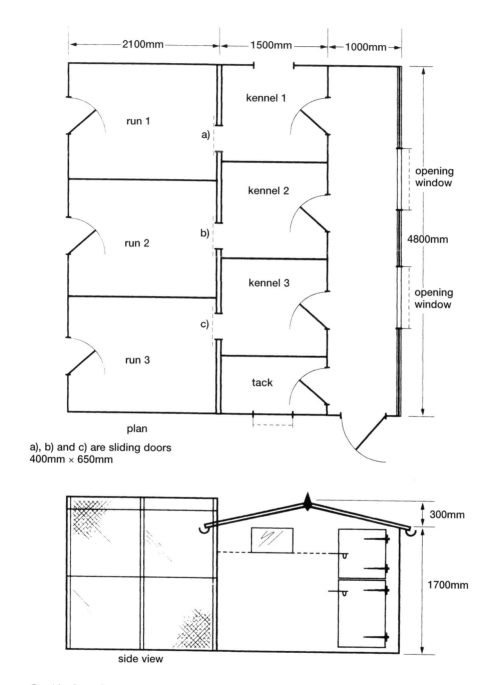

a), b) and c) are sliding doors
400mm × 650mm

Corridor kennel.

The height of the kennel roof should be at least 5ft 6in. (about 1.7m) at its lowest point. It is a matter of taste, but I think a double pitched roof is the least trouble to maintain, especially if it is of felted board construction. The roof boards should ideally be insulated with poly-styrene or fibreboard sheets. If you specify a wooden kennel make sure the boards are laid together tongue and groove (not ship-lap) to mini-mize draughts. The boards should be a minimum of ¾in (2cm) thick. Lesser boards are not strong enough to contain Labradors.

Again, it is personal preference, but I prefer a wooden construction to galvanized steel, brick or concrete; expense is usually a serious con-sideration and the last two are very costly although they are of course permanent and long-lasting. Wood feels warmer to the touch and suf-fers less condensation but it is less hard-wearing than the others. A stout concrete floor is preferable, and is easy to keep clean when it has been treated with a rubberized non-slip finish. There is also the advan-tage that wood appeals to the residents for its chewability. This is reas-suring even if it is not economical in the long run!

All kennels should have good-sized windows to allow plenty of nat-ural light. The end windows should open to give good ventilation in hot weather and they should not extend below 5ft (1.5m) from the floor, otherwise they will be within reach of the dogs' paws.

Inside the kennel the partitions should be about 5ft (1.5m) high and solid wood (or brick), not chain-link or steel mesh. This allows the occupants to hear each other but does not allow for direct contact. It is also easier to keep clean. The doors should open inwards and be secured by positive sliding bolts on the outside. We all know of the Labradors who can open doors: stable doors, front doors and even bedroom doors.

The kennel should be lit by two fluorescent tubes mounted well out of the way of broom handles or other equipment. If you intend to heat the kennels at a later date (not necessary for adult Labradors) you will need one electric plug socket per compartment fitted at a height of 6ft (1.8m) above the floor, well out of reach of the dogs. Heating lamps of the 'dull-emitter' kind, such as those used by pig breeders are eco-nomical and robust. These must be fitted at the height recommended by the manufacturer.

The dogs should be able to enter their runs by 'pop-holes' leading from the kennel compartments. The pop-hole should be fitted with a sliding door, operated by a wire running to a handle at the front of the dog run, so that the compartments can be closed up at night to prevent draughts and to keep the dogs in during bad weather. The runs should be made from 1½in (40mm) square, heavy-duty, ⅛in (3mm) thick weld-mesh fastened to stout angle-section steel supports. There should be a door at the far end of each run to allow access for cleaning. The surface of the run should be inclined away from the kennel to allow good drainage. At the bottom of each of the outer walls of the run should be built a low wall about 2ft (60cm) high. This wall will allow the dogs to lie out of the wind on their wooden pallets. Also, the walls facilitate better cleaning of the run because muck and leaves can be swept clean-ly away instead of lodging in the weld-mesh.

I think it is essential for dogs to 'feel the wind in their hair' but pro-longed exposure to draughts will lead to weight loss and rheumatism. Hence, the kennel should be sited so that the runs are on the leeward side relative to the prevailing wind. Generally, this would suggest the south side, except in coastal areas where there may be frequent south-westerlies. Before deciding on the site of a kennel try to envisage the location from the dogs' point of view. They like to be able to see some human activity when they are in their runs, so if you can cater for this, while avoiding the direction of the cold wind and the potentially hot summer conditions, you will probably satisfy all parties.

Over the years, we have all tried different kinds of kennels. The dogs have adapted well because, basically, all they require is a warm bed and a dry, draught-free run under cover. If you should be fortunate

Sh.Ch. Squire Harvey of Allenie, born 1980, by Sh.Ch. Stajantors Honest John ex Stajantors Pearl.

71

enough to have a spare stable or out-house to convert, or a cleaned-up pig-sty, the main thing to remember is that, generally, these have too much head-room which will lead to a significant heat loss in winter. The solution is either to install a false roof of hardboard supported on a light timber frame, or to build a double-bed box about 4ft (1.2m) square by 5ft (1.5m) high in each compartment (dimensions as before). The bed box should have a hinged front panel about 1ft (30cm) deep to allow access for cleaning.

Bedding

Most kennelled labradors are bedded on straw, even if it can be a haven for 'wildlife in miniature'. I have found that, provided the straw is good quality wheat straw (not barley or oat straw) and the bed is regularly sprayed (monthly) with a pest deterrent especially formulated for the treatment of bedding, there is not a problem with his method of bedding. However, avoid bales that contain an abundance of wheat husks and grain, both of which have sharp points which can cause them to lodge in the dense coats of black Labradors and might initiate a sore place. (For some reason yellow Labradors seem to be less troubled by this than are blacks.) Other useful bedding materials include paper 'straw', which is obtainable in large bales. Newspaper is a cheap alternative although sometimes the ink gets on to the dogs' coats; having said this, shredded newspaper is excellent for puppy boxes where it has to be changed frequently. I would not recommend using old clothes, old blankets or rugs, mainly because they are extremely difficult to keep clean and positively encourage the breeding of fleas and other pests and crawlies.

It is worth pointing out here that even if you keep your Labrador indoors, it will be necessary occasionally to treat his bedding and surrounding areas with a suitable insecticide: all dogs will at some stage pick up a flea.

Food Storage

If you keep a number of Labradors, it is most economical to buy your dog biscuit and complete or 'all-in-one' foods in bulk. The same advice is true for frozen foods, such as minced tripe, although you will of course need a separate freezer for storing it. Fresh food, such as marrow bone and minced meat can also be frozen. In the case of dry foods you must use new resealable airtight containers or you will attract all manner of vermin. Full-sized heavy-duty plastic dustbins make good containers because the better-quality ones have well-fitting lids and do not have crevices that attract dirt.

Cleaning

The usual daily routine starts with cleaning out the 'bedrooms' first thing every morning: minor accidents are cleared up, bed straw fluffed or renewed and water pots rinsed out and refilled. (Usually the eldest Labrador will accompany me to see the job's done correctly!)

During the week it is best to follow a strict routine for daily cleaning. I call it; beds, bowls, walls and floors. Thus, on Monday the beds are brushed clean and refilled with fresh straw; on Tuesday, each water bowl is scrubbed out with hot water before filling with fresh water; on Wednesday, the walls are cleaned of mud and other splashes; on Thursday food supplies are checked and notes made for the monthly order; on Friday, the floors are cleaned, hosed down and sprayed with a strong disinfectant, after which fresh wood shavings are scattered to give a thick carpet on the concrete, and the kennel is termed 'turned round' ready for the weekend.

The kennel roof and guttering should be checked for leaks each spring and the compartments cleaned and painted to a height of about 4ft (1.2m) with white emulsion paint. Often a kick-strip is painted with black bitumen paint about 12in (30cm) high around the base of the internal walls.

Managing the Kennel Residents

In a kennel, dogs and bitches impose their own hierarchy which makes for stability and establishes a 'code of behaviour' for all the kennel members to follow. This makes it possible for the residents to get on with each other and will mean that a good equable temperament will be passed from generation to generation. If you have a joint boundary with a neighbour whose dog may have a dubious nature or a penchant for 'visiting', erect a thick board fence to prevent your dogs from being disturbed unnecessarily. The added privacy will also stop the occasional stray or farm dogs from unsettling your Labradors by 'baiting' them through the wire. It may start as innocent play but if not controlled can develop into a nasty game. If it is allowed to continue it will ruin your dogs' temperaments by making them feel threatened, with the consequent arousal of your dogs' guarding instincts, which can lead to aggression. My advice is, don't let it happen – erect a fence first!

Do not exercise your dog when you know you are likely to meet an unruly, aggressive guard dog or a snappy sheepdog. Use another route for your walks. You and your dogs will not improve the aggressor's temperament, rather the reverse, because Nature does not work that way. For the same reason, avoid the training class which has a battery of shrieking toy-dogs just inside the door. Such displays are no benefit to a young puppy. Try to treat all your dogs the same when you are handling them individually, but, remember to respect their hierarchy and pack instincts. In this way you will reduce the chances of jealousy arising. However, *you* must be the pack leader, but, beneath you will be the 'shop foreman' or 'ward sister', (the top Dog or Bitch). He must be backed up in his decisions and likes and dislikes. In general, dogs are more tolerant and relaxed, but bitches are sticklers for protocol! Do not be tempted to impose your own views about who should be placed where in the hierarchy. Dogs do not understand 'fairness' in the way that we do, and your interference will only encourage confusion and resentment. So, allow the top bitch to choose her kennel mate (and sometimes her kennel). She will be fed first, exercised first and be the first to have her straw changed. Subservient to her will be the 'second bitch'. She will have her seasons quietly and cleanly (so you may have trouble detecting them). She may even come into milk to assist her superior if the litter is large. Provided that you and your family, especially the very youngest members respect your dogs' chosen arrangements you will not sow the seeds of jealousy in the kennel.

Labradors like to have their own places to eat, where they are not disturbed. But they need not be enclosed, often each will have his or her own corner of the run or kennel. Try to keep them to their own places. Similarly, all dogs have their own toilet areas for preference. If you can impose on their choosing, try to influence them away from the entrance to the run and the least accessible corners of the kennel!

Another important consideration for the Labrador owner who has a number of kennelled dogs is noise. You must try to keep this to a minimum, even if you live in the middle of fifty acres of orchard! An established breeder and judge of Scottish Terriers gave me some good advice some years ago: 'Dogs that can't see people, don't bark.' As a rule, this is true: if you have a joint boundary like a good high wall, a stout fence or a thick band of trees between your dogs and the general public, it will cut down the normal noisy excitement of feeding times and also prevent your dogs from being excited unnecessarily by outside disturbances.

Kennelled dogs do not bark during the hours of darkness unless they are upset and disturbed by sights or sounds that they do not

Time to take the Diant washing in.

understand. If the barking continues for more than ten minutes or so, you will have to find out what is wrong. It may be only a minor incident – perhaps a starling trapped in the corridor or a dripping tap causing a wet pool in one of the dog's compartments – but it could be an emergency. My advice is: always check it out.

Kennelled dogs need a good walk or a run in the paddock twice per day, even if the weather is cold and frosty. The dogs should work up a good pace and return relaxed and smiling. Put them in their kennels and allow them to cool down slowly in their straw beds: do not put them straight into their runs where they will chill off, especially if there is a cold wind blowing.

Exercise Runs

Whether or not the dogs are kennelled outside, many Labrador owners set aside a paved or concreted area that the dogs can use as a common exercise run. These are extremely useful for confining dogs for short periods of time while you are out, while allowing them the freedom that cannot be given them indoors. Ideally, such a run should be about 20ft (6m) by 20ft (6m) and have a surrounding fence at least 5ft (1.5m) high. In one corner there should be a small covered area which will give shade or some protection from the rain when needed. It is also essential to have a good-sized drinking bowl fitted in a holder and replenished regularly. The gate, which might be of the tennis court type, should have a good sliding bolt or stable latch with a safety hook provided. This ensures that the dogs will be safely contained, without being shut in while you are out. The overall siting of this run is important and the suggestions regarding the positioning of the kennel set out above should apply.

Diet

The adult or adolescent dog over eighteen months old needs a good maintenance diet to keep him healthy and active. From now on breakfast may be reduced to a 'token meal' of say, eight or ten dog biscuits. Don't forget to give him fresh water every day. He should have his main meal at 5 p.m., or thereabouts, to suit your routine. This feed should consist of about 1lb (500g) of meat, plus the other essentials, mixed in with soaked biscuit. He will enjoy an occasional hard-boiled egg or a little grated carrot. Do not be afraid to reduce the quantity of food by half a cup or so if he appears to be putting on weight.

By now your dog should have a nice 'rounded' appearance, not fat and yet not thin. A pretty good weight check is to stand over him and feel his ribs through his coat. You should just feel the slight corrugations of his ribs below his skin with your fingers. If you cannot feel his ribs at all, he is a little too 'well-covered'. If you can see his ribs, he is too thin.

Vaccinations

All dogs must have a series of vaccinations to protect them from the five most common canine infectious diseases. These are: distemper (or hard-pad), hepatitis, leptospirosis, parvovirus and kennel cough. Consult your vet as to the best time to give the injections and follow his advice. Different practices use different methods. Usually the first shot is administered at about eight weeks old followed by a second shot at fourteen weeks. A booster injection will then follow-on twelve months later and annually thereafter. Do not make the mistake of thinking that a puppy's first injection will protect him for life. Although your vet will probably remind you when annual booster injections are due, it is up to you to make sure that your dog has continual protection.

Grooming

Twice weekly each Labrador should have a good grooming. If you have more than one dog, each will soon learn to know which is 'his' day. Brushing should start behind the ears and continue down the neck, along the back and over the flanks, then the hindquarters and tail. Work using firm strokes in the direction of the coat and cover a small area at a time. It's rather like polishing a car! After brushing, use the velvety side of a 'hound mitt' or alternatively a good quality yellow duster, to polish him up, again, with the direction of the coat until you have a nice sheen.

Do not be tempted to 'rake' his coat with a metal comb as you will only succeed in removing the dense undercoat, which is his insulation layer. Do not use a wire 'slicker' brush, the sort that has a flat hard-backed handle, as this also will tear out his undercoat if used regularly.

Twice per year a Labrador will shed his coat during a moult. Dogs tend to do this more gradually over a period of weeks compared to bitches, who can yield large handfuls of fluffy down in a matter of days. When this happens, your dog will feel much nicer (and your house remain tidier) if the dead coat is gently combed out each day.

Claws

Finally, check that his claws are neat and not overgrown, especially the dew-claw. This latter may need attention from time to time as it does not get much wear in the normal course of events, although working Labradors do use theirs for scrambling over rocky terrain. Standing a dog on a low wall or low garden table will allow you to check the length of his nails. If you cannot see any gap as shown in the diagram, ask the vet to clip his nails. Alternatively, you could increase the amount of road-walking he is getting and check again in a couple of weeks.

Health Checks

Use the grooming routine to check your dog for any signs of ill health. See that his ears are nice and clean and that his eyes are clear and free of any discharge. The occurrence of even a little coloured discharge in the eye corners is often a sign of infection (sometimes in a tooth!) and should be checked out by the vet if it persists for more than a few days. Be very careful when cleaning the ear and avoid using cotton buds or any similar item to probe the canal. If the ears are not clean and pink,

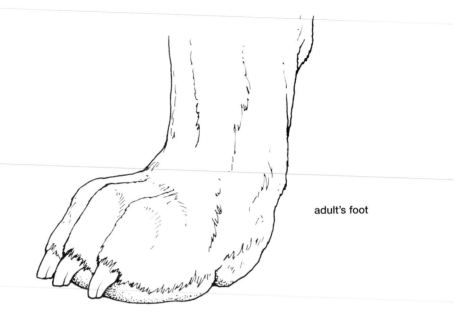

adult's foot

Stand the dog on a flat surface; if you can see daylight under the nail tips, they need no trimming.

obtain an ear wash and a bottle of drops from your vet and follow his instructions on their use.

Dogs and Bitches

There are some simple guidelines which should be followed in the keeping of dogs and bitches. These are not hard and fast rules, because all dogs' personalities are different and each has his own likes and dislikes. However, as a rule dogs may form close friendships, sometimes inconvenient ones (I know of one who fell 'in love' with a horse). Old dogs will share their beds with younger dogs on their own terms, provided that they are not stud-dogs used with bitches in season in the same kennel. The same applies to old and young bitches. However, I think that dogs and bitches are at their happiest when kennelled together, seasons permitting. However, never kennel two litter-sisters or yearling brother and sister together, because they are sneaky and will play rough games in which nobody knows when to stop. Eventually they will create ructions when you least expect it and they could injure themselves.

Mrs Gwen Broadley of the famous Sandylands Labradors advises: 'Never kennel more than two adult dogs or bitches together or they will form a 'pack'. And, as in any pack, the strongest will elect itself leader of its own free will and this process may lead to conflict.'

Bitches in Season

In an ideal kennel, dogs and bitches are kept separately and cannot see one another. Traditional hunt kennels operate this way and the temperaments of the inmates are second to none.

Bitches in season should *not* be exercised off premises from the third or fourth day onward. The bitch's scent, which increases in strength as the days progress, will attract every male dog in the neighbourhood. Eventually, they will form a choir on your boundaries and give you their version of the Hallelujah chorus at nightfall. Every night! The owners of these Lotharios will get into the habit of telephoning you to find out their whereabouts. This is not a recommended way of widening your circle of friends and acquaintances.

Confine your bitches to the exercise run or the garden whilst they are in season. Bear in mind that they will still be attractive and possibly fertile to dogs until the twentieth day or even later. Allowing more than one bitch to use the same ground will encourage them to come into season one after the other, and in time synchronize to the extent that they will get their seasons over almost in the same time period, thus creating less work for you and allowing possible matings to be better planned in the future.

Although owners of a single bitch will not have to contend with preventing an unwanted mating with a kennel- or house-mate, there is still the risk that she may come into contact with other dogs in the area. It is essential, therefore, that you are vigilant at all times and ensure that she is never left unsupervised. Any determined male will seize the slightest opportunity that presents itself and chain-link fencing is no protection!.

Should a mismating occur take the bitch to your vet as soon as possible and have her injected to terminate the pregnancy. This should be done within twenty-four hours of the pairing. However, subsequently, the bitch's next season should be more concentrated than before. She will be sexually more active and more eager for attention. So, you will have to guard her extra carefully each season from now on! These bitches are known as 'hussies', for they really are beyond the pale.

Castration and Spaying

Spaying a bitch involves the complete removal of the ovaries and the uterus. As a result, one of the basic reasons for owning such an animal, the breeding of puppies is lost forever. It is a major operation, requiring a general anaesthetic, and so it should not be contemplated lightly. However, there may be good veterinary reasons for this drastic step, such as the removal of tumours, cysts (of the ovaries) and the consequences of infection. Recurring false pregnancies, which cause her distress, are also a good reason. In my view, 'cosmetic spaying' either to save the owners the bother of heats, or worse, to assuage the guilt an owner may feel at preventing a bitch from having puppies are not good reasons.

However, there is a lot of folklore connected with spaying, and in particular there are four myths that should be dispelled immediately:

1. It is not necessary for bitches to have one litter 'for the good of her health'.
2. It will not stop her seeking out dogs periodically and teasing them.
3. It will not necessarily ruin her coat or cause her to grow idle and fat (She will do that anyway if you spoil and over-feed her.) And,
4. Spaying is unlikely to alter a bitch's temperament. If a bitch is spayed there is no reason why she should not continue to be a lovely faithful companion, just as affectionate and obedient as she always was.

In contrast the castration (or neutering) of a dog is comparatively straightforward in that it involves only the removal of the testes, which is achieved via a small incision that heals quickly. And unlike spaying, castration might be contemplated for three good social reasons:

1. To help to reduce hyper-sexual behaviour and thus to make him more manageable and less likely to develop an aggressive nature, particularly towards other males.
2. To reduce his tendency to wandering, which is linked to (1) above.
3. To render him sterile if he is no longer required at stud and accidents would be highly undesirable.

However, castration should never be viewed as a licence for a dog to wander at large and go where he will on the grounds that 'he can no longer do any damage'.

Eng. & Ir. Ch. Oakhouse Glenarem Classic, born 1970, by Sh.Ch. Sandylands Garry ex Glenarem Wilkamaur Cascade. Photo taken when he was twelve years of age.

The Older Dog

As long as your older dog remains healthy and active, there is no reason why he should not continue to live as full a life as his younger counterparts. However, it should be remembered that he will not be as lively as he was in his youth, and his wish to take things a little more slowly and to enjoy more rest should be respected.

Since the older dog uses up less energy, he is more prone to weight gain, although this is entirely unnecessary and can easily be avoided by introducing a diet that is lower in protein. There are many excellent low-protein complete foods on the market, which have been especially formulated to meet the specific needs of the older dog. However, as with the introduction of any new diet or foodstuff, the change should be made gradually to avoid causing gastric upset.

It is very important to continue to exercise the older dog, although he will probably want to take shorter walks. Older dogs are of course more prone to arthritis or rheumatism and you should keep an eye out for any signs of discomfort or stiffness, which may indicate the onset of one of these conditions. Many older dogs will also develop fatty lumps under the skin, which more often than not are painless and harmless. However, it is worth asking the vet to check any symptoms you notice; and it is in any case a good idea to take your older dog for a regular check-up. The older dog is more likely to develop dental problems for instance, and a regular check-up will reveal any such conditions that would benefit from some attention.

Remember also that the older dog is more susceptible to chills and the effects of bad weather. If he is living in kennels, make doubly sure that his accommodation is free from draughts or dampness, and do not allow him to become wet during exercise without drying him thoroughly immediately afterwards.

While your old dog may typically enjoy the company of younger ones, he should nevertheless be provided with a haven to which he can retire and find peace and quiet when he does not feel inclined to join in the boisterous games of the other dogs. Similarly, he should not be expected to 'compete' with them for food. Since he will probably be slower in eating his ration, you will need to protect him from opportunists who might have an eye on his food bowl.

The older dog will probably need to relieve himself more often. Unless he is housed in kennels with constant access to an area set aside for the purpose, it will be necessary for you to let him out more frequently, and also to make sure that you do not leave him for as long a period as you might have been able to in the past. A well-trained dog will be extremely reluctant to soil his bedding or any other part of the house, and his efforts to avoid doing so will cause him considerable distress. It is up to you to ensure that he does not have to suffer it.

It will be apparent from most of the above that the management of the older dog is really a matter of common sense. As long as you remain aware of his gradually changing needs and physical condition, a mature dog can approach old age with dignity, and enjoy a healthy, happy retirement.

However, there will inevitably come a time when you look at your old Labrador and it will cross your mind that the end is approaching. With many owners, it is more often instinct and their intimate knowledge of their dogs rather than any apparent physical symptoms that tells them this: perhaps an expression of weariness. Maybe he is lying in an unusual place (for him that is). Our old boy sat in the middle of the lawn, facing away from the cottage, with his head in his paws. Of course, it is always hoped that the end will come to him in his kennel or in his bed, peacefully and without pain. In which case, a practical mind would lay him gently on some newspapers or an old sheet to preserve his dignity for burial because after death fluids are released as the muscles relax. However, most dog owners will at some time find themselves having to make a difficult decision, and ask the vet for euthanasia to prevent further suffering.

Euthanasia

It is a painful decision to have to make, to have a dog 'put to sleep', but I do not subscribe to experiments aimed at prolonging life when it is evident that other faculties are on the wane, nor to subjecting an elderly dog who has reached the decent age of nine or ten to an investigative operation on the half chance of gaining him one or two extra years. I still believe in the good advice given to me thirty years ago: 'Leave well alone while they have a good appetite and sleep soundly; otherwise grasp the nettle and make a firm decision.' A dog would thank you for this last caring touch. As old 'Negger' Sharpe, who used to run in trials for the Midlands in the early 1960s, said to my father-in-law, 'Them as bring 'em into this world should not be afeared of helping 'em out. It's least you can do.'

When a beloved Labrador has died, many non-doggy friends will say, quite sincerely, 'Never mind he was only a dog; now you'll have more time for something else!' Except to us there is nothing else. Or, some will say, 'Go and get another dog. Get something different.' And yet no one says 'Go and get another Uncle or another Grandma'!

Research carried out in the USA shows that animal bereavement is very real and causes shock, denial and often actual pain. The shock may not be so great for the more 'professional' owners, such as show-goers or trainers because, more often than not, they are extremely busy people who are distracted from the immediate sense of loss by the demands that the other dogs in their kennels make upon their time and energies. The death of a pet is often much less traumatic when there are other dogs, or if you belong to a Labrador club where you meet friends who have had similar experiences. The more frequently one has to accept the fact that dogs have only a limited time with us may help to mitigate the pain. But it still hurts! And, people who lose their one and only pet do need space, more respect (but little fuss) and often a *lot* of time. The friendship of other pet-owners is vital. A common reaction to the sense of guilt is to feel sure that you will never want another dog. No two dogs are the same, so it is true that you can never 'replace' a much-loved pet. But think positively: you have much to offer, and can give a good home to a new dog. You are highly qualified for this; the fact that you are reading this is ample proof of that.

6

Training

All Labradors are capable of being trained in basic obedience and are a great deal better for it. Labradors and their immediate ancestors have served at the side of their owners, in one kind of role or another, for several hundred years. As a companion they have plenty of 'dog sense', a strong will to please and an inherent retrieving ability. What is also important, is that you, the owner have that same 'dog sense', and a will to understand the canine mentality!

Labradors are one of the most versatile breeds, whose combination of intelligence, strength and good nature provide him with the potential to perform his many varied roles. However, in order to realize that potential, good training is essential, and the basis for this is mutual respect and understanding. So even if you do not intend to train your Labrador to an advanced standard for competition or work in the field, it is important for you to appreciate some of the behavioural and physiological differences between canines and humans so that you can at the very least build a rewarding and stress-free relationship with your Labrador.

Understanding Your Labrador

A Labrador, like all dogs, is a pack animal. He needs the security of a 'pack leader' (you!) and the companionship of other animals, including humans, in a kind of extended family. A dog needs a framework for his life and a set of guidelines, without which he is not a happy dog. If you keep more than one dog, one will be submissive to the other, but it is essential that you are 'on top' of both, so that in the event of a conflict you will be able to prevent a serious fight.

A dominant bitch will use growling and eye contact to control her puppies, but remember that while punishment for any misdemeanour is swift, it never goes beyond a light nip. Thus, physical contact is not part of any dog's normal behaviour as far as discipline is concerned.

Only when there is an instinctive bid for power within the pack, does the behaviour become physical. A dog's instinct is to please you, which means that he can be trained to carry out tasks that he may not want to do naturally: giving up the 'prey' that he has hunted, is one example. A dog wants a pack leader that is stronger and more intelligent than he is. You must ask yourself whether you are strong enough (and intelligent enough!) to train a dog. In many families it is the female of the species who makes most of the decisions and is therefore 'dominant'. You will do well to recognize who has the stronger will in your family, because that person will earn the respect of your Labrador far more easily than the 'second in command'.

It is also necessary to understand that dogs do not reason in the way that humans do. When a dog is closely associated with a loving and caring owner he will often appear to understand not only what his owner would like him to do but what he would prefer him not to do, based on what he has been taught, and this might appear to demonstrate reasoning powers. However, when you start to train your Labrador it is better to assume that he cannot reason, and therefore you must stick to a few simple direct commands with simple objectives.

Body Language

In order to make himself understood, your Labrador will employ a wide variety of body signals. He will use his mouth, eyes and ears to indicate whether he is feeling submissive or dominant. The set of his neck, his action and the angle of his tail can all be changed at will. By studying his posture and facial expressions you will soon be able to detect what mood he is in. Do not ignore these signs because they are part of his language.

Generally speaking, a loving, submissive demeanour is easy to read. All parts of the body are set physically low: head bowed, tail down, and so on, and the expression is low-key and soft. Conversely, aggression is indicated by a high physical posture; head up, tail up and a hard bright expression in the eye. If ever you are confronted by a dog adopting this stance your response should be: avoid direct eye contact, do not turn your back on him but make minimal movements in order to, very slowly, reduce the height of your posture; never be tempted to run. By doing this you will appear to be less threatening and thus reassure the dog that there is no reason for his defensiveness to stimulate his aggressive reflexes.

Soft Mouth

An essential feature of the Labrador is his 'soft mouth', by which is meant his ability to carry in his mouth fragile living creatures, be they fish or fowl, without harming them with his teeth. The construction of his neck and the set of his jaw allows him to swim with his quarry tenderly but safely held. Through careful tuition plus a degree of in-bred aptitude, the Labrador can distinguish between food prepared for his consumption and shot game which he has been taught to retrieve to hand.

The working requirements for a soft-mouthed Labrador Retriever are explained in more detail in Chapter 7.

Most dogs are not able to control their mouth muscles very well, although they can bare their upper teeth in fear or apprehension, or their lower teeth in a submissive 'grin'. It is often thought that this teeth baring is a 'conditioned smile', but a true canine 'smile' is a turning up of the corners of the mouth as with a human grin. This facial expression is never seen in the wild; it is a feature of the domesticated dog and is an expression much favoured by the Labrador.

Humans can change facial expressions by employing the orbicularis muscles which dogs do not possess. Thus, Labradors will chew with their mouths open, which is very bad manners and as we all know, their mouths 'leak' considerably!

Sight

Your Labrador's eye is fairly similar in construction to that of a human being, but there are a few significant differences. The canine eye has virtually no ability to recognize colours as we see them but he can distinguish a wide variety of 'grey levels' with, it is thought, a high degree of contrast. The dog's eye also responds very quickly to small variations in movement, which in the wild enables a dog to detect a potential threat – and also potential prey – from some distance away. So, when you communicate to him over a long distance, he will recognize accurate hand movements above most other methods.

However, at close range, it is suggested that, compared to us, dogs tend to be near-sighted because they have never needed to evolve the mechanism for the recognition of high detail. Their superiority in hearing and scenting has been enhanced at the expense of their overall sighting ability. As a result, a Labrador will recognize the sound and especially the outline of his human partner but he relies on scenting for checking that he has the correct person close-up, especially if both have been parted for some time.

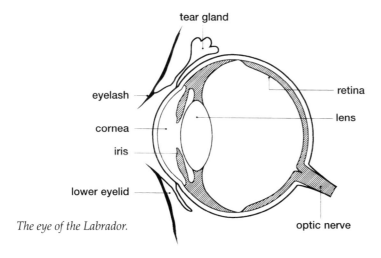

The eye of the Labrador.

Compared with a human being, your Labrador is well equipped for night vision via his in-built system of retinal reflectors. His ancestors found this essential for hunting, which was often carried out in the late twilight hours. It is this component of the cornea which allows the eyes of dogs (and cats) to appear to glow in the dark.

Sometimes when the optical muscles are very relaxed, a fine membrane (often called the 'third eyelid') can be observed in the inner corner of the eye. In some breeds, the third eyelid is more noticeable. This is thought to be a remnant of a protective eye cover employed by his very primitive ancestors, who led an almost 'seal-like' existence and spent much of their lives in the water.

Smell and Scent

The scenting ability of the Labrador, (in common with the majority of other dogs) has evolved to a high level. We human beings can distinguish many types of widely differing scents and smells. But our reaction is strongly influenced by the sensation of taste, which the dog does not have to the same extent. The dog's nasal cavity is much larger than ours, and this yields a considerable area of sensitive scent-detecting tissue. Hence the Labrador can detect very faint scents, probably one hundred times fainter than any that a human nose could recognize.

The Labrador's brain appears to be able to compartmentalize different types of smells, some of which he appears to remember individually. A trained dog can follow a specific scent through an area in which it would not be noticed by a human nose owing to the presence of a stronger overlying smell. This unique and subtle sensibility enables it to be taught to differentiate a chosen scent from the surrounding smell. In this way, the Labrador picking up for his handler, will hunt for his quarry using his memory of the smell of pheasant coupled with the previous sight which he may have had of its trajectory. A well-trained dog will ignore the scent of hare borne on the wind in the same locality.

During training or retrieving tests, it is virtually impossible to avoid tainting the 'dummy' with a human smell. The Labrador uses traces of this scent to locate the dummy and often confirms it is the correct one by taste and visual means.

Hearing

The hearing range of a Labrador is far in excess of that possessed by a human's ear. For example, although we can hear the top note on a piano, which produces a sound frequency of just over 4,000 hertz, a young fit Labrador dog can easily hear up to 35,000 hertz; and some Russian research workers have claimed that a dog can detect frequencies of 100,000 hertz which is in the realm of radio frequencies! It is interesting to note that many diverse breeds of dog have evolved different ear shapes, even though, technically, their hearing abilities are all virtually the same.

The Labrador's hearing makes it easy to train him to the whistle, whether of the audible or high-frequency 'soundless' type, and this method of control may be preferable to the human voice, since a whistle cannot express frustration, not to mention exhaustion, which the dog can recognize also. It is also worth mentioning that, owing to his excellent hearing ability, there should never be a need to shout at your Labrador!

Simple Sounds
A dog learns to associate simple sounds with your pleasure or your displeasure. And, he knows which you would rather have. Dogs can be fearful of what they do not understand and they can easily be upset by noise, especially when they are below par for reasons which we may or may not be aware of. This is why you must take great care not to frighten a puppy in the early stages of training.

The simple sounds that a young Labrador understands are those that he has learned from his mother. A bitch in the nest will make friendly soft noises, mews and grunts, and give tender licks to her puppies. In the beginning you must talk to a puppy quietly and handle him gently so that he learns the same security and trust as he had in the nest.

A Sixth Sense

There have been many instances where, it is claimed, dogs have used a 'sixth' sense to detect some impending danger and, by giving an early warning of it, saved the lives of their owners. We have already shown that Labradors, in common with many canines, have some faculties which are much more highly developed than ours. It is therefore not surprising that they can detect the smell of burning more easily than we can. And the same may be said of their hearing: your Labrador can hear your car arriving a good distance away; not only that, he will easily differentiate between the sound of your car and your neighbour's car by the change in its sound pattern.

Additionally, Labradors are creatures of habit and love a settled lifestyle. They are very susceptible to even tiny variations in routine. Thus when his regular routine is disturbed, as sensed by subtle changes in the sounds which he has become used to and perhaps coupled with a perceptibly different human scent, it is not surprising that he can give a low growling warning of an intruder in the garden.

Basic Commands

Take a little time each day to train your Labrador in the basic steps of obedience. The shortest time spent – even as little as five minutes every other day – will do an immense good for his ego, because it tells him you care. And that matters very much to him. You must try to develop his abilities. These basic commands have already been outlined in Chapter 4 for the new owner of a puppy. Now it is time to consider their use in more detail. If he is not to feel insecure in his station in life, you must establish that you are his 'pack' leader. An obedient dog is a happy dog and a much closer friend of his master's than a canine delinquent.

An essential training aid is a pocketful of tasty titbits, biscuit or meaty. When you are in your training rig, this pocket should always be primed and ready.

When you have a young dog in the house, he will often start to pester you for attention. This can be difficult to deal with, but you must

Correctly fitted check chain.

not give in to it. This is an important part of establishing yourself as pack leader: the leader dispenses attention when he is ready, not because a subordinate is pestering. The best way to deal with this form of attention-seeking is to *ignore* it completely; although it can be difficult, you must persevere and he will soon get the message.

Another basic rule for Labrador training borders on heresy for the average dog owner. This is: if you want to train a Labrador seriously, *never* throw tennis balls or sticks for him to retrieve. Actually, when he is older (three or four years of age) he will know the difference between work and play, and the rule can be relaxed!

When he is about four months old, begin to teach your Labrador six simple commands, one at a time. Concentrate on his mastering the following: Heel, Sit, Leave, Down, Stay and Come. Always use the same words for the same task and try to keep the tone of your voice the same also. Do not growl; speak to him quietly and firmly. For this training you will need a medium weight 'check-chain' on a strong clip lead

90

(thick rope or broad webbing) about 30in (76cm) long. Make sure you put the chain on correctly so that it loosens when you slacken it and tightens if he pulls.

'Heel'

Start with the command 'Heel'. Slip the loop of the chain over his head and encourage him to walk with you. In the first instance, let him walk of his own free will and sniff around the garden. He should barely be aware of the lead at this time. Do not pull him in any direction. Let him do the walking and get used to you being there with him. Once he is used to you, tug him gently as you guide him but avoid getting into a tug-of-war. If he starts to play up, stop. Give him lots of praise and encouragement and a titbit. That is the end of the first day's lesson. Leave it at that.

When you have repeated the above, daily, for a few days, you will find that he is enjoying the 'company of two'. Now he is ready to go for a short, proper walk. Put on his lead as described above, and as you set off give the command 'Heel' quietly and firmly. At the same time give a gentle tug on the lead and walk him quietly on your left hand side. Try to restrain him to your heel gently if he is distracted, but do not yank at his neck. Repeat the walks over about three weeks until he has got the hang of it. Praise him every time he returns home.

At the same time as you are teaching him to walk to heel on the lead, encourage him to walk with you in the garden, or in some other enclosed space, without the lead. You must allow him to go his own way for a short time at the beginning, then join him, give the command 'Heel' and entice him to follow you, rewarding him when he obeys. Try to reward every positive action he makes when you are training him. Never scold or smack him; he will not understand you. Make much of his positive progress and ignore his misdemeanours as much as you can.

'Sit'

Teaching a Labrador to sit is fairly easy once you have mastered walking to heel. On the word 'Sit', push his bottom gently but firmly to the ground with your left hand while holding the lead in your right. Repeat the procedure a few times on each walk when an appropriate place, such as a kerb, presents itself. Give him time to sit and think what he has done before you reward him with praise, 'Good boy'. If you have him in the house with you, make him sit before you feed him.

Hold his neck gently and put his rear on the floor as above; tell him to 'Sit' and give him his meal. Thus he will associate the command 'Sit' with a reward (his dinner in this instance), each time it is given.

'Leave'

The command 'Leave' is required to indicate that whatever he is doing should cease! 'Leave' should be accompanied by a firm tug on the lead. With practice, the check-chain can be used quite gently so that the tightening action makes sufficient noise to warn him 'Leave'. If you are confident, he will soon learn to ignore other dogs because he is confident in your control.

A necessary skill that you must learn when training your Labrador is that of 'heightened anticipation', which is a pompous way of saying 'be ready for anything!'. When you have a dog in your charge, whether it is a baby puppy or a sensible adult, you must keep your wits about you. A dog's reflexes are so acute that should they be startled or deliberately provoked they will be in 'overdrive' or 'escape mode' before your civilized poise has even considered giving way to consternation. For example, if you have to cross a busy road, do so where there is good vision for both you and the dog to see and hear, and where traffic, albeit moving swiftly, is predictable. There is nothing worse than the instantaneous roar of an engine to an unsuspecting animal. If your exercising routine could take you past a farmyard, beware of the friendly farm collie. Four out of five will let you pass with a wary eye, the fifth will try to snap at your heels. If you must go that way, try a 'dog free' dummy run first.

'Down'

If you want your Labrador to rest in one place until you need him, put him at the Sit and let him settle. Then, take his front paws and gently ease him down to the lying position with the command 'Down'. He will resist you at first, but do not force him. If it is not working, do not get into a wrestling match! Wait until he is about to drop of his own free will and give the command 'Down' as he does so. When he is down (even if he is going to lie down by himself) your praise will encourage him to link the action to the command. Many trainers do not teach Down as a command because they do not think it is necessary. They consider that Sit should suffice. And bearing in mind that a dog has limited 'vocabulary' it may seem best to teach another word that is more appropriate to your lifestyle. However, if you venture into the realm of Obedience competitions the command 'Down' will form part of the tuition structure and can be mastered by any Labrador.

'Stay'

The command 'Stay' allows you to leave your dog after he has obeyed either 'Sit' or 'Down' and still has your attention. This is a difficult act for a dog at first because instinctively he wants to follow you and he will note the tone your voice adopts in order to recognize what you want him to do. If you employ a different tenor in your voice (even a little hint of a reprimand in it) it will jolt him slightly, even to the extent of making him think that you do not want him near you (which is true, for the moment). Therefore, on the command 'Stay' (you must use a sharp tone of voice) he will remain either at the Sit or Down, whichever position he has assumed earlier. This requires a fair degree of practice and you must be very patient. Give him a couple of days at least between sessions for learning different commands so that he does not become stale.

'Come'

This is the very beginning of retriever training. To start with, you will need a length of light cord about 20 feet (6m) long. The best place to get it from is a ship's chandlers or an agricultural merchants. Attach the cord to the collar and let him walk to the extent of about eight feet (2.5m) away. Call him with 'Come' and get his attention. Then gently draw him towards you. He will respond if you make a fuss of him. Give him a titbit when he comes to you. Gently keep him in front of you and avoid letting him tie you in knots. After each return, put a light slip-lead on him so that he gets used to it. Repeat this exercise a few times until he begins to understand what you want of him. In subsequent days let him go to greater distances until he is reliably returning to you at the word 'Come!' for praise and a treat. Provided that in the beginning, you work with him in an enclosed space, you can then let him off the cord.

Make sure he will come to you obediently before you let him off the lead in a public place. If you have any doubts, keep him on the slip-lead. Take great care when you are walking him where there are sheep with lambs. An inexperienced Labrador can quickly turn a bit of fun into a full-blown chase if he is given the chance. Once he has experienced the thrill of 'hunting' he will never forget it and is ruined as a retriever.

Learning to Retrieve

When your puppy is about five months old and has gained a fair degree of obedience to the six commands, most especially 'Sit' and 'Heel', you can start to train him to retrieve seriously. If you start too early, he may not have finished teething, so you must check, or have checked, his mouth to see that it has no sore places. If you start before he is ready he might use the training dummy as a teething toy.

If you are very keen and intend to work your Labrador at a high standard, and enter Field Trials and Working Tests, you should seriously consider having your dog trained by a reputable professional. Otherwise, if you practise together and persevere you can be successful, taking one step at a time, and make a decent retriever for yourself. Thereafter, he will be perfectly good as a rough-shooting companion, and he should be able to enter a Working test and compete without the fear of making a complete fool of his owner. However, do beware of becoming complacent: dogs have a habit of showing you up if they are feeling 'that way out'. I still have painful memories of the peals of laughter ringing across the gravel pits as an unseen retrieve turned into a widely observed swimming lesson.

Should you be very fortunate and have good contacts with the shooting fraternity, it is possible that you could be invited to 'pick up' behind the guns at a recognized shoot. For this you *must* have a dog who will behave and is biddable and reasonably proficient. Shooting grounds are at a premium and once you are accepted at an established venue you must do your level best to honour the invitation with a decent performance.

Usually, a professional trainer will only take a dog that is fairly raw and has not developed traits and faults which are almost impossible to undo. So, you must decide at a pretty early stage which way you want to go. You will have endless fun in training a dog for yourself but your attainments may be modest.

Once you have entered the fascinating world of working a Labrador, you may think that he has an aptitude for it, and want to try him in competition. If you have progressed this far, it is likely that you will have joined a club that holds training classes. Do not be tempted to 'jump in at the deep end' and send off lots of entry fees for nominations to run in a field trial. Find out about the retriever working tests that take place in your area and go along and watch. Field trials are run under actual 'shooting day' conditions. That is to say, the dogs are very well trained and obedient (or should be!) and they will be asked to retrieve freshly shot game.

There is also a tendency to think that a good working dog is one that is almost automatic in its response, submissive in its obedience and arrow-like in its action. Personally, I would rather have a dog that can think a little, make a little mistake, work out the correct solution and return exhausted but triumphant. But that is only my preference. Don't let us lose the precious canniness and game-seeking that Labradors have intrinsically, bred in from generation to generation.

If you decide that you would like to train your Labrador to competition standard, I would advise you to dig more deeply into the literature. There are a number of excellent books available (*see* Bibliography). What follows here is an outline of some basic techniques and procedures.

First Steps

To begin with you must train your Labrador to come to the whistle. You must instil this in him from an early age. If this is your first attempt at training, buy a simple black plastic whistle, one that is fairly robust. Do not be tempted by a 'silent' whistle or an exotic type of caller, it is better to hear, and be heard, in the beginning.

It is never too early to train a promising Braemar puppy.

95

Carry the whistle when you are out exercising the dog in the early stages. When you have him loose, call him using the command 'Come', and as he trots towards you, give two or more 'dit-dit-dits' on the whistle. Avoid making a sound like a whistling kettle; it amuses other people unnecessarily. When he comes to hand give him a titbit, (although this will not be necessary later on). Soon he will routinely return to you on hearing the signal 'dit-dit-dit' on its own.

Start by letting him retrieve something old and worn that belongs to you and that he can relate to you, such as an old gardening glove or a woolly dummy made from a pair of dark socks, rolled one inside the other. Throw it for him and let him play a little game. Ten to one he will take it in his mouth and carry it. Then, he will probably take it to bed. Next, you must stand by his bed and take it from him, gently. Don't let him maul it. Greet him and make a fuss of him; telling him how clever he is. Play this 'game' for a few days but only two or three times each day or he will get bored and look for another diversion.

For the first few times he will return to you but try not to part with his prize. Encourage him to bring the glove or socks to your hand, and make him let go by pressing his muzzle gently at each side at the back of the teeth. Plenty of praise and fuss will make him realize how important the glove is to you.

It is essential to get two or three good dummies to train with. These can be bought at good gun shops or obtained through a Retriever breed club, or you can make them for yourself. You can make a good dummy from a short length of carpet about 8 × 10in (20 × 25cm), rolled up and tied with string in two places. This should be covered with canvas or denim cloth and sewn up tightly so that it is fairly watertight. A short length of cord tied to one end is useful for throwing with, but this must not be more than, say, 6in (15cm) in length or it might get in the way. A typical dummy should weigh about 12oz (400g) when dry.

If you put a couple of strong rubber bands on a dummy from the beginning, you will be able to cover it with rabbit fur or a pheasant wing when you and your dog are ready for more complicated retrieves. It is not recommended to use pigeon wings on a training dummy, because these wings contain a high proportion of fluffy feathers which can upset a youngster, and even cause him to choke. These can be used later, when he has become more experienced. Don't try to economize and make a test dummy from slippery synthetic material even though it might claim to have good waterproof qualities. A smooth slippery surface would cause a novice Labrador to bite harder in order to cling on to his prize because it is now very important to him and, as a result, he could develop an over-strong grip – a 'hard-mouth'. Any signs of teeth marks on a bird that he might retrieve in the future would be heavily penalized by a Field Trial judge.

Several things that you will need to learn about and understand in the process of training a Labrador are concerned with the great out-doors. The smell of wet, cut or trodden grass is easy to detect, as are the smells of wet leaves, beet fields and mown hay. If you can smell one of these then you are downwind of the source. If there is a hare sitting upwind of you, you will not get the scent of him but your Labrador will. (And, more important, the hare will not get the scent of either you or your dog.)

Being able to sense the direction of the wind and the 'lie' of the scent, even if the wind is but the slightest zephyr, is very important when training a Labrador. Moist or humid days seem to aid scenting, and also the production of conflicting smells. Icy cold, frosty days, where the humidity is frozen from the air, carry little scent. Be aware of your surroundings right from the start, when you begin to train your dog.

Next, you must have somewhere to train. Pick a field of fairly short grass, free from animal droppings and far enough away from the road and buildings that you will not be disturbed. You must of course get

Ch. Brigburn Zenny, born 1991, by Fulbeck Fantail ex Haverton Tawny Pipit at Brigburn.

97

permission from the landowner before you enter his land. Be professional about it. Call on him and ask his advice. Explain to him politely what you hope to do and let him meet your Labrador. Many farmers will welcome meeting a potentially useful pair of hands, and you may be called on at straw time. But in any case, all farmers appreciate a sensible dog that is trained and under control. Remember to leave the field as tidy as you found it.

Lesson 1: Seen Retrieve

For the early lessons you will need a whistle and a couple of dummies without any fur or feather on them. Put your Labrador on a light slip-lead. (Incidentally, you must set aside a good hour for these first lessons, so that you and your pupil can 'commune with nature' undisturbed.)

In the same way as you started with the glove or the sock, take the lighter of the two dummies and tease him with it. Start by throwing it a little way away and with encouragement and praise he will enjoy bringing it back. Should he take it into his head to run off with it, do not get annoyed or impatient. Let him explore with it for a few moments. He may be distracted momentarily, by a butterfly or even a passing Tornado jet fighter, which might cause him to drop it, in which case, wait your chance and pick it up unobtrusively.

When he has had the dummy for a minute, give a quick 'dit-dit-dit' on the whistle to get his attention and then start to walk away. Usually, he will follow and come to you. If so, much praise and petting are in order, because he has done his first *real* retrieve for you.

The above first retrieve is a very intensive course of study to a young Labrador. Let him have a couple of days rest afterwards to think about what he has done, and let it sink in. It is important to be relaxed about the success of these early days. Try to end a lesson on a high note, with plenty of praise – even if you have done most of the retrieving!

Lesson 2: 'Sit', 'Get on', 'Lost' and 'Give'

The second lesson begins with a refresher of Lesson 1; a dummy, thrown a short distance, which your Labrador will return to you. Do this a couple of times; but do not be upset if he wants to play instead of work. Slip him on the lead and walk twenty or thirty paces and repeat the lesson.

The next step is to stand still holding the slip in your right hand with

Nemo (Priorise Bespoke) shows how it's done.

him on it, and make him sit on your left-hand side. Then walk six or eight paces and make him sit again. With your dog at your side, sling the dummy high in front of him so that he can see it land. He will watch it bounce and set down and he will 'mark' where he thinks it is in his mind. Without wasting time, let him off with the command 'Get on!' As he gets to within sight of the dummy, call out 'Lost', or 'Hi Lost' and, hopefully, you will see him pick it up in his mouth. Give him a 'Dit-dit-dit' on the whistle to get his attention and let him bring it home. 'Give' is the signal to give up the dummy – which must be obeyed! Praise him fulsomely if he brings it to hand, and pop it in the inner pocket of your jacket. Now put him on the slip-lead. If the retrieve is less than perfect – and it probably will be – turn to go, pretend to tie your shoe, coax him and whistle him (only once) and abort the lesson for today. However, always end on a high note, even if it is not the one you wanted to hear! Praising him for a good 'sit' on the way home will do.

Should he return to you like the proverbial boomerang and make to circle behind you, do not be impressed and do not scold him. Drop to your knees and pretend to scratch the earth, and study the spot of grass in front of you. His curiosity will bring him to you. Next time, arrange

A good retrieve to hand.

it so that you are in the corner of a field or in a narrow alleyway between fence and trees, say, before you send him off to carry out the retrieve. Keep the misdemeanour low-key and he will not repeat it.

When he makes a good retrieve, walk a little way to another part of the field and let him do a couple more. Praise him, and carry the dummy home, prizing it, like a puppy, to show him that he has done well.

Lesson 3: Walk to Heel, Unseen Retrieve

The essential part of the third lesson is the basis of 'walking up', that is, the part of a field trial where new ground is covered by the competitors with their dogs in pursuit of fresh game. For this the dogs must walk

100

quietly and to heel and learn to stop and lie down when commanded.

The above is achieved by repeating the basics of Lesson 2, namely, carrying out a few good retrieves from a sitting position on a slip-lead. When he understands 'Sit' and 'Get on!' (i.e. 'Go further away and seek'), 'Lost' (You're in the right place!') and 'Give', he is ready to learn to walk off the lead. As I said before, get the conditions right, avoid being seen easily and so interrupted. Let him commune with you on your little walk between periods of work. Slip his lead off, talk to him and keep his attention. Don't try to go too far before you give him a firm command to sit. Replace the lead and repeat the retrieve. Now is the time to vary the retrieves; try dropping the second dummy into the hedgerow whilst he is busy retrieving. When he has returned the first dummy, walk a few paces, make him sit, then turn to face the way you want him to travel and command 'Get on!'. If he seems unsure, walk nonchalantly in the general direction of the dummy and 'draw' him along with you. Ten to one he will find the hedgerow, and thus can only go up or down it. Draw him in the right direction until he is near enough for the command 'Lost!'. If you have kept enough distance between him and you he will complete this 'unseen retrieve' without more ado. Praise him to the highest! Then walk with him at your heel, basking in your approbation.

The practice of walking quietly to heel, then sitting waiting for something to happen can be ingrained in his mind as you build on more and more difficult retrieves. Steadiness is everything in a fine retriever, although 'running in' to retrieve before the command may be forgiven by judges, for the more elementary competitions. If you can stop it before it starts, you are in with a chance. However, you certainly will not be able to progress to higher things without a 'bomb-proof' steady dog. Also, when you are training, if you get any sign of whining from your Labrador, it must be stopped with a severe reprimand. This, like unsteadiness, or a dog out of control, is a major offence. All judges will exclude a dog which whines or appears to be out of control. Do not let your dog be responsible for a field full of carefully reared and placed pheasants taking wing in a spectacular fashion. Neither of you will be popular.

Lesson 4: Fur, Feather and Water

Now is the time to spend ten or so minutes with one normal dummy and a realistic one (which has a rabbit fur or pheasant wing strapped to it). It is essential to divert your dog if he becomes too interested in

*A dripping Ch. Lawn-
woods Midnight Folly
waits for the next test.*

the latter varieties. Do not let him worry a realistic dummy. Straight away, tease him with the normal dummy, remove the real one and restart the sit and walk routine. Don't make a big deal of his mistake, try again later with an unseen retrieve using the real dummy, standing nearby to retrieve it before he realizes the difference. Eventually, using a combination of controlled confusion, excitement and praise, he will bring anything back to you, provided that he recognizes the scent of it and links it to your praise and pleasure.

As you vary the retrieves with short and long throws, seen and unseen quarry and different dummies, you must be on the lookout for a stream or pond which you can bring in to the natural retrieving scene. By carrying a dummy through water, even a few inches, he will get used to working in wet conditions and provided it is not too deep he will take it in his stride. Combine his inherent curiosity with a little guile. Sometimes, an innocent walk with another more experienced retriever will encourage him to take to the water and swim. By now he will know when he is 'off duty' and a fun swim to retrieve a stick might just get him going. Provided that it is made fun at first, he will soon learn to enter water without a second thought. However, the sea is another matter. It has strange things called waves which can surprise a youngster, and in the extreme could put him off aquatics forever! It is better for him to learn in a calm pool or lazy stream.

Lesson 5: Directed Retrieves and Gunshot

For the fifth lesson you will need a selection of dummies, two with fur or feather, two or three plain ones, a shot rabbit in its skin (from a game merchant) and a friend with a shotgun.

The first objective of the exercise is to encourage your dog to bring back your piece of game (i.e.dummy) which you choose for him while ignoring any other. The second objective is for him to learn to accomplish a retrieve and associate it with the sound of a gun. If both of these objectives are approached in a structured and unhurried manner you will be successful.

Placing your Labrador at the Sit, stroll a good few paces away and throw two dummies in fairly quick succession, one to his right and one to his left. At the same time, give him the command 'Get on!'. As he decides which one to go for, stick out whichever arm corresponds to his direction of travel, and move a few steps in the same direction. When he retrieves the first dummy encourage him to bring it to you with whistle or call. However, should he set off for the second dummy also, command him to 'Leave' (or use a short loud whistle blast, 'Dah!'). Give him every encouragement to come to you and ignore the second retrieve. By varying the positions of the two dummies, you will, over a period of two weeks, but no more than three times per week, get him to take the dummy you choose. Once he has got the idea that you want one, and one only, of the available dummies, you may progress to several dummies, some seen, some unseen. Here, he must wait until you are ready to send him, and then choose the correct one to retrieve. However, don't be too strict in the beginning, a good retrieve on a 'near miss' may be his best attempt. He will improve as his experience widens.

When you are confident that he can pick only one of, say, three dummies, he is ready for a little confusion. Commence by sending him for the farthest of the three and when he is about one-third of the way there, signal your friend to hurl the rabbit across or towards his path and as near the ground as is possible. A gap in the hedge with a bit of open fencing will allow the thrower to remain concealed. At first the pupil will be tempted to get the bunny. This must be prevented by a call of 'Leave' or a whistle blast, as above. If he should succumb to

103

temptation, dissuade him quietly, regain the bunny and carry on without any more interruptions for the day.

The final part of the lesson involves introducing the sound of gunshot before you ask him to retrieve. Again, he should be quiet and sitting comfortably. The gun should be located about 150yds (135m) away from you downwind and fired into the air. Take care that there are no stock or public roads within 300yds (270m) of the shooter (in-lamb ewes, young horses or milking herds, and so on). Try out the gun beforehand in the area in which you wish to test your dog. It is amazing what odd reverberations and echoes can be generated from the unlikely corners of rickety old barns or unassuming rocky outcrops. Do not let such noises put off a young Labrador. Let him do a couple of seen retrieves before he hears the gun. When he does so, send him off and encourage him to bring back his prize with much praise, as before. If he shows no reaction to the sound of the gun, repeat the exercise with the shooter about 100yds (90m) away. A few days later you will be able to shoot more closely, but for the purpose of training keep the gun at least 50 to 60yds (45–55m) distant, downwind, and always fired downwind so that the sound is carried away from you.

Lesson 6: Sounds and Semaphore

The tests set out in Lessons 1 to 5 above should now be carried out in reverse order, mixing a little from one with a little of the other, so that you cover the basics of seen and unseen retrieving. Some work should be done in fairly deep undergrowth or cover, some in open fields and some again in woodland. The water tests should be carefully stage managed; it is no good dunking a young Labrador and expecting him to enjoy it. Err on the gentle side and avoid pressurizing him. In the first instance, let him meet the water with other dogs that are already swimming, to give him confidence. If you are suspicious of his reaction to gunfire, leave it for a few weeks before you try again with a smaller bore gun such as a .410 or a .22 blank fitted in a 12 bore using an adaptor. As for 'surprise' hares or rabbits, keep them to one per week at the most.

When your dog is retrieving steadily, making a few mistakes but (it is hoped), realizing that he is, and being able to take your corrections, now you can gild the lily by training him to obey either the whistle, or your hand signals. As you and he progress, you will start to combine them both naturally. This will give you a much greater range and enable him to relate to you when he is down in a deep gully or behind thick woodland.

Ch. Fabracken Comedy Star, born 1979, by Sh.Ch. Martin of Mardas ex Ch. Poolstead Pin Up of Fabracken.

At the command 'Get on!', he will run away from you; when he gets in roughly the right area of the fallen bird you can signal one 'Dit' on the whistle, which tells him 'Lost' or 'Go seek'. Accompany this whistle with your right hand held high, palm to the front. A variation of this is, when you do not want him to proceed any further in that direction, signal one loud blast 'Dah!' (hand held high, palm to front, as before). This means 'Stop' or 'Leave' and await orders.

If he runs out of steam and looks back to you, or maybe he is lost, you can send him farther out with another single 'Dit' ('Go seek') accompanied with a high hand signal giving a forward motion (flat hand, palm front, motion forwards).

To bring him back to you, bird in mouth, whistle 'Dit-dit-dit' as he starts his return journey. If he looks as though he is going to stray from the direct route, repeat the whistle once to correct him. Do not 'pipe him aboard'!

The help of a mature and reliable older dog is very helpful when training a youngster to obey direction signals, whether given by sound or sight. Let them run together. Explain to the older dog that he is to 'Take the baby with him, and show him what to do'. You may smile, but provided you are in control of the 'Senior prefect', you will get the desired result. In addition, in the normal course of retrieving practice and even on exercise runs, giving the whistles and / or direction signals as explained below, whilst he is moving in the correct direction will help him to associate your commands with his responses. If you have hidden two dummies on either side of the field, as he chooses to go towards one of them, give the appropriate signal (no more than twice) and let him make the retrieve. Your praise will boost his learning of both the signal and the retrieve together.

To send him from left to right, the called command is 'Come by!' The hand signal is made, palm to the front with the right arm outstretched and the whistled command is 'Dahhh-dit!' with the 'Dah' lasting almost to the count of three and the 'dit' short and sharp.

Bringing him from right to left is done by using the command 'Get over!', sometimes abbreviated to just 'Over'. As before, the whistle mimics the command, but this time the beats are reversed, 'Dit-dahhh!'. The accompanying hand signal is made with the left hand, palm to the front and left arm extended.

Often it is to your advantage to wrap a white handkerchief round either hand. These will make your hand signals more distinct when you work your dog at a distance. However, don't forget that it is the *directional movement* of your hands that he will see best, so try to catch his eye with your signal when he looks back for a direction.

When you begin to train a dog for the first time, work together, learn together and play together. Try to progress slowly, and don't be in a hurry to try something new until your Labrador has mastered the basic commands. Make haste slowly. Mary Roslin Williams summed it up, 'A little work does little harm, too much work does the damage'.

Electronic Aids

I am not in favour of the electronic guidance and control of Labradors (or any dog for that matter). I think the use of electronic shock transmitters via training collars, applied to gun dogs in order to 'sting' them into obedience is a very retrograde step. The very act of introducing an external voltage near to the spinal column which might interfere with the delicate natural neurological impulses of the canine nervous system is abhorrent to me. The Labrador's hearing ability is vastly superior to man's; his antennae are perfectly tuned; his scenting and seeking capabilities have been developed over a thousand years of research. If you cannot obtain satisfactory results using your Labrador's natural abilities, you will get better results with a radio-controlled model aeroplane.

7

The Working Labrador

Obedience Competition

If your Labrador shows an aptitude for obedience, in the sense that he enjoys pleasing you and you feel that you want to progress along these lines, you should consider joining an obedience class. I say 'consider' because the standard of teaching at dog training classes can vary enormously from place to place, so you must first visit the club and take a look at the type of work that is being carried out. Find out whether the dogs are being taught with their owners in a regulated and structured way. It may be that the club is run by fairly inexperienced people and has become a therapy refuge for canine drop-outs and those with bad temperaments, commonly called 'behaviour problems'. If this is the case, go home and watch television. You will have enough problems of your own invention to deal with, without learning any new ones.

Contact your local canine society (or the Kennel Club) for details of training classes approved by them. Find out whether there are classes for pre-beginners and beginners before the dogs are progressed on to Novice and Class 'A' training and above. Visit them and watch what the dogs are doing and whether the instructor is confident and sympathetic. (It is not pleasant to find that you and your sensitive Labrador are being subjected to the pressure of competition before you are both ready.) On joining such a club, you will find that *you* will be trained in the first instance; later on you will learn to train your dog.

Obedience Shows

These shows enable you to take part in obedience competitions at different levels of proficiency. Remember that shows run under Kennel Club regulations do not permit dogs under six months of age to take part and no dogs other that those officially entered may be present. During the show you must keep your Labrador on a slip-lead at all times except when competing, and no food (not even titbits) are allowed.

*Sh.Ch. Lasgarn Ludovic, born 1972, by Ch. Sandylands Mark ex
Lasgarn Louisiana.*

Obedience shows fall into three types: Open (open to all dogs registered at the Kennel Club), Limited (limited to club members' registered dogs) and Exemption (for both registered and unregistered dogs). Classes are for Pre-beginners, Beginners, Novice and Class 'A', 'B' and 'C'.

To be eligible to compete in a Pre-beginners class you must not have won a 1st prize. Points (maximum shown in brackets) are awarded for each manoeuvre in the test: Heel on lead (15); Heel free (20); Recall from Sit (10); Sit one minute (10); and Sit two minutes (20). Thus a total of 75 points are available.

The Beginners class is limited to those who have not won two 1st prizes above the level of the pre-beginners class. The tests include those shown above for the pre-beginners plus an added Retrieve test which is worth 25 points. Beginners' dogs are expected to carry out all the tests with added smartness and positioning. Marks are awarded to a total of 100.

Class 'A', 'B' and 'C' tests are more advanced and increase in difficulty. The tests include those listed above plus dumb-bell retrieving and temperament tests, scent discrimination (using a cloth 'marked' by the hand of the handler), and Sits and Downs carried out with the handler out of sight. Full details are outside the scope of this book, but once you progress towards this level you will be a fully-fledged member of the training club and, it is hoped, well on your way to the big ring at Crufts.

Often, Obedience shows are held in conjunction with other events, Open shows and Breed shows, for example.

In order to qualify a Labrador as an Obedience Champion in the UK, three Obedience Certificates need to be won under three different judges when competing in obedience classes run under English Kennel Club rules. Alternatively, Championship status is awarded to the dog that wins the Kennel Club Obedience Championship.

Agility

Agility competitions have become very popular in recent years and now feature at some of the big Championship shows in the UK, including Crufts, and are also popular in Australia and New Zealand. The competitions are informal and are open to non-pedigree dogs provided that they are over eighteen months of age. Having said that, agility competitions held under Australian rules are quite formalized and are limited to pedigree dogs only. Nothing included in the tests must endanger the safety of dogs, handlers or spectators.

Agility tests are regarded as fun competitions, designed for the enjoyment of the competitors and their dogs, and have a lot of spectator appeal. In essence they are similar to show jumping competitions for horses. The dog and handler must negotiate a series of obstacles of varying difficulty in the shortest time. Generally the fun is fast and furious and the excitement of the 'run off' in the final is heightened by an enthusiastic commentator.

The classes at Agility competitions begin with Elementary (for exhibitors who have not won a 3rd prize or above) and progress through Novice (for winners of two 1st prizes), Intermediate and Advanced to Open class.

The course area must be at least 35 × 35yds (32 × 32m) and contain at least ten obstacles, which might typically include hurdles, fences, brush fences, tables, gates, tunnels, weaving poles, ramps and see-saws.

The dog's performance is marked according to the number of faults accumulated in each round. Clear rounds (no faults) are then run against the clock to decide the winner.

If you intend to compete with your Labrador, I would advise that you join a club where the facilities for training will be available. Some of the obstacles can be dangerous to an inexperienced dog and handler and should be properly constructed. It is very important to teach your dog the correct way to negotiate each obstacle. Once a wrong approach is learned it is very difficult to correct. You must teach your Labrador to jump hurdles on command, tackle the tunnel slowly at first until he knows it inside out, sometimes literally. Similarly, weaving poles need to be negotiated absolutely right first time otherwise you will lose valuable seconds.

Flyball

Flyball competitions will appeal to some Labrador owners in spite of what I said earlier regarding training and tennis balls! In essence, Flyball is a team knockout competition which gives a lot of enjoyment to spectators and participants alike. The Flyball 'box' is placed at the end of a course of four hurdles. It contains a simple spring catapult mechanism, not unlike a clay pigeon launcher, which can be triggered by a dog's paw. Once the trigger is pressed, a tennis ball is released into the air with a set trajectory.

There can be a number of teams competing simultaneously. There are four dogs in a team, plus a couple of reserves. Each dog in each team must jump the four hurdles, one after another, and trigger the ball. He must then catch the ball and return over the hurdles with it in his mouth. As he crosses the finish line, the second dog may go. The first team to have its last dog over the line wins the race.

Flyball competitions are becoming quite popular in the UK but it is not such an advanced sport as it is in America, from whence it originated. Competitions are now controlled by the Kennel Club and the interest generated at Crufts shows that the sport has a promising future.

Most Labradors take to the game readily, because they are natural retrievers. Once they learn the Pavlovian trick of triggering the ball, they will jump the obstacles in their stride. However, at first they must be taught to activate the box trigger when the box is empty of balls, otherwise they will scent the ball and retrieve it directly from the catapult – it's quicker that way!

Licensed Working Trials

Working trials are held under Kennel Club rules for dogs to demonstrate a high degree of training and control in handling. Essentially, these trials are advanced forms of obedience testing, using the basics described in Chapter 6, to which have been added jumping, steadiness to gunshot and nose-work (searching and tracking). Understandably, Working Trial stakes enable the training and abilities of a dog with its handler to be tested to the limit. Dogs must be eighteen months of age to compete and, obviously, bitches in season are ineligible.

Working Stakes

There are several kinds of working stake: Companion Dog (CD) stake, in which the dog must show a high degree of control both free and on a leash; be able to remain sitting for two minutes and at the 'Down' position for ten minutes; show good jumping abilities; retrieve a dumb-bell and carry out an elementary search for a 'marked' object.

The Utility dog (UD) stake involves all of the test criteria employed in a CD stake, but the standard is higher and the dog must also show that he is steady to gunshot and able to track a prepared scent. Working Dog (WD) and Tracking Dog (TD) stakes extend the scope of both The CD and UD stake exercises described above, with the accent on agility and nose work. These tests show progressively increasing levels of difficulty. The Patrol Dog (PD) stake is the most comprehensive test for the combined abilities of dogs and handlers, and includes: testing the dog's ability to take directions over various distances; speaking (barking) on command; quartering; a test of courage; search and escort duty and recall from pursuit, and detention of a 'criminal'.

A Kennel Club working trial certificate will be awarded to any dog winning a TD or PD stake at a Championship Working Trial by winning 70 per cent of the total marks available. A dog winning 80 per cent of the marks will be awarded the qualification 'Excellent' (Ex).

The following wins in TD or PD stakes are needed to attain a Working Trial Championship title: two Trial Certificates gained under two different judges where 70 per cent (or greater) of the marks has been obtained in each exercise group; an Excellent qualification for the stake.

Gun Dog Working Tests

Labrador working tests are intended to simulate the conditions of a shooting day or field trial in a controlled way. The Kennel Club has guidelines which should form the basis of the tests and it is stressed that the safety of the dogs is paramount (many of them and their handlers will be learners and anything might happen).

Success in a working test is only a taste of things to come. To be a true worker, a Labrador must be able to retrieve freshly shot game, fur and feather, on a properly organized shoot. Working tests are only really good practice for dogs and handlers, nothing can simulate the combination of a fast flying bird, a well-aimed shot and the nose and ability of an efficient Labrador for excitement, suspense and satisfaction, in that order.

Naturally all dogs competing must be Kennel Club registered and bitches must *never* be brought to a test in season. Although prizes are awarded to the winner and for second and third place, there are no formal qualifications or 'letters' to be won at a Gundog Working Test. (These should not be confused with working trials or stakes described earlier, and at which Working Dog Certificates (denoted WD) can be gained.)

You and your Labrador will be tested at a drive (when you wait for the dummy birds to fly over) and he should be able to walk steadily at heel. The retrieves are done on standard dummies, used in all forms of retrieving practice. Usually, your club secretary will advise you on the best kind. For some tests cold game, pheasant or hare (usually well thawed out) may be included.

The basic test is the marked retrieve. For this the Labrador must mark where the dummy has fallen and, when ordered by the judge, you must send him to retrieve it, preferably in a straight line there and back. You are allowed to direct your dog with discreet signals or whistle if he needs it.

Similar to the above test is the water retrieve. For this your Labrador must have had plenty of swimming practice with the dummy. Marks will be awarded for an efficient retrieve, quietly carried out. Either of the aforementioned exercises may be done as marked retrieves or they may be 'blind' (hidden in cover earlier in the day, or floated across the surface by one of the test stewards). In which case you must send your Labrador with a 'Get on' so that he runs in the direction set by the judge; you must then direct him to the 'bird' with as little display or noise as possible. I know how difficult this is, when a Labrador suddenly becomes sorely afflicted with with temporary blindness and total deafness! Or perhaps he has remembered it is past his lunch time. All retrieving tests may be accompanied by gun-fire which is timed to coincide with the sight of the 'birds'. Shots must be carried out within 50yds (about 45m) of the retrieves.

Working tests are broadly divided into four types: Puppy, Novice, Intermediate and Open. A Puppy test is for any dog or bitch between the age of six months and two years on the day before the test. A Novice test is for dogs and bitches that have not won: any Field Trial award including Certificate of Merit (COM); 1st to Reserve in an Open test; 1st in a

Working Test winner, Silver Larch of Nazeing. (Pedigree, see Appendix.)

Novice test; or 1st in a Puppy/Novice test. An Intermediate test is for dogs not having won 1st in an Intermediate or Open test or any award in a field trial including a COM. An Open test is open to all dogs.

Remember that all who take part in country sports usually do so on private land. As such you are a privileged guest of the owner and also of the people who live in the immediate neighbourhood. Always have a great respect for their property and avoid any damage to fences and hedges. Do remember to thank your host personally after the test and also thank the judge or judges and the organizers who have worked hard behind the scenes. And, if you are a good sport and congratulate the winners and their dogs, you will be welcomed when you return another day.

Do not forget that your dog has had a busy day too. As in training, try to end the day on a high note and let him carry a dummy back to the car.

Field Trials

Field trials for Labradors, which are run under the rules of the Kennel Club, fall into four categories: Open, for dogs to gain Championship

Ch. Midnight of Mansergh
makes a perfect retrieve to
the hand of his owner
Mary Roslin Williams at
a field trial.

qualifications; All-aged, for all dogs without age restriction; Novice, for dogs not having won 1st, 2nd or 3rd in an Open stake, or 1st in an All-aged or Novice stake; and Puppy, confined to dogs born not earlier than 1st January of the preceding year to the trial. The number of runners in an Open stake is limited to twelve per day, and for a Novice or other stake sixteen per day.

In essence, the trial should be run as nearly as possible to an ordinary day's shooting. The basic requirements are that the dogs shall be steady while being shot over until sent to look for game, and they should be able to retrieve the game tenderly to hand from either water or land. There are some faults that will result in a dog's disqualification from taking any further part in the proceedings: whining or barking during the test, running in, chasing or being out of control, failing to enter the water, losing game and demonstrating a hard mouth (crushing a bird by excessive pressure). Unsteadiness, slack work, noisy handling and 'eye wipes' (game picked up by a second dog) are considered to be major faults.

The judges will give credit for a demonstration of natural game-finding ability, good nose and positioning, style, quickness and quietness in handling and delivery of a bird.

114

Stakes

As with working tests, good, stout, warm weatherproof gear with capacious pockets is a must. The stake will start with the birds being driven towards a line of guns by a team of beaters. The beaters, often with the keepers, make their way, a white flag at either end of the line, through the wood or covert. The judges or stewards for the trial stand in between the guns who are stationed well apart. The entered dogs and bitches, with their handlers wait fairly close to the judges, usually two to a judge. The steward sends new handlers to the judges as they request them.

When the birds break cover and fly upwards and over the line of waiting competitors, the guns volley and then fall silent. The end of the drive is usually signalled by a whistle or horn blast. The first judge asks No.1 competitor to retrieve the first bird, say a pheasant lying at the edge of the cover. The handler must then send his Labrador, who should return with the game firmly in his mouth and deliver it to the handler's waiting hand. The process is repeated with each competitor, and the judges take note of the style and neatness of the retrieves and also any faults and mistakes.

Depending on the performance of the dogs in the first drive, the judges together decide which competitors deserve to carry on to the next drive. The dogs' retrieving ability is then re-tested on a new batch of pheasants or other game. This time the level of difficulty of the retrieves is somewhat higher, as game left from the first drive may still

Ch. Groucho of Mansergh retrieving a duck.

be lying around and may, or may not (according to the judge's instructions) be retrieved by the dogs. Sensible dogs with good memories are
obviously off to a good start!

If a handler sends his Labrador out on a retrieve and the dog fails to
locate the required bird even though he appears to be near it, he may,
after time for a little direction by hand signals, be called back by the
judge and the next competitor's dog can be sent out for the same bird. If
his performance is successful and a good quick retrieve is accomplished,
the second dog is credited with an 'eye wipe' of the previous dog.

If the trial moves over to a new piece of ground, it can be heartbreaking to see a fine retriever who has done well so far, fall for the
'trap' set when a hare who has been lying doggo behind the line, suddenly pops his head up. Many a prize has been lost, as the hapless handler watches his charge set off in pursuit in a spectacular fashion.

After the third and fourth retrieve, the final is run off between the
last two dogs and the judges will confer and declare the winner.

Field Trial Champion qualifications are confined to wins in Open
stakes. A prerequisite of completing a trial satisfactorily is that a
Labrador must sit quietly during the drive (whining is a cardinal sin!)
and enter water readily for a retrieve. In order to gain his title, a
Labrador must win: The Kennel Club Retriever Championship Stake;
or two 24-dog stakes held over two days; or one 24-dog, two-day stake
and one 12-dog stake held over one day; or three 12-dog stakes.

In Australia, the types and kennel lines of Labradors used for both
show and field trials are pretty much the same, in contrast to the UK
where types and lines may vary widely.

There are three kinds of field trial competition in Australia: Retrieving, Fieldwork and Obedience; all are conducted under Australian
Kennel Club Rules. The Retrieving trials may be of two kinds:

1. Cold game (often pigeons), which must be retrieved following the
sound of gunshot. A Novice field test consists of several kinds of
retrieve: on land, over water and into water, plus walking to heel and
steadiness to gunfire. A Restricted stake employs longer and more
complicated retrieves. Wins in an All-aged stake will earn Championship points. In Australia, all National Retrieving trials held in all
States conform to the same set of rules.

2. Shot game (often rabbits). In these trials, the dogs work in pairs. They
are carried out in a 'duck season' which extends from autumn through the
winter months. The retrieves are often carefully contrived and demand a
higher degree of control than would be required for rough shooting.

116

Aust. F.T.Ch. Strangways Goshawk, by Driftway Sandpiper ex Strangways Nightingale. (Owner: Mrs Guest, Australia.)

There are similar types of test carried out generally in Europe, Scandinavia and Finland where many show-oriented folk work their dogs in order to gain a Championship qualification in a field trial. There are three kinds of trial carried out in Denmark. These tests fall into three broad groups, and are fairly representative:

1. Trials using hunted and shot game.
2. Trials using cold game.
3. Cold game tests exempt from DKK rules.

Field trial dogs must be well-balanced and should look like a typical Labrador as described in the Breed Standard. They should be well trained but able to hunt and retrieve using their own skills and be capable of being aided by the handler. There are a few professional retriever trainers, but the majority of participants are owner-trained.

In Germany, special retriever tests are organized by the German Retriever Club using only cold game. The club also holds training courses for interested owners but 'hard' training methods are avoided.

In South Africa, there has recently been an increase in the number of show dogs competing in trials and the general standard is now very high.

Trials are controlled by the Kennel Union of South Africa Liaison Council which is empowered to run Puppy, Junior, Maiden, Novice, Open and Champion stakes. Obviously, the degree of retrieve and the necessary control of the owners increases with the age and the experience of the Labradors as they progress from Puppy stakes to Championship level. Most of the competing dogs are owner-handled and so the trial world is a close community. The Retriever Club runs training courses for dogs and there is a great deal of interest in these.

In the USA, most of the Labrador clubs in each state hold working tests. A certificate of working ability is granted by the Labrador Retriever Club, Inc., the parent club of America. This body is empowered to award the AKC (American Kennel Club) title WC (Working Certificate). Field trials have been established in the USA since the mid-1930s. In these, great emphasis is placed on the speed of the competitor's dog, his marking ability, and his facility for handling in blind retrieves. Most of the dogs are professionally trained to a high standard, but amateur stakes are held also for owner-handlers whose dogs usually have nevertheless been trained professionally.

Am. Ch. Braemar Heather CD WC, born 1977. (Owner: Mrs Borders, USA.)

Hunting retriever tests, which were instituted by the AKC in about 1980, are held for amateur handlers. These assessments are not as difficult as 'pure' field trials. Hunting retriever tests do not qualify dogs for any AKC titles but, being less formal, they enable the dogs and their handlers to gain invaluable experience in the field. The gamebirds used may be pigeons, upland game or duck, or any combination of the three. Performance in the HR tests are graduated in difficulty from Basic Working to Excellent. For the last mentioned, the dog must carry out seen retrieves on three separate birds which must be picked on land, and two birds retrieved from water. Blind retrieves with some decoys and interruptions (such as by hidden game) must be carried out effectively. The dogs may be quietly encouraged by their handlers and must show good positioning ability and obedience to their controller.

Rough Shooting and Hunting

If you intend to go rough shooting, it is imperative that, first, you know how to handle a shotgun safely and responsibly, and that you acquire an understanding of the countryside that will enable you to help preserve it. If you get to know intimately the habits of the birds and animals you intend to hunt, you will be able to get well in range and kill cleanly and efficiently. Wounded game must be caught and dispatched quickly, and this is when a good Labrador is invaluable. In addition you must respect the farmer and his livestock, and avoid damaging fences and crops. It goes without saying that you must have permission to shoot from the landowner. If he is a decent chap he might have a troop of girl guides camping out. He will not be pleased if you scare them out of their wits. And, neither will they!

Never attempt to rough shoot without a thorough knowledge of safety procedures. Always keep your dog in your sight and close to you unless he is carrying out a retrieve. If you cannot see your dog, the gun's safety catch must be on.

Before setting out rough shooting as a novice, it is worth having a few hours tuition and practice at a clay pigeon shooting range. There are many clay pigeon shooting clubs and it is a lively and challenging sport with a good social atmosphere.

If you intend to shoot or pick-up regularly, join a field sports or shooting society, which will provide you with all there is to know about safe shooting and the rules governing the sport, and also the relevant information on shotgun certificates and game licences.

Dress and Etiquette

For working tests, rough shooting or field trials, wear sensible outdoor clothing, bearing in mind that the shooting season often falls in the wettest and coldest part of the year (in the UK, at least). A warm jacket is essential, and useful if it has a large inside pocket for storing spare dummies, cartridges, and so on. Wear strong, well-fitting shoes or wellington boots with soles that provide a good grip. It is also worth bearing in mind that as well as being practical, warm and comfortable, dress should be sober and unobtrusive. Incidentally, in a formal shoot, never wear a cartridge belt (the implication being that your host can provide only twenty-five birds for you to shoot!)

Even if you are lucky enough to have permission to rough shoot at any time, always contact the farmer, gamekeeper, or the landowner himself, and ask if it is convenient. Never shoot 'blind', that is where the vegetation might conceal houses, public footpaths or roads. Always leave the land as tidy as you find it. Always thank the owner and manager as often as possible and try to offer them something from the bag. Similarly, at field trials or working tests, always thank the host personally for allowing their grounds to be used. Without the help and support of such committed people the appreciation and testing of the true nature of the Labrador would not be possible.

The Labrador 'Civil Service'

Guide Dogs for the Blind

Some training of guide dogs was attempted in 1819 in Vienna, but it was not until after the First World War that formal training began, this time in Germany. In 1931, a trial training scheme was carried out in the UK, and in 1934, The Guide Dogs for the Blind Association was founded in London and a training centre was established.

From the start, German Shepherd Dogs (Alsatians) were bred almost exclusively for the purpose, but today, Labradors, Golden Retrievers and crosses of both breeds, together with some German Shepherds, form the basis of the breeding programme.

The training of Labradors and other retrievers as guide dogs usually starts at about eleven months old. The Labrador temperament is ideal although he does have his disadvantages too, one of which is gluttony!

120

Guide dog Raybooth Midge with her proud owner.

The basic training takes about nine months, after which the young dog must be 'paired' with his new partner: the one who will rely on him totally, and literally put his life in his hands. This is the difficult part and the one that tests the skill of the trainer to the limit: there is more to it than than just effecting a physical match of 'big man equals big dog'. The temperaments and personalities must complement each other so that both guard and guarded can be ready to face a new life together.

Dogs for the Sick or Disabled

Of those Labradors that do not attain the high standard necessary to be a guide dog for the blind, some are given specialized training to enable them to lead very useful lives, not the least of which involves the giving and receiving of much love and attention. As well as giving constant support and companionship to a disabled person, a trained Labrador will provide a degree of personal protection. More sophisticated tasks such as barking on hearing a telephone, opening doors and operating switches give inestimable help to their grateful owners. That a Labrador has the ability to learn to open door latches, and gain access

121

Guide dog 'Major'.
(Rep. by permission of The Guide
Dogs for the Blind Association.)

Dog for the Disabled 'Jack' poses proudly in his harness and jacket. (Rep. by permission of
Dogs for the Disabled Association.)

so that he will get a nice reward, will come as no surprise to Labrador breeders all over the world.

Two other excellent schemes – the Pro Dogs Charity and PAT (Pets as Therapy) – give sick, elderly and disabled people, especially those who lead a lonely existence, the benefit of contact with loving dogs which they would otherwise be denied owing to their circumstances. There are now about 6,000 PAT dogs visiting hospitals, children's homes and hospices throughout Britain.

The Hearing Dogs for the Deaf scheme trains dogs to respond to different household sounds, which might include fire alarms, telephones, door bells and alarm clocks. Labradors who do this work act as the ears of their owner as well as faithful companions. The result is a great increase in the confidence and independence of the deaf person.

Search 'Sniffer' Dogs

The first official police dogs used in England were employed about the year 1909 to assist the railway transport police in detecting vagrants sleeping in the carriages and rolling stock. The dogs were not formally trained but used their noses and provided a guard for their handlers against any possible aggression! The use of dogs by other police forces soon became widespread and the Bloodhound, among other breeds, was trained for the job. In 1945, Labradors were employed by the Metropolitan Police for duty in Hyde Park, London and a dramatic cut in the crime level was the result. Labradors, together with other Retrievers, German Shepherds and Spaniels are especially trained to seek out a variety of 'quarry', which might include firearms, explosives or drugs, lost persons and, periodically, buried bodies. The dogs and their handlers work as an efficient team who are available to cover any eventuality. In the UK, the basic training of the dog and his handler is provided by a very rigorous twelve-week course operated by the RAF. An advanced course is aimed at detecting arms and explosives.

The success of these 'super sleuths' is evidenced from time to time by reports in the national newspapers when large amounts of illegal drugs or caches of weapons are seized. A Labrador named Jake became Ireland's top sniffer dog when he brought to light a drug haul worth over £9 million at the port of Rosslare. In fact, he was proving so successful that last year he was kidnapped for a period, perhaps by the thwarted drug dealers. Fortunately he was rescued unharmed. Subsequently, he was honoured by a 'Devotion to Duty' medal which was presented to him by the PRO Dogs Charity.

RAF 'Air Dog' carrying out a building search. (Rep. by permission of RAF Newton.)

Labrador 'Jake', Ireland's top sniffer dog receiving his 'Devotion to Duty Medal' a PRO Dogs award. With him are Handler Crosby, Customs Officer Lally and Mike Boulding of Dog World.

8

Showing

The first show for pedigree dogs was held in 1859, some fourteen years before the foundation of the Kennel Club. The first show organized by the showman Charles Cruft was held at the Royal Agricultural Hall, Islington, London in 1891; in 1942 the Kennel Club took over the running of Crufts and held the first show in 1948.

A useful dog is a prized possession and a handsome, useful dog enjoys being admired. It only requires a slight 'shove' in the direction of a show to get the novice dog owner to venture into the ring. Unfortunately, though, it is not often realized that a novice exhibitor can be encouraged to advance too fast too soon and, instead of learning the art (for that is what it is) of preparing and presenting a dog and enjoying a little success among relaxed company, the desire to 'take on the world' overcomes them and, unless the are very lucky, they quickly become disappointed.

Ringcraft

If you have a nice puppy, you may well take him to show training classes or 'dog school' as it is sometimes called. You can get the name of the training organiser from the secretary of the canine society in your area. However, before you commit yourself and your dog to a course of lessons, watch a training session on your own and make your mind up first. You may find that the training is swamped by a group of lovable but unruly animals in the throes of 'socializing' sessions. Or you could be enrolled in beginners' obedience which is excellent training but not appropriate for a novice exhibitor with a Labrador. My advice is to take an interest in what is going on, have a cup of tea during the break and ask a lot of questions. All dog enthusiasts are friendly and willing to set you off on the right track if first you are patient.

On the first evening you attend a ringcraft class, let your Labrador take you into the hall, specially if he is still a puppy. If he hesitates at the door, because it is new to him and very strange, do not force or drag him; wait until a suitable, confident dog arrives with his owner and follow them in. In extreme cases you may have to carry him into the hall. Thereafter, keep him close to you, refuse to be cajoled into joining the class in the ring; rather, let him just watch the proceedings. In all probability he will grow so inquisitive watching the other dogs that he will forget his reserve and enjoy a little attention.

At first, do not put any pressure on him to learn. You should learn to present or 'stand' your dog in front of the 'judge', adjusting the lead so that he stands away from you but looking at you. He should stand four-square on his feet with his head level and his ears relaxed. Being a Labrador, he will wag his tail enthusiastically if you show him a titbit. Usually, the judge will approach him head on, examine his head and open his mouth to look at his teeth. Keep your Labrador at a distance and let him meet the judge. (If you shorten his lead by 'winding it in' he will feel crowded and try to back away.) As the judge looks in his mouth, try to keep your dog's attention with the titbit, at the same time place your left hand at the back of his head to steady it. The judge will then proceed to inspect the front, hindquarters, coat and tail of your Labrador, paying great attention to the last two features if he is a 'gundog man'.

The Labrador should stand four-square. Sh.Ch. Follytower Pandora at Rocheby, born 1989, by Poolstead Pretentious at Rocheby ex Follytower Jill Too.

With the appraisal completed, the judge will ask you to move your Labrador either back and forth or anticlockwise in a triangle. Your dog will soon learn to enjoy this exercise and show himself off. With the dog on you left hand side, you give him the signal to move off, 'Get on'. You must adjust your pace to his so that he moves smoothly with his back level and without bobbing his head. You will be surprised at the speed at which he can trot and the amount of ground that he can cover. Watch his action closely and at the same time adjust your speed so that you negotiate the turns together. When you return, present him to the judge side on. As you are dismissed, give your Labrador the titbit as a reward.

In subsequent sessions, whether he has done well or not, give your dog plenty of praise and encouragement. It is very important in all forms of training to let him leave on a 'high note' and wanting more of the same. Incidentally, you will find that he is quite tired on the day following a training session, so do not be in a hurry to put him through it again. Let him take his time and think about it for a day or two.

Do not fall into the trap of ringcraft for the sake of it. It may be very nice to have an evening off, but remember that to him it is his evening on, and a very exhausting one at that. If you persist in flogging the same routine, week in, week out, he will become tired, then bored and, finally, very bored. And, in all probability he will lose the desire to show.

Types of Show

The Match

Most canine societies that organize dog training classes set aside an evening when they hold a 'Dog Match'. This is usually the first level at which one can gain dog showing experience with an element of competition. Matches are held under Kennel Club rules and only dogs owned by members of the canine society may take part. At a canine society match the dogs can be of any breed registered by the Kennel Club. The number of dogs taking part is limited to a maximum of sixty-four.

Competing in a match is very simple because, like a soccer cup 'knockout' competition, the judging is by elimination of one dog against another. Sometimes, adults and puppies compete separately. Each dog handler receives a number card and waits until he is called to present his dog to the judge. This is the first heat. If you are lucky you may be competing against another retriever. (If not you will have drawn the most immaculately prepared Lhasa-Apso in the room!)

The judge then examines and moves each dog in turn before declaring the winning number to the steward. When all the dogs have been assessed, the second heat is played by calling all the first heat winners to compete in pairs as before. The winners of this and subsequent heats are chosen in turn until one remains unbeaten. This dog is then declared 'Best in Match'.

Exemption Shows

Once you have begun to train your dog and attended a few classes you can start out on a bit of 'fun showing'. Exemption dog shows are run by charities, and are so called because the exhibits may (or may not) be unregistered with the Kennel Club and so the show is deemed to be exempt from the usual regulations. Additionally, both pedigree and mongrel dogs can take part, although the rules specify that up to five of the classes must be for pedigree dogs only. This is one of only two types of show (the other being the Primary show) which exhibitors can enter as they arrive on the day.

After the judge has examined all the dogs he will place them in the following order: 1st, 2nd, 3rd, Reserve, Very Highly Commended (VHC) and sometimes Highly Commended (HC). The fourth place is termed 'Reserve' because in the event that any higher-placed dog is disqualified, the Reserve would assume third place.

All dogs over six months of age can show at an Exemption show provided that they have not won any award that could count towards the title of champion under Kennel Club rules, or have won a Junior Warrant (see later) or an Obedience Certificate. Although success at Exemption shows will not earn you a Challenge Certificate or count towards qualifying your dog for entry into other shows, they are extremely useful for novice handlers (or novice dogs) to gain some valuable experience in the ring.

Limited, Sanction and Primary Shows

Eventually, you and your Labrador will be introduced to shows run either by a local canine society or a Labrador breed club. At these shows you will find that entry into the classes is more complicated. Separate classes are provided for minor puppies (6–9 months), puppies (6–12 months) and juniors (6–18 months). For older dogs a form of 'handicapping' is applied. Simply put, the more you win the higher the class you must enter. The more common classes are: Maiden (for dogs not having won a 1st prize); Novice (dogs not having won three 1st prizes); Tyro (five 1st prizes); Debutante (dogs not having won one 1st prize at an Open or Championship show); Undergraduate, Graduate, Post-Graduate and Limit classes (as for Debutante, but three, four, five and seven 1st prizes respectively). The top class is the open class, which is open to all. Sometimes classes are provided for Beginners (owner not having won 1st prize), Veteran (for dogs over seven years old), Stud-dog (which must include two of his progeny), Brood-bitch (which must include two of her progeny) and Brace (two of the same breed shown as a pair). Some of the shows will include Variety classes where dogs of more than one breed can compete.

The shows themselves are limited to dogs with different levels of achievement. Thus, the highest class at a Primary show is Maiden, for dogs with little or no experience of showing. Sanction shows are for more experienced dogs. The highest class is Post Graduate. Limited shows offer classes covering the full range outlined above, but entry is limited to owners who are members of the organizing society or club.

Open and Championship Shows

Classes held at Championship and Open shows have the same basic qualifications for entry as those for Limited and Sanction shows, which I have already listed above. However, because these shows are intended for the exhibition of dogs and bitches of the highest quality, the qualifying wins 1st, 2nd, 3rd, and so on, relate to places gained at Open and Championship shows only. Classes for puppies, juniors and veterans have age qualifications identical to those for Sanction shows.

Challenge certificates for the best of each sex are awarded only at Championship shows. A dog or bitch winning three Challenge Certificates under three different judges may be awarded the title of Champion (or Show Champion, if he is a gundog without a Show Gundog Working Certificate) with the approval of the Kennel Club. One certificate must be obtained when the dog is over twelve months old. Dogs that have not won three Challenge Certificates may enter the Limit class. Champions and show Champions must enter the Open class, which, as it states, is open to all.

Junior Warrants, for dogs aged between twelve and eighteen months, may be awarded following a succession of wins at both open and Championship shows. Three points are awarded for a 1st prize in a breed class at a Championship show and one point for a 1st prize at an Open show or at a Championship show where Challenge Certificates

Sh.Ch. Croftspa Hazelnut of Foxrush, born 1983, by Sh.Ch. Ard-margha Mad Hatter ex Foxrush Caprice of Croftspa. Holder of record for number of CCs won (45). (See Appendix for pedigrees.)

are not offered. Field trial classes are provided for dogs that have won prizes, i.e. Diplomas of Merit or Certificates of Merit at field trials.

Some Championship and Open shows are run on what is termed the Group System. Most kennel clubs classify dogs into groups, which roughly correspond to the different kinds of work or purpose for which each dog was originally bred. The UK Kennel Club has six group classifications: hounds; gundogs (to which Labradors belong); terriers; working ; toys; and utility.

When the judging of all the Labrador dogs has been completed, the class winners, if they have not been beaten in subsequent classes, compete for the dog's Challenge Certificate. Similarly, all the unbeaten bitches compete for the bitch's Challenge Certificate. The Best of Breed is then chosen from the dog and bitch Challenge Certificate winners. The competition for Best in Group (the gundog group in the Labrador's case) brings together all the Best of Breed winners, plus the winner of the Any Variety Not Separately Classified classes held for dogs without a breed classification at the show, to be assessed by the group judge. Winners in the group are placed 1st to 4th place. The winners of 1st place in each group then go forward to compete for Best in Show.

Open class winner at Crufts, Olympia, 1976.

1st.   *Ch. Timspring Sirius (out of picture).*
2nd.   *Eng & Ir. Ch. Oakhouse Glenarem Classic.*
3rd.   *Ch. Ballyduff Marketeer.*
4th.   *Ch. Follytower Merrybrook Black Stormer.*
5th   *Stanwood Puckwudgie.*

Crufts

Championship shows and the larger Open shows may be held over two or even three days. At the present time only Crufts, the Kennel Club's Championship show extends over four days. Entry for Crufts is by qualification at a recognized Championship show. At the present time, qualification for Crufts is achieved by wins in the following classes at Championship shows where Challenge Certificates are on offer: 1st and 2nd place in Minor Puppy class; 1st and 2nd place in Puppy class; 1st and 2nd place in Junior class; 1st and 2nd place in Post-graduate class; 1st, 2nd and 3rd in Limit class; and 1st, 2nd and 3rd in Open class. Winners of Challenge Certificates and Reserve Challenge Certificates also qualify for Crufts.

The Stud Book

Every year the Kennel Club publishes a 'stud book' which contains a record of all the major winners at Championship shows, field trials, working trials and obedience tests. It also lists the sex, colour, date of birth, owner, breeder and three generations of the dog's pedigree. All dogs have to qualify for entry into the Kennel Club Stud Book by virtue of their wins at Championship shows or in recognized trials. The places gained and the classes for qualification vary with the number of dogs in competition in the breed. This information is published annually. Currently, Labradors may qualify for entry into the Stud Book by winning either 1st, 2nd or 3rd place in the Limit and Open classes at a Championship show or 1st to 4th awards inclusive, or diplomas of merit at Field trials held under Kennel Club Field trial regulations. The winners at Championship Obedience classes (Class 'C') also qualify on winning a 1st, 2nd or 3rd prize.

Entering a Show

Before you enter a show, you must be sure that your dog is in good health and has been inoculated against the canine diseases (In the UK and most other countries, it is an offence to enter a dog if you suspect that he is suffering from even a mild infection of, say kennel cough.) Also, your dog must be registered at the Kennel Club. If he is still a puppy he must be at least six months old on the day of the show and if his name on his pedigree is still in the process of registration or transfer from the breeder to you, you must style him: Name Applied For (NAF) or Transfer Applied For (TAF).

Complete your entry form carefully, and check which classes your dog is eligible to enter. You may find that your dog is eligible to enter more than one class, Puppy and Maiden for example. He may also be

The correct show stance. Sh.Ch. Trenow Briar Rose, born 1986, by Joline Inkling of Follytower ex Trenow Minuet.

eligible for the Novice class, but you must weigh up the odds against his winning this, as he could be in competition with older dogs that have won two 1st prizes.

In the beginning, do not be influenced totally by your peers around the ringside. Make your own mind up where and when to show your dog and don't be afraid to stick your neck out and try an experiment. Don't limit yourself to local shows, either: try those that are a little outside your immediate area. Pay little heed to judging 'form', imagined preferences and tales of woe. The vast majority of judges are not fools and you still have a long way to go. It is up to you to keep it interesting. Trust in your own judgement and don't be afraid to lose. When you have a 'new' dog, choose a wide variety of judges, all-rounders (i.e. those qualified to judge a wide variety of breeds), breed specialists and novices. Don't be afraid to enter as a 'beginner', because that is where we all start and if your dog is good enough you may win first prize and that will be that. You have moved up one rung already!

As your show technique improves and your Labrador matures and begins to look forward to his fortnightly show outings, move him up into the harder classes. Don't be a 'mature graduate' for too long: stick your neck out again and see how he does. You might be surprised.

Show Preparation

It is in your own interest to brush up your ringcraft technique in the week before the show. Develop a routine of 'Stand', 'Teeth' and 'Move' at home, but do not overdo the rehearsals or your dog will become bored and stale. Twenty minutes per dog, two or three times weekly, is quite enough.

Labradors are trained to show with a piece of cooked liver or sausage titbit as a reward after each step in his showing routine has been carried out correctly, or near enough correctly. So, take up a practice position as though in class. Stand your Labrador four-square on a loose lead, head level, ears relaxed, tail wagging ('Good-boy', titbit); then both of you relax. Move into judging position: stand him four-square as above for the judge to examine him (titbit). Move him in a triangle, stand again, return to first practice position ('Good boy, titbit); then both relax.

Learn to handle your dog properly in the ring. Well-run ringcraft classes will help in the early stages of your showing, but there is no substitute for a once-a-week practice. These wise words were said to me once, 'You will teach your first dog; your second dog will teach you; but you will not win together until you are on your third dog.'

Lenches Pickle, born 1987, by Sh.Ch. Poolstead Pocket Picker ex Lenches Felicity, standing four-square on a loose lead.

Learn to handle your Labrador in the ring. (Paignton Championship Dog Show.)

Show Equipment

Labradors are best shown on a light, nylon slip-lead about 43in(110 cm) long and ⅜in(10mm) wide. Obtain a couple of these so you will have a spare with you. Also, a light soft rope slip-lead is useful for leading him to and from the car park, because it makes it easier to handle your dog when you are loaded up with bag and baggage. It also keeps the show slips clean for the ring!

Buy yourself a stout tack-bag similar to a sports holdall. In it you should have: show passes, car parking slips, catalogue vouchers, bench chain and collar, soft brush, medium-hard brush, hound mitt, towel, damp flannel, two show slips, a plastic bottle of mild disinfectant, band-aids, a small pair of blunt-nosed sharp scissors (in case you forget to neaten the tail beforehand), a light plastic water bowl for his drink and a small bag of titbits. Personally, I do not like waist slung bait-bags, because they remind me of nose-bags for cart horses, and Labradors are not cart horses. Some judges disapprove of excessive baiting of Labradors in the ring because it spoils their natural expression (which should be good-tempered, not ravenous).

Not all shows have ample seating, so a lightweight fisherman's folding stool will come in useful. Some of these are conveniently made to fasten to the handles of your show tack-bag.

Grooming

Keep your Labrador to his regular feeding routine and go through his grooming ritual two or three times in the same week. Prepare his coat by brushing it with a medium-sized stiff-bristle brush, starting at the neck and working down over the shoulders, back, haunches and tail. Do not forget to brush his legs and chest, but do not be too rough. Finish off his coat with the corduroy or stiff velvet side of a hound mitt. Work in the direction of the lie of the coat hairs. This will impart a nice bloom to his appearance. Clean his ears with a drop of cleaner obtainable from the vet, but do not probe his ears with 'cotton buds'. The removal of any deep or stubborn deposits should be attended to professionally. It is a good idea to wipe his eyes gently with a soft handkerchief before you enter the ring.

The only trimming a Labrador should require is a neatening of the final tail hairs to remove any untidy twist. Occasionally the feet whiskers appear untidy around the nails and these can be removed with care to give a rounded appearance.

Labrador coats should be short and dense and feel fairly hard to the hand. This last is due to the natural oils in the coat which help to give it its weather resistance. It will serve no purpose if you bath out these oils before a show, even if you feel the bath will enhance the cream 'flashes' in a yellow coat. The judge will detect the soft texture as untypical of the Labrador. Similarly, beware of coat preparations that are not water-based, because under recent Kennel Club rules, many substances once used for preparation now are not permitted in the show-ring.

Do not be afraid to show a Labrador who bears an 'honourable' scar, such as a scratch obtained in the course of his training. If he is sound and his coat and make are right he will not disgrace you.

Dress

The type of dress worn for showing Labradors is governed largely by personal preferences and the time of year. Nowadays, winter shows are held in large exhibition halls or sports and leisure centres, which are invariably well-heated, so you must be prepared to show your dog in smart casual indoor clothes. As the exhibition of Labradors usually involves a fair amount of running about you will not need to be clad in your heavy, oiled-cotton, outdoor coat. At the height of summer, you will probably wear smart but casual summer clothes, and for outdoor shows take with you a light waterproof jacket.

At the Show

When you arrive at the show, buy a catalogue, which will list the names, addresses and bench numbers of the exhibits, and the entries in each of the classes. Check your ring and bench number and, if you have a puppy dog with you, consult the ring plan so that you know the location and number of the Labrador puppy ring. It does not hurt to stretch his legs after a car journey, while you seek out the ring before you put him on his bench.

The Kennel Club rule is that the dog should not be absent from his bench for more than fifteen minutes at one time unless he is competing. This allows you to exercise him when necessary and prepare him for the ring. The benches are raised individual compartments consisting of wooden baseboards separated by metal partitions. The baseboards are supported on wooden trestles. A typical bench for a Labrador would be 27in(69cm) wide by 36in(90cm) deep, and about 18in(45cm) off the ground. This provides a convenient seat for both dog and exhibitor. When the dog is on his bench he must be secured to the metal ring provided by a strong chain clipped to his collar. Benching chains can be bought from the dog show accessory stalls which are found at most Championship shows. Only the dog's exhibit number may be displayed above the bench together with a small card bearing the owner's kennel name and address.

Give the pup a drink and settle him on his bench and keep him warm. He must be safely chained, not too tightly but secure enough to stop him wriggling off, sit closely with him and let him rest. In the case of an inexperienced dog or young puppy, do not leave him unattended. If you must leave the bench, arrange for a good friend to watch over him for a few minutes.

Ten minutes before judging is due to start, get your dog off his bench and give him a good brush and polish from head to tail and wipe his eyes. Walk quietly to the ringside and keep your eyes open. Watch for the judge to enter the ring; he may instruct his steward on how he wants the dogs to be moved. Listen for the steward to announce your class.

Arrange to have your dog standing when judging begins. Sh.Ch. Tibblestone the Chorister, born 1985, by NZ Ch. Carpenny Chateau Cranspire ex Sandylands Forever Amber at Tibblestone.

Once in the ring, take your place in the line of new dogs indicated by the steward. Choose a patch of level ground or, of you cannot avoid a sloping part, face your dog up-hill and do a quick practice 'stand'. Keep your eye on the judge because it does no harm to have your dog looking 'together' when he takes his first glance around the ring. If there is time let your puppy relax and sit if need be until the judge begins his first circuit of inspection. Arrange to have your dog standing by the time the judge is looking at the dogs about two or three before you.

Be alert and aware. No one breed is full of perfect exhibitors. Occasionally you will find examples of 'gamesmanship'; much of it is largely unintentional but persistent offenders can be annoying. If you allow yourself a reasonable amount of space for your dog you will be able to minimize most of the problems posed by close neighbours, such as those who may not give you enough space to allow you to get your dog's neck at the right angle, and 'coverers' who take an inner ring position in the crowd, thus coming between your dog and the judge. If you feel you are being placed in an impossible situation, it is quite in order quietly to leave the line and find yourself another place nearer the end, but this must be done without fuss.

Do not talk to the judge unless he speaks to you to ask a question or give you direction. When you are asked to move your dog – usually in a triangle – listen carefully to make sure you know which way you are expected to go. If he asks you a question about your dog, answer it politely, and concisely; do not go into lengthy explanations about anything.

If you do not win a place in the winner's line-up, leave the ring quickly and without fuss. Remember that whatever the outcome, you must have nothing but praise for your Labrador. He was probably showing with all his heart. Don't be put off by failure; it will be a constant companion, so you may as well recognize it. Try to see where you are going wrong. Is your dog too thin or too fat compared with the others in the class? Did he stand nicely for the judge or did he welcome him like a long lost friend. Did the judge really see his teeth? Did you both move together in the 'triangle'. Is your dog's coat fully grown in or 'slightly on the blow'. (Spit on your hand and run it down his back and flank: are there any loose hairs?).

Eventually your dog will win a place in the winners line-up. Or, he may be pulled out in the 'cut' (the selection by the judge of a few promising dogs from a large class). If the class has over fifteen or twenty dogs, and you are in the selected seven or eight, this is a 'moral win' in my estimation, and may be a sign of things to come.

We all see the well-known exhibitors who seem to win most times with a dog just like yours. You will eventually learn why this is justified more often than not. Experienced breeders do not waste expensive entry fees unless they are confident that the dog they are going to show has what it takes and is in the best possible condition. Also they know, from bitter experience, that no one is going to gain a place at a Championship show with a Labrador who has not got a kind, intelligent expression in his eye, a good thick overcoat concealing a dense second coat and a good typical otter tail.

You enter for the judge's opinion; be prepared for it and be prepared for a little constructive criticism. Try to think before you open your mouth to speak about the other dogs. Listen to yourself when you are chatting to your friends at the ring-side. Be a little suspect of the 'gleaming nuggets' of inside information offered. Time will tell whether they are true or not. It is unusual for Labrador exhibitors to be unfairly critical or catty, it does not somehow become them in the company of Gundogs. The vast majority of the exhibitors will want you to enjoy yourself and have a good day with a good dog, but be prepared for some jealousy because no one is perfect! You should be patient because your dog also has a lot to learn; a show dog is not just any old dog, and he will soon tell you this, in his own way. Be very proud of his little achievements and don't forget to tell him so.

Remember, when you are in the ring at a Championship show you are literally on view to the dog world as a whole. Just one little grub can make a whole apple bad, so be polite and courteous in and out of the ring, even if it hurts! When you have been showing for a couple of years, be kind and patient with newcomers and their unruly, boisterous dogs. Be friendly, smile as you enter the ring and smile as you come out. There's always another show – and it's only a bit of fun, after all.

Show Quality

Our first 'show dog' was a red Cocker Spaniel called Willy, after whose acquisition we resolved to show dogs seriously. Three weeks before the show, which was to be held at Nailsworth, we took our spaniel to a gentleman 'breed specialist' to have him properly stripped out. He did not enjoy this at all. (I don't think that either of them did!) When the great day arrived, Willy behaved abominably in the ring and refused to have his teeth examined by the judge. Shame-faced, we left the venue resolving never again to waste our money and time on such a futile pastime. On the way out, a seasoned exhibitor tried to encourage us to persevere. She complimented us on the preparation of Willy's coat, and especially the beautiful feathers on his feet.

The point which I am trying to make is that you will not know whether you have a dog of 'show quality' until you show it. And you must be prepared to be disappointed. One of the sorriest sights an experienced exhibitor is called upon to witness is the procession of lovely (and some not so lovely) pet Labradors into the show-ring. It is no use trying to fool oneself into the trap of 'try, try, try again'. It does not work. I hear the cry that the exception proves the rule. If you do try, and keep on trying eventually you will win, and possibly win well. But that does not give you a better dog, but rather, a false dawn. Unfortunately, such a win encourages one to persevere further, even to the extent of breeding from such a dog.

Having said this, it is also time to say that one or two failures does not mean that you do not stand a chance of success. If you are honest with yourself in your assessment of your dog and more experienced

The Yellow Labrador Club Championship Show, 1986, the last show to be judged by Mrs Gwen Broadley (Sandylands).
Best in Show – Ch. Kupros Master Mariner.
Best Bitch – Sh.Ch. Croftspa Hazelnut of Foxrush.
Best Puppy – Tibblestone the Chorister (later Sh.Ch.)

people in the breed encourage you to persevere, you will eventually find all the initial disappointment worthwhile.

Showing Around the World

Australia

Each Australian State, with the exception of the Northern Territory, has a Labrador Breed Club which is affiliated to the Australian State Canine Council.

The Labrador Standard for the breed in Australia is that of the English Kennel Club, which is very helpful to visiting judges from the UK.

In Australia, the show classes are as follows: Baby class; for dogs and bitches aged three to six months; Minor Puppy class, for dogs and bitches aged six to nine months; Puppy class, for dogs and bitches six to twelve months; Junior class, for dogs and bitches aged nine to eighteen months; Intermediate class, for dogs and bitches aged eighteen to thirty-six months; Novice class, for dogs and bitches not having won 1st prize at an Open or Championship show, (baby class excepted); Graduate class, for dogs and bitches not having won a CC; Limit class, for dogs and bitches not having enough points to win a Champion title; State bred class, for dogs and bitches native to the state in which the show is held; Open class, for any dog or bitch.

Aust. & NZ Ch. Black Shadow of Veralea, born 1990, by Cambremer Thatcher ex NZ Ch. Mascot Rayners Game (Owner: Mrs Dunstan, Australia.)

Ch. Attikonak Khatrine with Progeny group winning BIS at Malmö
International Championship Show (All breed). (Owner: Mrs Ek, Sweden.)

Follies Viscountess, born 1986, by Int. Nor. Ch. Mallards Clay
Basker ex Follies Pink Witch (Owner: Mrs Kaitila, Finland.)

142

Scandinavia and Finland

For simplicity and as an example of the Scandinavian practice, I will take the Danish show scene as typical. The Danish Kennel Club (DKK) holds thirteen shows annually under FCI (Federation Cynologique International) and NKU (Nordic Kennel Union, comprising Denmark, Finland, Iceland, Norway and Sweden) rules, where Challenge Certificates (CCs) are competed for. Also, several international shows are held where International Beauty Certificates (Certificate d'Aptitude au Championat International de Beauté, (CACIB) may be awarded.

In general the Labrador Standard for the breed on the Continent is accepted as that of the country of origin (in this case the English Kennel Club Standard).

All dogs are 'graded' against the Breed Standard in each class. The grades are 1 (very promising), 2, 3 and 0. Those graded 'very promising' compete against each other and are placed, finally, 1st, 2nd, 3rd and 4th. The winners may compete against the 'very promising' in the Youngster class. The overall winner of the show gains the CC provided that they also have passed an obedience test under DKK rules. To qualify as a Danish Champion, a dog or bitch must hold three CCs and two prizes in the Open class at a 'B' Field Trial.

In Finland, show dogs must be registered with the Finnish Kennel Club (FKC) and the shows are organized by the FKC or the Finnish Retriever Organization, both of which also publish breed magazines. All Finnish shows are held under FKC rules. Forty-two breed shows are held on average per year, plus two International shows with CACIBs on offer, and two speciality shows which award CACIBs also.

Dogs are first judged individually and then a critique is written which may be published in the breed magazine. As is common in Europe and Scandinavia, prize ribbons are awarded to the class winners as follows: red – Excellent, 1st; blue – Very Good, 2nd; and so on. All first-prize winners are then assessed as a group and the winners placed 1st to 5th. The judge can award a Certificate of Quality (SA) to those that he thinks are worthy or he can refuse to award any at all. All the SA winners then compete in the Best Dog or Bitch class where the winners are placed 1st to 5th. In this competition, the 1st winner is awarded the CC if he is not a Champion already or is under two years of age and having already won two CCs, in which case the CC may be awarded to the next dog that qualifies for it. For the title of Champion to be awarded, three CCs are required to be gained under three different judges. At least one CC must be won after the dog is over two years old.

France

There are no rules prohibiting any Labrador from showing provided that he has a pedigree. However, in order that a dog may be bred from, both dogs must pass an examination by an approved breed judge, a test called 'Confirmation'. The judge assesses the type, size, temperament, bite (including number of teeth), testicles, and so on. This can cause some discussion among breeders as many of the judges are 'all-rounders' rather than breed specialists.

The French show scene is divided into three types: National Championship shows; International Championship Shows; and the Labrador Breed Club Championship show. At all Championship shows, the Challenge Certificate (CAC) may be awarded to winners in the Open or Champion classes. The Best of Breed is chosen from winners of all the classes (Puppy class excepted). CACIB and Reserve CACIB awards may be given at international shows only, and may be gained by the winners of the Open, Field Trial and Champion classes. However, if the dog considered by the judge to be worthy of the CAC (or CACIB at an international show) is already a French Champion, the CAC (or CACIB, as appropriate) is awarded to the dog in reserve place.

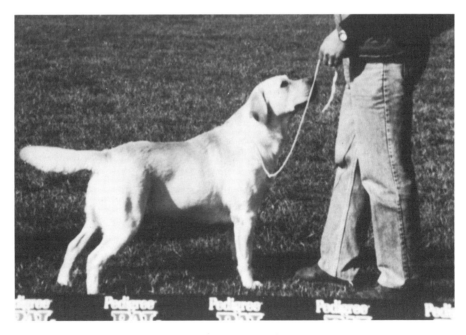

Swiss Ch. Gladlab Chase Me Charley. (Owner: Mr Gad, France.)

To gain the award of French Champion, a dog must win (under three different judges), a CAC at the Labrador Club of France Championship show or a French Championship show, plus a CAC at a French National show, plus a CAC at a French International Show, plus two Field Trial Awards. All these awards must be won within two years of gaining the CAC at the Labrador Club of France Championship show or all is lost. The award of International Champion requires two CACIBs won in two different countries under two different judges, plus a Field Trial award. One year and one day must elapse between winning the first and second CACIB.

The organization and control of Labradors is in the hands of the Labrador Breed Club, which has the power to recommend judges to the French Kennel Club for all shows including Championship and International Shows. Surprisingly, few breeders and exhibitors find any opportunities to learn ringcraft in France.

Germany

At present there are no facilities for show training in German Labrador clubs. It is recommended that a new owner should contact the breeder of their puppy for showing hints. As the breed is still in relatively small numbers in Germany, there are only a few breeders who own more than five or six dogs and there are no professional handlers for Labradors shown under the rules of the German Kennel Club (VDH).

At German Championship shows, there are two different titles of Champion to be won. The first is a VDH (Kennel Club) Champion, for which the dog must win four CACs under three different judges with two of the CACs won at an international show. A year and a day must elapse between the first and last qualifying awards. The second is the title of German Champion (under Labrador Club of Germany (LCD) rules), for which the dog must win four CACs, or three CACs and two Res. CACs in the same time span as above.

CACs are awarded to each sex provided they are entered in the classes higher than the youngster class. If a youngster wins three CACs under three different judges he would qualify for the award Jugenchampion. At international shows the best exhibit in each sex may win a CAC and a CACIB. A winner of a CACIB in both Germany and another country may claim the title of International Champion on passing a hunting test, provided that one year has elapsed between the first and last CACIB wins.

145

All dogs are graded against the Breed Standard in each class and each receives a written critique. The grades are; 'Excellent', 'Very Good' and 'Good'. Those 'Very Good' and above compete against one other and are placed finally, 1st, 2nd, 3rd and 4th. The winners may compete against the 'very promising' in the Youngster class.

South Africa

Approximately twenty shows are held in the Johannesburg and Witwatersrand region each year. The other shows, which number about a dozen, are held near Cape Town and in Natal. As the distance between shows is very great 'back to back' shows, held by two or three breed clubs at the same venue, are fairly common. Hence two or three sets of CCs are on offer on consecutive days. CCs are offered at single breed (speciality) shows and All-breed shows. Five points are needed to qualify for the title of Champion. CCs are worth either one or two points each, depending on the size of the entry of dogs.

The Labrador Standard for the breed in South Africa is accepted as that of the county of origin, so in this case the English Kennel Club Standard is used. All shows and dog events are held under the rules of the Kennel Union of South Africa (KUSA), which has the authority to approve and appoint judges. Stewards may get training tuition and information from the Stewards Association of the Transvaal.

The United States

The American Kennel Club controls all aspects of dogdom in the USA. The Labrador competes in the Sporting Group for purposes of classification. Most of the Labrador breed clubs in the different states are 'show' organizing clubs, although many also support obedience and hunting tests. Working certificate tests are held annually. The running of Field trials are the main prerogative of the retriever clubs.

Many of the dogs in the USA are professionally handled in the ring. Because of the large distances between venues, many shows are arranged in a 'back to back' circuit, as in South Africa, with two or three shows held over consecutive days.

Championship shows are sanctioned by the AKC. To gain Championship status, points are awarded relating to the total entry of Labradors, on a scale set by the governing body. Also, according to the region it is in, a dog must acquire a total of 15 points including two 'major' (3 to 5 point) shows to become a champion.

Am. Ch. Braemar Duggan, Best of Breed, National speciality Show, California 1979 – Judge Mrs Satterthwaite GB. (Owner: Mrs Borders.)

The regular classes of the AKC are: Puppy (for dogs aged six to twelve months); twelve months to eighteen months old, champions excluded; Novice (for dogs aged six months and over, whelped in USA, Canada, Mexico or Bermuda, and who have not won three first prizes, or one or more Championship points); Bred-by-Exhibitor (for dogs over six months old, bred in the regions stated for Novice, and who must be handled by the breeder or immediate family member); American-bred (for dogs over six months old, whelped in USA as a result of a mating in USA); Open (for all dogs aged six months and over); Winners (for dogs of the same sex who have won 1st prizes in the above classes).

The Labrador Standard for the breed in North America is different from that of the English Kennel Club Standard in that the points are more detailed and desired heights (maximum and minimum) are specified.

147

9

Judging and Stewarding

All dog show organizers and committees rely on good stewards to help organize the smooth running of the show. Gate stewards are invaluable for checking the dog passes at the entrance to the ground and, more important, checking dog passes at the exit so that the dogs are with their correct owners as they leave.

Ring stewards are there to check that the exhibitors and their dogs are in the correct class and ring. Also they assist the judge to deal efficiently with the exhibits and to try to follow the timing of the show. Generally in the UK, stewards are unpaid at the smaller shows, although some Championship Show Societies pay modest expenses, but stewards always get a free lunch, plus light refreshment during the day and free passes to the show.

Before the judge commences, a steward will prepare all the paperwork, prize cards and rosettes, if these are offered. A good steward will not interfere with the judging of the dogs, but must assist the judge

Sh.Ch. Balrion King Frost, born 1976, by Sh.Ch. Sandylands Clarence of Rossbank ex Balrion Royal Princess.

with his judging book, check that the numbers worn by the owners of the exhibits are correct, and that all the dogs transferred from an incorrect class have been authorized. He makes the exhibitors aware that judging has commenced and sometimes he will visit the benches to check.

During the judging, the steward is responsible for ensuring that dogs at the ringside do not interfere with the judging of the class, that photography is not intrusive, and that exhibits are not attracted from outside the ring. He will also arrange for the results to be taken to the secretary's office for collation.

At the end of each class the steward hands out the prize cards to the winners, notes the results on the appropriate forms in the judge's book and writes them on a blackboard for all to see. It is the steward's responsibility to ensure that Challenge Certificates and Reserve Certificates are completed and signed by the judge.

In Great Britain no paper qualifications are necessary to become an efficient show steward. In some other countries, such as the USA, Finland and South Africa, stewards may get formal tuition and information from their own Kennel Club or, in the case of South Africa, the Stewards Association of the Transvaal. In Finland, formal training is given by The FKC and qualification is by examination. Ring stewards at American shows are appointed by the show organizers and must prove to have a sound knowledge of judging procedure, breed classification and rules. There is no formal training for stewards in France or Germany; all are volunteers obtained from Club members. Some canine societies in the UK hold day seminars for aspiring stewards, but the greater part of a steward's education begins in the ring, usually as an assistant to a more experienced person.

You may meet some interesting characters stewarding the dog ring, and it is an invaluable way to gain more experience of different breeds and to learn what is required of a judge.

All dog show societies welcome offers of assistance from apprentice stewards and are only too pleased to encourage them. Stewarding is a very good way of getting to know the pros and cons of a breed and the sight of some very good dogs, too. It should be a part of every potential judge's portfolio, in my view.

When you have been committed to the breed for a few years, you may receive a letter inviting you to judge, say, eight classes of Labradors at an Open show. This is a sobering experience because with power comes responsibility, and you must ask yourself if you have the temperament to accept judging Labradors as a test of your ability to assess the breed impartially and objectively. And, more practically, you have to ask if you have the physical stamina to be able to make an objective judgement after judging the hundredth Labrador, when you might dither over placing the first.

If you accept the appointment you will have set out on a solitary path, because you will be a judge-in-exhibitor's-clothing at every show you attend, and from now on you will regard not only Labradors but all other breeds with a different, more critical eye.

It is true to say that some people – and I respect them very much for their honesty – truthfully admit that they could not enjoy being a judge. They understand the nature of the change it would make to their hobby, and if you are one of these, you might skip the rest of this chapter and enjoy your showing.

Judge's Records

When you have received an invitation, you must usually reply within fifteen days. Check in your diary that you are available. Keep a file of all your appointments and judging correspondence, and keep all your judging books together. As your experience widens, keep a record of the shows that you have judged; this should include the name and type of show, the date, and the number of classes, dogs, entries and any absentees.

In the letter of invitation it will state any conditions that you must fulfil under the rules of the Society. For example, in recognition of your acceptance, the Society might request that you refrain from judging Labradors for a period of six months prior to the show, within a radius of eighty miles of the venue. You must adhere rigidly to these conditions. Also the Society will inform you whether they would be prepared to pay any judging fee or travel expenses and, in case of a long-distance appointment, whether overnight hotel accommodation will be provided. It is entirely up to you whether you ask for travelling expenses, but in my estimation, it is bad form to demand a fee for judging your own breed.

Once you have accepted a written appointment, you are then party to a legal contract to judge. If, for any reason, you are not able to keep the appointment, no matter how unfortunate the circumstances, you must contact the secretary of the show at the earliest opportunity and confirm your predicament in writing.

Qualifications

In the United Kingdom there are no formal or written qualifications necessary before a novice judge may enter the ring. Judging appointments are by invitation only and are subject to the approval of the organizing society or breed club. However, approval to award Challenge Certificates in the United Kingdom may be given only by the Kennel Club. In order for approval to be sought, the prospective judge must complete a questionnaire listing his prior judging and breeding experience and any other relevant information (including seminars, committee service, and so on). The Society is then at liberty to confirm or deny the appointment on the basis of the information submitted. It serves no purpose to submit a questionnaire to the Kennel Club if there is insufficient evidence of judging experience. Approval will only be *considered* if there is a minimum of at least five years' judging of Labradors at Open and Limited shows, including a Breed Club show, listed. Also, the number of dogs bred or owned by the petitioner and entered in the Stud Book must be stated. You should note that future invitations will not be approved until the first appointment has been completed without a formal complaint being received.

In the USA judges are appointed by the AKC and must meet certain key criteria; for example, sufficient breed knowledge, good ring procedure, impartiality and ethical behaviour.

The expression tells all. Beechcroft Talmarc Tartan. (Breeder: Mrs Wiest, USA.)

151

For Australian judges, training schemes and written examinations covering the history, standard and purpose of the breed of dog in question, are organized by the local Canine Council in each state.

In Denmark, France, Finland and the majority of the continental countries, judges are approved by examinations held by the Breed Club and the appropriate Kennel Club. To qualify as a show judge in Denmark, the candidate must first sit an examination set by the DKK. Selection for shows is done by recommendation by the Labrador or Retriever Club. In the judging, each dog must be assessed and graded individually and receive its own critique stating the good and bad points.

Finnish judges must pass an examination set by the FKC to qualify for judging shows in the whole of Finland. The Labrador Standard for Labradors in Finland is accepted as that of the country of origin, in this case the English Kennel Club Standard. For show stewards, formal training is given by the FKC and qualification is by examination.

Judges at German shows are approved by the Kennel Club VDH following a written examination. It is usual for a new judge to have completed several appointments as an assistant to a senior judge in the ring.

In France, judges are approved by examinations held by the Breed Club and the Kennel Club. As a rule judges do not breed commercially. All dogs have a written critique which is presented to the exhibitor after the show. These are rarely published.

The Labrador Standard for Labradors on the continent in general (FCI rules) is accepted as that of the country of origin, in this case the English Kennel Club Standard.

Integrity

Do not place yourself in any position, socially or professionally, where you could be suspected of soliciting a judging appointment. Quite aside from anything else, a temptation to disregard future legitimate proposals for such a person to judge will reside permanently in the collective memory of the panel. Pushing to judge is counter-productive.

When you enter the ring, do not stare at the exhibitors as they take their places. Instead, concentrate on the dogs as a whole and try to get a feel for the standard of the class. Avoid the temptation to look at who is entered; concentrate on judging the dogs. Above all, don't panic and try to recite the Breed Standard in your head; instead, repeat to yourself 'temperament, type and transportation' (the three Ts). Then let the dogs judge themselves. By that I mean, take each exhibit one at a time; the true Labradors will shine out like stars. Do not allow your judging to become fudged by trying to 'get by' by guess or by gosh, and then rely on your wits to get you out of a fix at the end of the day. This does not work because you cannot produce a Best of Breed from a row of mediocre unbeaten dogs. Neither is it fruitful in the long run to rely on putting up the Establishment, well-known faces or club officials. It is not unknown for experienced breeders to try out their second- or third-string dog (knowing full well the limitations of their stock) to see what you will do with it. Rely on your knowledge, and put each dog in his correct place with respect to the other exhibits. If a dog is the best, put him at the top; if not, don't place him. Avoid the temptation to share out the prizes. Do not be afraid of repeating yourself when putting dogs of the same type from the same kennel in first place, sometimes, seemingly, over and over again. If they are the best dogs, so be it! Stick to what your eye can see and your hands tell you.

Finally, a word from Mrs Gwen Broadley, who said, 'If you have to think twice about it there must be a reason'. Hence, take care, don't place it.

Dress and Etiquette

To a certain extent, a judge should present himself in the ring like the good Field-Marshall. After all, you are on parade and should set a good example. Also, possibly a hundred Labradors are going to assemble for your inspection and all will be (or should be) in their best 'bib and tucker', smartly brushed and polished. It is only fair that you should return the compliment. A gentleman should wear a jacket and tie (the latter can be tucked into the shirt, out of the way, when in the ring), plain trousers and comfortable shoes (but not trainers, in my opinion). I would suggest that because judging Labradors involves getting close to a lot of hairy, oily (possibly muddy) Labradors, a great deal of standing, a certain amount of bending forward and a lot of walking up and down, ladies should avoid navy blue or black suede, high stiletto heels, seductive perfume, exceptional décolletage, 'second skin' leather trousers or taffeta skirts, or any combinations of the above. Do not mock, I have seen it!

It is essential for everyone's peace of mind that you arrive in good time for a judging appointment. Give yourself at least thirty minutes to visit the comfort station, have time for a coffee and to collect your thoughts. Do not be tempted to go straight out to the ringside or you will give your stewards and the exhibitors heart failure thinking they have missed an early start. Collect your judging book and rosette or badge from the secretary as soon as you arrive and enquire where you will meet your ring steward. Unless you are instructed otherwise by the secretary, commence judging in the ring promptly at the published time. You can always take a little extra time over the first class (but only the first class) to allow for last-minute hold-ups, but you must make up this time rigorously so that you do not get behind. Twenty minutes lost before lunch becomes forty minutes after lunch, which is impossible to recoup.

Do not invite your children or other relations or close friends to watch you judge from the steward's table. Even if you do not think they will distract you, other people, especially the exhibitors, may think that they will. Do not be tempted to join in general conversation with anyone in the ring, especially not the exhibitors. However innocent such an exchange may be, it will give other exhibitors, and for that matter other officials, reason to question your impartiality. In any case, no exhibitor will expect it from you, however familiar you may be with that person on a social level outside the ring.

Be polite and courteous at all times, remember to thank your stewards.

Assessing the Dogs

You must know the standard description of the breed, know how the standard was drawn up and how its implications affect the looks and performance of the dog today. Nowadays, not all Labradors have the opportunity to carry a hare or swim from a boat, although many of them do. But they must have the neck and shoulder construction to enable them to do the former, if required, and a deep chest and otter tail to enable them to do the latter.

Temperament

The Standard requires a Labrador's temperament to be: 'Intelligent, keen and biddable, with a strong will to please. Kindly, with no trace of aggression or undue shyness'.

The guide to a dog's temperament lies in his eyes, the set of his ears, his overall stance and the angle of his tail. When you are called on to judge a Labrador, his approach should be relaxed and good-tempered

Temperament: intelligent, keen and biddable. Charway Hope of Abbeystead.

with an affectionate response to your touch. Sometimes he will tend to 'fly' his ears (hold them slightly puckered at the fold and fairly high up on his head) at first. This is because he is initially excited and slightly unsure of his situation. His own 'Top dog' is offering him to another 'Top dog'. How would you feel? Nervous? Like a promotion interviewee, I think would best describe it.

When he senses from your tone of voice that you approve of him, his ears should hang normally close to his head, his expression should be soft and kind, his body stance should be relaxed, yet potentially agile, and his tail should be animated but not a blur. It should certainly not be erect and quivering.

Breed Type

'A Labrador should look like a Labrador and nothing else'. So said Mary Roslin Williams. There are certain fundamental characteristics which a Labrador must have in order that a judge will know immediately that it is a Labrador. Good strong evidence of these characteristics or points is known as breed type. Adversely, the evidence of characteristics which are intrinsically part of the type of another breed are

155

highly detrimental in a Labrador and should be penalized in judging. Furthermore, if the points relating to the other breed or breeds are strong enough to outweigh some of the Labrador characteristics then this should cause the judge (at least in thought if not in deed) to disqualify the exhibit from competing. In practice, this means that the dog is discarded at the earliest opportunity.

The Labrador can be traced back to different types of ancient dogs. As a group, retrievers carry the seeds of hounds, mastiffs, pointers, Newfoundlands and possibly sheepdogs. These roots go back to the Labrador's geographical origins. Over hundreds of years a purebred Labrador has been evolved by careful breeding and in-breeding. At the same time, randomly and, in more recent times, deliberately, the Labrador has suffered inter-breeding by owners desirous of changing its looks to give more (or less) substance, or to alter its conformation, or to 'tune it up' for extra speed. The last was achieved by crossing it with a quicker, more elegant dog, such as a pointer or even a Greyhound.

Thus, on entering the ring a Labrador judge is presented with what is a refined pudding with ingredients produced by good recent line-breeding based on an ancient recipe made up of out-crossings of Foxhound or pointer, plus a generous portion of Flat-coated Retriever, a good helping of Golden Retriever and a sprinkle of Chesapeake or Curly-coated Retriever. Occasionally, the pudding may contain spicy bits of Bloodhound, Greyhound, Elkhound, Setter, Rottweiler, and even Doberman; some of these may come bubbling to the surface.

Labradors
A Labrador must be short-coupled, broad in skull with a defined stop; broad and deep through chest and ribs; broad and strong over loin and hindquarters. He must be good-tempered, intelligent and kindly in his expression. He must have a rounded, thickly clothed tail, tapering towards the tip, described as an 'otter tail'. A judge of Labradors must know these breed points like the back of his hand.

An exhibit must be penalized if he *strongly* reminds you of any of the breeds mentioned below because in an ideally purebred animal such characteristics are breed faults.

Foxhounds
Foxhound blood is characterized when the head shows a lack of stop, the front is upright and atypically muscled with fore-chest strongly defined, and the feet are extra tight like a cat's feet. Foxhounds stand slightly higher at the withers and have a pronounced stern (tail)

General appearance: strongly built, short coupled, very active; broad in skull, broad and deep through chest and ribs; broad and strong over loins and hindquarters (from KC standard).

Breed points (*italic*) are shown in the diagram below. Typical descriptions used by judges in critiques are shown within quotes ('…').

'Well-set ears', i.e. rather far back on head, is good.

Eyes: medium size, expressing intelligence and good temper; brown or hazel.

'Nice clean cheeks with good length of muzzle.'

'Good depth of chest.' But note: for correct conformation of body, depth 'A' must always be *less* than length of reach of neck 'B'.

'Good correct front.' Note: vertical line of leg must lie between 'x' and 'y' (x = breastbone, y = point of shoulder blades).

'Good reach of neck leading into well laid back shoulders.'

'Nice level topline.'

Otter tail: thick at base gradually tapering towards tip; medium length, thickly clothed. 'Rounded' appearance.

'Good angulation.' Good turn of stifle but curve must not be so rounded as to look like a sickle.

'Hocks well let down.' Good point for driving movement. Note: length 'c' is much greater than length 'd'.

'Short coupled' i.e. between ribs and thigh.

Coat: short, dense, feels fairly hard; dense, 'weather-resistant' undercoat. 'Good double coat.' 'Good bloom' i.e. condition.

'Good turn (curve) of stifle.'

'Good bone.'

'Neat (compact) feet.'

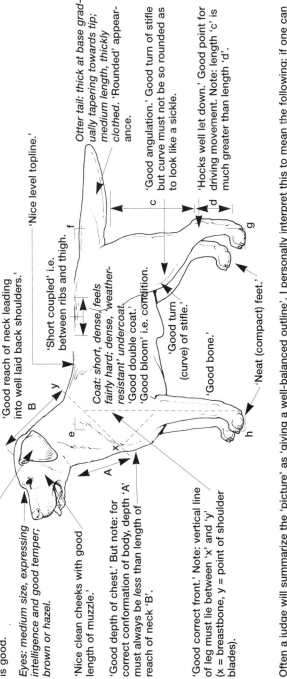

Often a judge will summarize the 'picture' as 'giving a well-balanced outline'. I personally interpret this to mean the following: if one can place the dog in a square as shown ('e' to 'h'), and if the length from 'e' to nose equals the length from 'f' to the tip of the tail, then the dog is well-balanced.

Points of a Labrador.

157

'A Labrador should look like a Labrador and nothing else.' Mary Roslin Williams. Eng. Sh.Ch.,Am.,Can.,Mex.,Bda Ch. Bradking Black Charm, born 1976, by Ch. Follytower Merrybrook Black Stormer ex Sh.Ch. Bradking Bonny My Girl.

carriage. Personally, I think that it should be a basic qualification for every Labrador judge to attend a Hunt Puppy show. Here he will see the seedcorn of the Foxhound breed. Failing that, go and see a typical meet of Foxhounds when you next get the chance, watch them greet the public with their lovely equable manner and then move off under the control of the whipper-in. You will appreciate their soundness and their breed points: the latter correct for them, not so for Labradors.

Greyhounds
Although an ancient breed, Greyhound traits in a Labrador are most likely to have arisen from relatively recent (twentieth century) out-crossing between the two breeds. Often this is done deliberately to achieve a faster moving, racier type of Labrador. The outcross is easily distinguished by its untypical (for a Labrador) head, from whence the snipiness may have originated, long hare's feet and a back that is arched. The above, coupled with a slender bone and a totally different tail, which is longer, thinner and whippier than a Labrador's result in an exaggerated slimmed-down version. (The Greyhound tail is designed for maintaining balance and rhythm at high speed. Followers of Greyhound racing will appreciate its

unique action.) Arising from this outcross Labradors at one time were prone to have an inch or two removed from the end of the tail for showing. Thus, it was the common practice for some judges to check for this bluntness with the thumb when examining Labradors in the ring. Any evidence of docking was then rightly penalized.

Bloodhounds

In the process of developing a useful retrieving dog, it is probable that the superlative scenting abilities of the Bloodhound made their contribution. The ancient Bloodhound was widespread throughout Europe long before Roman times. Manifestations of his influence may result in the occasional sight of a heavily wrinkled head and brow and loose eyes.

Spitz

Elkhound (or Spitz) features in a Labrador are usually denoted by excessive depth of coat with a finer, almost fluffy, undercoat. Also, as the coat is longer, it lacks the typical Labrador texture, which should be hard to the touch. In an extreme case, an over-curling tail will be present also.

Rottweiler

It is possible that the Rottweiler, a useful dog with origins going back to the mastiff-type war dogs of the Greeks, lies behind the coat variations or mis-marks – black and tan or white marks – that occurred around the 1930s and 1940s. Because the Rottweiler has a head of medium length, a defined stop, medium muzzle length, deep chest and a tail set similar to that of a Labrador in silhouette, he may be crossed in order to increase substance and even give a guard-dog temperament. However, such interbreeding produced a much more upright shoulder, an exaggerated width of chest and worse, a very untypical challenging expression due to the furrowed brow and coarser Rottweiler skull.

On a more positive note however, I venture to suggest that his contribution to the ancient origins of the Labrador would be to instil some brown pigmentation which, together with liver from later pointer crossbreeding, could be responsible for the lovely liver/chocolate colour of some of the present-day dogs. A serious judge must give credit to a Labrador whose typical chocolate colour is present without any of the more disagreeable features listed above.

Setters

In a poor specimen Labrador a Setter head is distinctive. This head is sometimes found in the larger spaniels and occasionally in other retrievers. It appears to be excessively long and lean, and the skull has a pronounced occiput. In addition, the ears are longer and of different shape and are set lower on the head.

Pointers
Moving on to more recent times, another outcross, the Pointer, is most recognizable by the make of the head, which also has a decided occiput and a dish-faced appearance. The leg bones are oval rather than sturdy and the loin is more arched. Obviously, a pointer has a totally different tail from a Labrador. It is much thinner and whip-like, which enables him to lash it from side to side when on the move, a Pointer characteristic.

Flat-coated Retrievers
Flat-coated Retriever outcrossing is often difficult to put one's finger on when judging black and chocolate Labradors. Flat-coats have a head of longer cast with a moulded appearance and much less pronounced stop. Usually, this head, together with over-feathering on forelegs, breeches and tail show up strongly in a profile view. However, the accompanying head and expression often appear typically Labrador from above and in front, except that the eye placement is not quite the same. In these circumstances the judge has to work for his living!

Golden Retrievers
Golden Retriever characteristics are a flat and wavy coat of distinctive length in cream or gold; dark brown eye colour; good neck, leg and tail feathering and a deep chest, but lacking the barrel ribbing of the Labrador. Compared to the Labrador he stands very slightly 'longer-cast' although he is a short-coupled dog. His chest is slightly more ribbed back and in my view, because of this extra length his hind action is more like a swinging action from the hip than the trotting action typical of the Labrador's movement.

Chesapeake Bay Retrievers
Occasionally one will come across Chesapeake Bay Retriever features when judging Labradors. I have included these because it is popularly (and reasonably), assumed that his closest ancestors are the Flat-coated and Curly-coated retrievers, the latter of which give him the typical close-waved 'perm' to his coat. As both the above carry liver (chocolate) coloration, it is not surprising that an untypical amber eye, head shape and coat texture sometimes come through in poor specimens of chocolate Labradors.

Curly-coated Retrievers

The Curly-coated Retriever claims the Irish Water Spaniel (himself an ancient breed of Spanish origin), the Poodle (from whence he gets his curls) and the Labrador as his close ancestors. Therefore, it is not surprising that his distinctive coat features infrequently manifest themselves in a so-called purebred Labrador. Blood will out, as they say.

In earlier English versions of the Standard of the Labrador, the faults used to be listed: for example, no undercoat, feathering, snipiness, large ears, tail over back. At a later date, any tendency to 'fault-judge' on the basis of the above was discouraged by replacing the list of specified faults by a generalized statement including the words 'departure from the points should be a fault . . . . regarded in exact proportion to its degree'.

In my opinion, and certainly at Championship show level, a Labrador should be heavily penalized if any of the breeds discussed above appear to be present in his make-up. In one's assessment, such characteristics must be regarded as Breed Faults and thoroughly untypical of a purebred Labrador. In which case no such exhibit is worthy of a winning place. Furthermore, if all the exhibits are of the same ilk and carry obvious breed faults, the judge must withhold the prizes. This is obviously very important where qualification for the Stud Book or Crufts is at stake.

However, I would not suggest that an aspiring or novice judge should try to store all of the above in his head. The reason I have tried to find explanations for their existence is so that when so-called 'non-Labrador' traits appear I hope they will ring a bell and help him make an informed comparison against other dogs rather than rely on a decision based on instinct.

Kennel Type

When a Labrador is being judged in the ring, the breed points are the first things to be assessed. That is why you see the judge walk slowly round the class looking at all the entrants. The first impression will give him a very good idea of the standard of the Labradors and the level of the quality of the class. Obviously, a Junior class will not necessarily contain 'finished' examples of the breed, but any feathering, lack of undercoat and mastiff-type heads, and so on, will stand out. With any luck, the Limit class should contain none of these features and the overall quality of the dogs should be much higher.

However, there will be some distinct variations in the exhibits; some will appear larger overall (although below the standard height of

22½in/57cm (in the UK) 24½in (in the USA) and have a slightly rangy appearance; some will be smaller, compact, rounded and often, but not exclusively, black in colour; others will appear ultra-short in coupling, slightly short of leg but have excellent neck placement and shoulders. And others will have strong bone, deep chests, short backs and tails set to perfection. The point is: they are all purebred Labradors.

The variations outlined above are owed to the breed-lines behind the kennels in which they originated. Labrador breeders have to start somewhere. This usually begins with the purchase of a brood bitch having a pedigree and physical appearance appreciated by the breeder. Hence, with the aid of good complementary stud-dogs, a successful breeder puts together a dog of the cast that he or she wants to see around the place. Eventually a kennel 'line' is established and, by dint of careful selection, avoidance of repeated mistakes and a fairly large slice of good luck, the puppies produced year after year will all have the same hallmark on them. Look at the pedigrees in the Appendix.

True in-bred kennel type is only achieved by a few. However, some excellent kennels come to mind, some of which are still showing in the ring today: Mrs Broadley's Sandylands kennel, whose 'background' dogs excelled in their conformation of neck and shoulders and lovely head proportions; Mrs Hepworth's Poolstead kennel, whose older lines were famed for a succession of lovely bitches; Mrs Rae's Cornlands kennel, which established a lovely line of really handsome-headed yellow dogs; the late Mrs Roslin Williams' Mansergh kennel (which really deserves a book to itself), whose dogs and bitches excelled in true thick black coats, the roundest of otter tails and the most biddable of temperaments; Mrs Satterthwaite's Lawnwoods kennel, whose bitches are renowned for their femininity of expression and the dogs for their substance and well-proportioned heads; Mrs Woolley's Follytower kennel, whose well-known Stormer is discernible in the neck and shoulders of the kennel's later dogs and bitches; and the late Mrs Docking's Ballyduff kennel (now in the hands of her daughter, Mrs Cuthbert), whose predominantly black line shows the distinctive head and ears and a good reach of neck.

To a sensitive breed judge who is truly in tune with Labradors, these points of kennel type occasionally shine through in the ring. Maybe they have arisen through different breeders' interpretations of the Standard. Perhaps the reason is geographical. Certainly, a dominant stud-dog in particular will put his stamp on his puppies.

Sandylands Kennel type

Sh.Ch. Sandylands Longley Come Rain, born 1974, by Sandylands Charlston ex Longley In Tune.

Sh.Ch. Ransom of Sandylands, born 1983, by Sh.Ch. Sandylands My Rainbeau ex Bonfield Lady. (Pedigree: see Appendix.)

Poolstead Kennel Type

Sh.Ch. Poolstead Preferential, born 1978, by Sh.Ch. Poolstead Problem ex Sh.Ch. Poolstead Preface.

Sh.Ch. Poolstead Pipe Smoker, born 1987, by Sh.Ch. Poolstead Preferential ex Poolstead Positive Mystery. (Pedigree: see Appendix.)

Conformation

Temperament, type and transportation; this is my shorthand for the three essential steps to be followed when judging Labradors. Temperament defines how a dog behaves, type is a summary of how he should look, and transportation is how he moves. Having discussed the first two in some detail we come to the 'engine and chassis' part of the process. How he moves presupposes that he has been constructed correctly in the first place, hence the emphasis on conformation.

Correct conformation for some breeds of dog can be defined in the Standard in simple arithmetical terms. Set proportions, for a Cocker Spaniel for example, from base of neck to root of tail compared with the height at the withers shall be equal; or distance from end of nose to stop should equal the distance from stop to occiput. (These are part of the Standard for the Cocker Spaniel.) There are no such precise definitions in the Labrador's English Standard. The only numerical qualification is that the ideal height at the withers should be in the range 56–57cm (22–22½in) for a dog and 54–56cm (21½in) for a bitch. This suggests to me that the conformation of a Labrador must be a question of balance and harmony rather than a rigid blueprint.

Correct Labrador conformation. Eng. & Am. Ch. Lawnwoods Hot Chocolate, born 1973, by Ch. Follytower Merrybrook Black Stormer ex Lawnwoods Tapestry. (Pedigree see *Appendix).*

I suggest that a good procedure for judging conformation is to examine the dog in the way that you would write the letter 'Z'. Hence, starting at the nose, look at the head and skull, then the eyes, ears, cheeks, jaws and mouth. Work down the neck along the back of the tail: assess the tail carefully. Moving to the rear of the dog, look at width of hindquarters, testicles, thighs, second thighs, hocks and stifles. Then, travelling in a shallow diagonal via the flank, assess the coat and undercoat, ribs, chest, shoulders and upper arm placement. Now, returning to the front of the dog, checking height at withers en route, examine depth of chest, forelegs, pasterns and feet, both fore and aft, as you complete the base line of the 'Z' (*see* diagram of points earlier in chapter).

Here I must stress that you must be *exceedingly gentle and careful* at all times when judging a dog, no matter how large or small the breed. There is a tendency to 'dig deep' with your fingers to prove to an exhibitor that you are searching for every muscle and bone placement. This is not necessary. Those most admired and respected of judges, Harry Glover, Joe Braddon and Percy Whittaker, were very light of touch but extremely accurate in their assessments.

For a start, you should examine the mouth and 'bite' of the teeth, which should be correct, as shown in the illustration opposite.

Taking the head of the dog in both your hands, it should have a 'flat' appearance. You will note: the nostrils, wide and set high enough to ride above the water when swimming; the jaw length, not too short, about the same length as the cranium; the eyes, which should not be round or prominent; the eye colour, brown or hazel, not too light, or boot button black; the set and size of the ears and the clean cheeks. Beyond the head, you will also have a good overview of a thick neck, broad back and broad quarters. The tail should be thick at the base and taper to a point. It should feel flat underneath. The hindquarters should be powerful with hard muscles, and second thighs well-fitted to the hocks, the latter appearing to be close to the ground rather than raised up (termed 'well let down'). Two testicles should be evident, neat and well-coated.

A feature which can give rise to some misconception is that of the coupling. The Labrador Standard calls for a short-coupled dog. This means that the coupling, the distance between the last rib and the muscles running from the upper thigh to the croup (rump), should be short. I think that the reason for this in a Labrador, is that a short coupling gives a construction for optimum strength as well as mobility. An exaggerated length of coupling, as in a Dachshund, allows the dog maximum flexibility for extricating himself from a confined space, whereas a Labrador (and other retrievers for that matter) require

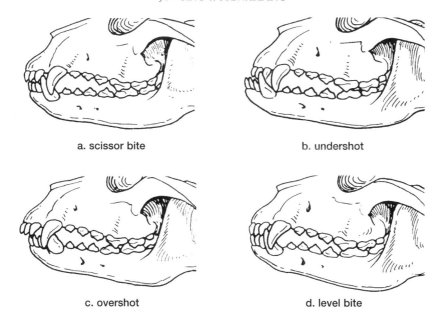

a. scissor bite   b. undershot

c. overshot   d. level bite

The teeth should have a correct 'scissor' bite, as shown in a.

strength and compactness in order to do their work in water or over rough terrain. So, the coupling must be short, but that does not mean that the Labrador is an ultra-short dog, because he is not. He is a rough-ly square dog with a good length of leg. A Fox Terrier is a short dog and so is a Pomeranian. Test the width of the coupling with the flat of your hand. For a man, it should be about the same width as the dis-tance across the knuckles.

A good way to check that the coat is deep and correct is to stand close to the dog, place the left hand on his flank and rake the fur against the grain with four fingers of your right hand. You will sense the hardness of the topcoat, see the undercoat (if there is any) and when the dog is sent away, you will see the imprint of the rake which you can use as a reminder later. But do this gently!

The ribbing should be rounded, but not like a flat-bottomed barge, because this would make him look wide in front. The ribs should extend backwards so that the coupling is short (see above). If you can-not feel any ribs underneath the coat(s) for the fatty layer between, then the dog is verging on overweight. He will probably also have a roll of fat at his neck.

The shoulders should be long and sloping. They should slope

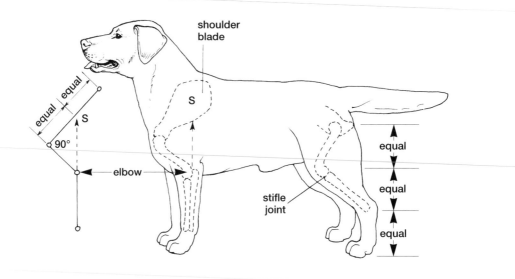

Shoulder placement and hind angulation.

backwards, with the upper arms sloping forwards as shown in the diagram. The angle between them should be about 90 degrees, as shown.

To check the placement of shoulders and upper arm, place your left forefinger on the point of the dog's left shoulder and spread your hand to its fullest extent. Your thumb tip should locate the region of the shoulder blade and your little finger will reach to or point to the elbow joint. Placing your head above the dog's shoulder and looking down the left leg, the dog's leg, elbow joint should be in line with the knuckle of your first finger. This is a rough, on the hoof, estimation of the shoulder/upper arm conformation which should give a good spring to the front suspension.

The upward movement of the elbow joint directed towards the spring point 'S' will work best when 'S' is located at about the mid-point of the shoulder blade. Hence the 90 degrees mentioned above. Now, returning to the front of the dog, it is possible to estimate his height using the top of your right kneecap to ground level (when you are wearing sensible shoes, of course). For me, that is about 22in (54cm).

At the front of the dog, examine his depth of chest and heart-room by placing your flat hand palm upwards, between his forelegs. Normally, there is little room to spare on either side but any cramping will

Shoulders long and sloping. Ch. Carpenny Bonhomie, born 1987,
Group winner, by Ch. Trenow Brigadier ex Carpenny Carmargue.

indicate lack of space. The dog's forelegs should look parallel, straight and sturdy, with the pasterns at a slight angle to the vertical. The feet, front and rear, should be rounded and well-padded. Some dogs and bitches splay their feet involuntarily, as though trying to get a better grip. A good handler will bring the dog up to show off his feet.

In the senior classes (from Junior onwards), I test the depth and texture of the pads by lifting up one of the front feet. I do not examine puppies' feet for fear of upsetting them. One can tell at a glance whether a puppy's feet are forming correctly and they can tighten up with maturity.

Returning to the hindquarters, compare the width of the rump with that of the chest. In Mary Roslin Williams' words, 'The arrow should point forwards'.

Next, from the side compare the depth of the quarters with the length of the hock. The former should be about twice the length of the latter (*see* diagram on previous page) and should appear curved but not excessively rounded. This has a direct bearing on the ability of the animal to move powerfully and correctly, because if the hock is high and the curve of stifle short, excessive pressure will be brought to bear on the hock joint when the dog accelerates.

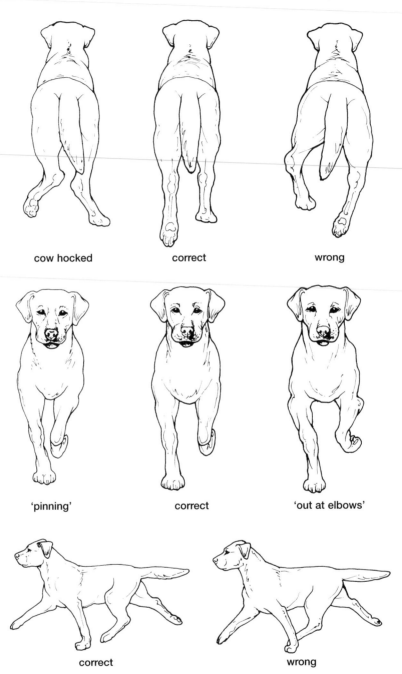

cow hocked   correct   wrong

'pinning'   correct   'out at elbows'

correct   wrong

Movement.

Movement

The Standard calls for a free-moving dog, able to cover adequate ground with a straight and true movement. If the judge sends him directly away from him in a straight line he should see nearly parallel action of the hocks driving the body. The feet should be placed regularly on either side of the line of travel. Not too close or overlapping (called tracking in some circles) and not widely spaced as though the dog was wearing a wet nappy. In motion, the hocks should move directly above the feet, as shown in the illustration.

A profile view of the dog's movement should indicate that he is covering adequate ground, which I interpret as the area necessary for his feet to be so placed as to keep his body balanced at all times. A dog that moves with little ballet steps (*en point*, as they say) would cover inadequate ground; conversely, a naturally bounding stride would cover excessive ground. If you can, imagine a dog moving out of doors with the sun directly overhead; the shadow of the dog will be cast on the ground. If the dog is moving correctly, his feet will never stray outside the area of the shadow and thus he will cover adequate ground. Also, if he is made correctly, his forward-moving rear feet should not overlap his backward-moving front feet.

The handler should turn the dog and bring him straight towards you. If he is obviously off course, move quickly into his line of attack so that you can see his rear feet between his front action. The front legs should move in a parallel fashion with his elbows neither held into his chest nor wide of his ribs. The reach of the legs should be fluid and positive. The pasterns should move in unison with the legs and not flap sideways or knuckle under when he puts on his brakes. On the whole the action should be tidy and economical, because if it is not he will use up a lot of excess energy when out for the day and may be prone to injury as well.

Flaws and Imperfections

A Labrador may be of good kennel type and have all the correct points and still lack minor points of excellence. No exhibitor is perfect – far from it – neither will their dogs be on the day. One would expect a show Labrador to have the breed points listed in the above paragraphs but, in fact, these can vary in quality and quantity, and Labradors can have flaws or failings in their make-up without being untypical. For example, the head may be broad but not broad enough to render the expression quite masculine enough for a male. Similarly, the jaw might be somewhat too short or not deep enough. The cheeks must be lean and clean, fleshy cheeks and jowls are not typical; neither is a furrowed forehead over a deep stop. (It reminds me of a Rottweiler's head.)

Eyes may be correctly coloured but of a slightly lighter shade than desired. Small flaws in dentition are a matter of personal taste, I find. Some judges will forgive slight unevenness, others will not tolerate anything less than a perfect scissor bite. For my part, a neat correct bite is a prerequisite for a win at a Championship show. However, an honourable scar, such as a single tooth missing from an otherwise good jaw, would not prevent me from placing a good Labrador in the line, but obviously he would have to yield place to dogs with complete dentition. To some, large ears are anathema; to others, provided the ears are set correctly and not excessive, medium-large ears are tolerable.

In general, the forelegs should be well-boned, but they can be over-stocky for a bitch. Shoulders can be less than perfectly positioned but they should not be upright; neither should the upper arm be vertical or near vertical; both are serious faults of conformation. In my view there is a sufficient number of Labrador stud-dogs which are entire and potent and of service to the breed and I would discourage any tendency to promote any dog minus one testicle (monochordism) or both testicles (cryptorchidism) for whatever reason.

Every dog and bitch is entitled to be, for example, out of coat, or carrying a little excess weight. Usually, a Junior class will contain a wide variety of 'adolescents'. Some will be advanced youngsters, well reared and covered (perhaps excessively so, but do not confuse fat with muscle!). These will look like real little Labradors (but will they still look typical in six months' time?). Others will look like 'Thelwell ponies', and yet more will look like stick insects. Generally, all Labradors will grow through the 'legs and wings' stage. In other words, they are typical of naturally growing animals, often leggy and obviously immature. As the judge, it is up to you which one you think is more correct for its age and therefore worthy of a prize.

In the senior classes, an otherwise well-made dog might have a lightish eye when you compare it with the colour of his coat, or he may lack chest depth, or a brood bitch could be forgiven a slightly poor topline. The above are examples of flaws which would lose a high winning place but not preclude a place further down the line, but this again would depend on the overall standard of the exhibits.

Imperfections might include honourable scars such as scratches, broken nails, shaved patches, pockmarks, 'rusty bits' and 'frosty bits'. Many of these are typical of the older dog or bitch. The question is what to do with them, honestly, in the context of the show. My advice is to try to ignore these blemishes if the three Ts are correct. In which order you should place a shaved leg, a scratched nose and a white blaze is for you to decide. You are the judge!

Excellence and Superiority

It is the duty of the judge, whenever possible, to pick a winning dog or bitch for Best of Breed, who shows excellent breed type and that little extra in style. After all this is the world of show dogs. The other exhibitors and spectators, especially those from overseas, have paid to see the best there is.

Excellence is difficult to qualify and impossible to quantify but it is definitely recognizable in the beauty of a purebred animal. I think that a dog judge has an extra edge if he can appreciate excellence in any form, be it in the world of antiques, music or dance. Do not be satisfied with the mediocre. Take a look at the best paintings of animals. Look at the paintings by Stubbs or Munnings in the National Gallery in London. Visit Amsterdam, New York, Paris, Venice and Sydney, if you can. These are some of the centres of excellence. It is not uncommon to find that some of today's leading canine experts have interests in other fields that require an educated eye, judgement and a knowledge of form.

An aspiring judge can learn a lot from studying the conformation of animals that have reached the top of their tree, and who have a style and presence which announces their superiority to the world. It is in the nature of the beast to know when he is unchallenged. Superiority in the wild, whether in the expression of a lion, the leap of a dolphin, or the flight of an eagle, is unmistakable. You may smile and think this is far from the world of gundogs. But I would disagree. I am reminded of the Jazz pianist Thomas 'Fats' Waller , who when asked by a lady, 'What is rhythm?' replied, 'Madam, if you has to ask, you ain't got it'.

Judging Technique

However you commence your judging career, you must develop sound judging technique. This will become a ritual performance which you will develop and refine with practice. As you increase your skill and experience, you will be expected to judge more dogs in less time. So, at an Open show you may be given five classes of Labradors, say thirty-five to forty dogs, and two hours or so to judge them in, but you will be expected to judge about a hundred dogs in the same time at a

*Nor. Ch. Jayncourt
Starsound.*

Championship show. And, in all probability, judging them will need a great deal more concentration than before as the quality of the exhibits will be higher.

A neat, confident and consistent approach to judging Labradors is essential if you are to finish on time. Before the show, estimate the time you will need to judge the number of dogs in your entry less, say, 20 per cent for absentees. The show secretary will send you a list of the number of entries you have drawn. One hundred dogs can be judged at a rate of approximately one dog per two minutes. If you estimate how many classes you should have completed in the first hour you will have an indication of whether you are judging slowly or quickly so that you can adjust accordingly. Bear in mind that the senior classes might require more than one pre-selection or 'cut'. If this includes moving each dog again – which it usually does – you will easily use up any extra time you have allotted.

Develop a set routine for a thorough examination of every dog in every class and do not forget to include dogs re-entered from earlier classes. They have paid for a second chance and you must give it to them. Judge the 'poor' dogs with as much concern and attention to detail as you give the good ones. Remember that every exhibitor has paid you the compliment of asking for your opinion of his Labrador.

A good routine should start with a steady tour of all the exhibits set up in the ring. The purpose of this is twofold: first, to allow the handlers time

174

to warm up their Labradors and get their concentration and, second, to allow you to get a general assessment of the quality of the class and to pick out which are Labradors and which are not. Each dog is then examined in turn and his soundness judged by his movement in a set pattern.

Go over each dog using the pattern described above (as you would write the letter 'Z'). Start at the nose, look at the head and skull, then the eyes, ears, cheeks, jaws and teeth. Work down the neck and along the back. Assess the tail carefully. Move to the rear of the dog, check the width of the hindquarters and coupling, testicles, thighs, second thighs, hocks and stifles. Then move to the flanks, assess the coat and undercoat, ribs, chest, shoulders and upper arm placement. Returning to the front of the dog, check height at withers if necessary, examine depth of chest, forelegs, pasterns and feet, both front and rear.

If you have a large number of dogs to judge you must be strict both with yourself and the exhibits. A simple triangle will allow you to see all you need to decide whether the dog is sound; movement going away, in profile and advancing towards you is all you and the handler should require. Economize on time now and you will have a little in hand to 'run off' the finalists. If they have got this far, they deserve it. The only exception I will make is for mistakes in moving owing to an outside disturbance, for instance, or in the case of a puppy 'taken short'!

Remember to examine every dog very thoroughly. Note in your mind's eye the very good points and the very bad, for example: typical expression, excellent correct coat, poor bone, poor feet. Should you have the misfortune to make a mistake before you have awarded the first prize in a class, stop judging, tell your steward that you need to reassess the dogs, and ask all the exhibits to set up again at the side of the ring. Then judge the dogs once more, placing them correctly. Do not make any excuses or initiate any conversation but give yourself a mental kick on the shins.

For your winners, pick out all those with a correct temperament and sufficient breed characteristics in head, coat and tail. You might recheck the expression, bite and movement only if you are unsure of an otherwise splendid specimen, otherwise repeat judging can waste a lot of time. Do not fall into the trap of 'fault judging'. By this I mean condemning a dog because he has a feature that you dislike personally even though the main breed points are basically correct but not emphatic. Put into first place the Labrador that fits the Standard most closely in your estimation.

Work closely with your steward and don't be afraid to check a ring number with him if you are unsure of a previous decision. He can look it up in his results book. Sometimes exhibitors wear a wrong number

175

by accident, which can lead to a terrible confusion later. Try to keep some of your class winners unbeaten because you placed them first for a good reason in an earlier class.

Never discuss, apologise for, or attempt to justify your placing at the ringside. Outside the show a serious judge will respect the opinions of his peers. You are never too old to learn, so take on board the advice of the senior judges and breeders. And think before offering your two-pennorth. Read all the books you can find on Labradors and the judging of all dog breeds, it is often rewarding to understand the all-rounder's point of view.

One final thought; do not smoke or drink, and *never* remove your jacket in the ring. You don't know who might be watching!

Judge's critique

When asked to judge Labradors, it is your duty to write a critique of the dogs you place first and second in each class and submit them for publication in the canine press. When judging abroad, it is also very much appreciated if you send a short essay on your major placings – Best of Breed, and so on – plus any observations and constructive criticisms to the secretary of the Regional Labrador Club for inclusion in the Year Book.

When you have placed the dogs and the prize cards have been awarded by the stewards, ask the first and second placed dogs to stand in front of the table. You can then make notes of their good and bad points in your judging book or note book. It is a good idea to develop your own short-hand for making quick notes. Thumbnail sketches are also useful if you cannot quite put what you see into words. For example, H+, C+, T+ will take care of the breed points in general, whereas: H+, De, CC+ and F- could be translated, 'Correct head, dark eye, super double coat, but her feet are not her fortune'. Or you may prefer to use a Dictaphone or tape-recorder. If you opt for this method you must practise with it first and get to know its peculiarities. Pocket recorders are foolproof, but then you are not a fool. Carry some spare batteries with you; note the time you have left when the 'low' indicator comes on and make sure you can read the spool indicator so that you know how much speaking time you have left.

I think it is good practice to sit at the table and make notes as the habit will stand you in good stead when you are required to judge in other countries under their rules. In many cases you will be required to comment on all the exhibits brought for your delectation, not just the winners. The individual critiques may not be long, but repeating the process for every one of perhaps a hundred dogs can be quite tiring. As a rule, your words are dictated directly to a translator who writes them down on the exhibitor's results slip, so the fatigue of writing is avoided.

Many British Championship shows have a computerized results service and are happy to give them to the judge after the show. It is then a relatively simple matter to type in your critiques of the winners.

In my view, it is not always necessary to list the essential breed points because these should be evident in your winners. However, a simple explanation of the minor differences between first and second place winners is always appreciated. Generally, I would avoid emphasizing any negative points, however well-intentioned, because these can always be open to misinterpretation. You have placed these dogs and bitches highly because of their excellence. Say what that is. Different dogs have different good points and also vary in balance, style and showmanship (or should it be showdogship?). Remember that youngsters are allowed to be immature and very often move and behave badly. Also, bitches may be on the edge of coming into season, or have false pregnancies, maternal undercarriage and so on, which are perfectly natural phenomena. I would not treat these as disqualifying faults if the three Ts are correct.

Do not allow yourself to list the faults to the exclusion of the virtues, even if the latter were a little short on the ground. On the other hand, no one wants to read a long paean of praise to the breed of Labradors. It is not necessary to write a critique with the Breed Standard open at the side. Try to make your observations short and to the point, between thirty and thirty-five words is a fair aim.

I find that it is very instructive to read the write-ups for other breeds. Some judges have a flair with words, others stick to the well-worn track. Try to understand what they are describing in the dog; it could apply to the 'difficult' Labrador that every judge will meet in his career. Read and mark the sense and insight written by the better 'all-rounder' judges. Many of them see the Labrador as the soundest breed in the gundog group. His attributes (and deficiencies) are there for all to see undisguised by a wealth of coat or skilful preparation.

In summary, I can think of no better words of advice to tender to a judge than those recounted by Mr Keith Hart of Landyke Labradors, who at the age of about fourteen accompanied his father to Scotland to help him show a team of dogs. These words of advice were offered to him by none other than Lorna, Countess Howe: 'When you judge the breed, and have summed up the coat, tail, balance and overall type, the final decision should be taken by the expression. In a Labrador it tells all'.

177

10

Breeding

Before deciding to breed from your Labrador, you must first consider seriously the reasons for your wishing to do so. Breeding carries with it considerable responsibilities, not only to your bitch and her puppies, but to the breed in general. Every good breeder will have the interests of the breed as a whole at heart, and will strive to improve – or at the very least maintain – its quality by producing sound, healthy puppies that will go on to live rewarding and comfortable lives with responsible owners.

So it will be immediately apparent from this that before you embark on your search for a suitable stud-dog for your bitch, you must be confident that you have the time and money to commit to the proper care and rearing of a litter, that you will be able to produce healthy stock that will contribute – rather than detract from – the quality of the breed in general, and that you will be able to find good, caring homes for any puppies that you do not want to keep yourself.

Having said all this, it must be added that for those who have the necessary time and commitment, breeding can be a highly rewarding and worthwhile occupation. And if, having considered all the implications, you are keen to breed from your bitch, your first step must be to assess her suitability for breeding.

The Brood-Bitch

Generally speaking, a bitch for breeding should be fit, neither fat nor thin and neither too young nor too old. The Kennel Club now suggest that seven years old is the maximum age at which breeding should be considered. As a rule, the optimum time at which to breed from your bitch is when she is about two or three years old. Most importantly, a brood bitch must have *excellent* temperament and she should not be noisy or excitable. She should be a good example of a Labrador Retriever as described in the Kennel Club Standard; she should have good teeth that meet in a scissor bite and she should, of course, be in excellent health.

178

Remember, you are hoping to produce up to ten replicas of your dog, and it is up to you to make sure that they will be a credit to you and to Labrador Retrievers in general. Indiscriminate breeding will help no one.

For the purpose of breeding on and establishing a line of a good Labradors it is essential that you start with a well-bred bitch from a good kennel. It is not enough that she appears to be a good example of the breed: you must be sure that you are consolidating and building upon solid foundations, laid down over a period of time by the original breeder. Which line or lines should be used in establishing your own line is, of course, for you to decide, but if you take the task seriously, ask a lot of questions, see a lot of dogs and bitches (and puppies), and follow your own preferences, you should end up with a Labrador that all can live with, which is the most important thing.

Health

Before proceeding any further, a visit to the vet is necessary to check the general health of your bitch and also to make sure, as far as it is possible, that she is free from hereditary defects. For example, for breeding purposes she must hold a recently issued certificate showing she is free from Progressive Retinal Atrophy (PRA) and Hereditary Cataracts (HC) (*see* Chapter 12). The certificates should be updated annually. The vet will also X-ray the hips of your bitch for evidence of hip dysplasia, which can lead to infirmity in later life. He will send the photographic plates to be 'scored' by a panel of clinical ophthalmologists. In the UK, this procedure is jointly supervised by the Kennel

Sh.Ch. Raybooth Socks, born 1981, by Rocheby Blue Boy of Raybooth ex Netherton Shadow.

Club and the British Veterinary Association. The hip scores should, in my opinion, total less than 16 (although 20 is acceptable in the extreme) because 16 is the average score for all Labrador Retrievers currently examined under the KC/BVA scheme. (Hip dysplasia and other hereditary diseases are discussed in more detail in Chapter 12.)

Wherever possible, scan the photographs in the Labrador Breed Club literature to satisfy yourself that none of the parents or grandparents show the scars typical of operations to correct entropian (*see* Chapter 12).

When you contemplate breeding a litter, whether it is with the intention of producing a good worker, a potential show specimen or a faithful companion, remember the three 'Ts' discussed in an earlier chapter: temperament, type and transportation (soundness). These are paramount considerations for both the dog and the bitch.

Choosing a Stud-dog

For the newer breeder, choosing a stud-dog might appear to be a potential minefield, but with common sense, perseverance, and some luck, most of the pitfalls can be avoided. For example, it is well worth spending a good deal of time gathering as much information as possible. Study the pedigrees of prospective stud-dogs (*see* Appendix), and accept any invitation to visit those dogs that might be suitable. Talk to the stud-dog's owner about his bloodlines and those of your bitch.

As with the bitch, the stud-dog *must* have an excellent temperament. Ideally, he should be a proven sire (that is, having already produced some sound well-boned puppies) and he should have good masculine looks, proclaiming the quality of his breeding. He will have been tested for – and be free himself from – the hereditary defects discussed above. However, don't reject a stud-dog because he has one superficial failing which you personally dislike. For example, a slight over-length in coupling or just a little shortness of the muzzle does not disqualify him from use at stud because, as with the bitch, the quality of the progeny will be owed as much to the dog's background breeding as it will to the stud-dog as an individual. So, if his grandparents appear correct in these features to your eye, the chances are that his progeny will be also.

Before looking at a stud-dog, compare the written pedigree of the stud-dog with that of your bitch. Remember that, for your purposes, a pedigree is not just an elegantly printed list of names: it is a record of a stud-dog's background, the 'ingredients' that have gone into making him what he is and, potentially, what his offspring will be.

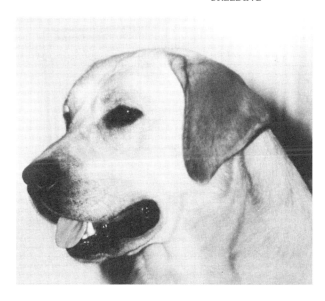

*Ruselton Kite, born 1980,
by Ballyduff Kestrel ex
Roncott Priceless Purdy.*

Note the colours of the parents and grandparents in the first three generations. If you are breeding blacks, do you want a chocolate in the litter? If so, you must consult with the colour experts in the breed. The mode of chocolate inheritance is calculable but by no means certain. When breeding yellows, is there a history of light pigmentation in the line? Such questions must be asked.

Stamp

In the second and subsequent generations of most pedigrees, an experienced breeder will note the 'marker' or 'dominant' dogs: dogs that have put their 'stamp' on the breed at various times, most frequently to good effect (though occasionally the reverse is true!). A good marker dog usually is, or has been, a prominent stud-dog, but not necessarily a top show dog. It is essential to locate these dogs in your researches and to use their influences to improve your type.

Their stamp and quality should complement those of your bitch. Such a dog may occur two or three times in the pedigree, and he usually has the following assets (and often several more): generally, he *tends* not to pass on any of the 'older' problems that have beset many breeders post-war, such as entropian or poor dentition, which are fairly uncommon nowadays. These dogs are sometimes known as 'gates', they let through to the next generation the best points but tend to keep back the bad.

181

Ch. Charway Ballywill-will, born 1978, by Bally-duff Spruce ex Charway Simona.

Usually a marker dog has produced quality puppies to similarly lined bitches in the past. If he has the stamp of the type of animal you would like to own and show yourself, breed from him, by all means. Try to combine your instinctive reactions with exhaustive research. In other words, it sometimes pays to let your heart rule your head.

However, even an experienced breeder cannot get all the best features transmitted to all of offspring. Life is not like that. To get the best from a well-planned mating, it would probably be necessary to 'run on' the whole litter (and maybe take out a second mortgage, too). However, for practical purposes I suggest that you retain at least two, or maybe three, puppies until they are six months old, by which time you will usually be able to see what you have achieved.

Line-breeding

Very often, a successful mating is 'lined' to one or two marker dogs (*see also* Appendix). This is known as line-breeding in order to perpetuate similarity of type (or 'homozygosity', in genetic terminology).

Below is an example of a lined pedigree. The marker dogs are Sam and Max. So, if Sam and Max are of similar backgrounds – perhaps even from the same kennel – then the pedigree is lined to that kennel: the kennel has provided the foundation stones on which the pedigree has been constructed. It can be seen that Hal and Bob are half-brothers, and Sidney and Sue are brother and sister.

In contrast, Rick and the dogs behind him constitute the introduced line. This is where, ideally, the breeder hopes to make small changes by the introduction of a new kennel line. In so doing the breeder hopes to make small changes in for example: conformation, such as a slight lengthening of the coupling; or to improve a rather plain expression. Also, the introduced line may be used to improve hunting ability or training aptitude.

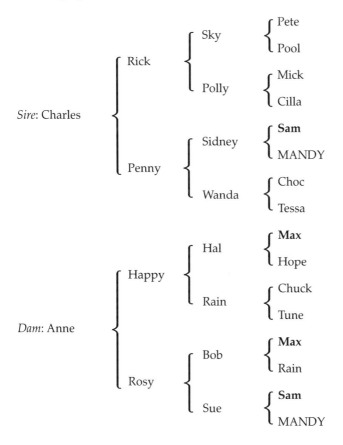

However, it must be remembered that these changes will be small, not only diluted by the other three-quarters of the pedigree which is 'carved in stone', but further diminished by the variability over the number of puppies in the litter. In other words, the introduced improvement will be swamped by a factor of three to one by the features already inherent in the breed lines and further reduced by four to one. I think this is an area where it is wise to make haste slowly.

In-breeding

Simplistically, in-breeding, line-breeding and close breeding are all variations on the same theme. It is a question of degree. In general, dog breeders regard mating half-brother to half-sister as in-breeding. These combinations should not be attempted by the novice.

When repeated relatives do not appear in, say, second, third, fourth and fifth generations of a pedigree, the resultant progeny is often called an 'outcross' by the cognoscenti. Strictly, as we have seen in earlier chapters, all Labrador Retrievers can be shown to share a few common antecedents. Examples are shown in the Appendix.

I think that breeding with a Labrador Retriever to get a certain 'look' on the progeny is like trying to unravel a multi-stranded rope by teasing out the threads one by one. One hopes that, finally, the chosen strand will be stronger than the others.

Breeding Coefficient

When you have selected a dog for your bitch you might want to check, by comparing the two pedigrees, the degree of in-breeding that would be produced. A breeding number or coefficient has been devised by Sewell Wright. This was discussed at length in *Dog World*, in an article on successful show dogs compiled by Simon Parsons.

The breeding coefficient (F) is expressed as a percentage. For example, where F = 0%, no relation is indicated; but where F = 100%, a brother to sister relationship is indicated. Union between first cousins gives F a value of 6.25 per cent.

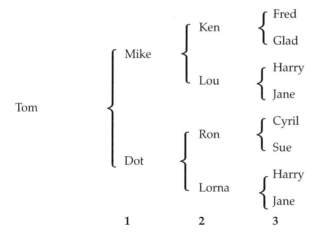

Lorna and Lou are sisters and Mike and Dot are first cousins. The coefficient (F) is calculated by assigning 1 to the parent's column, 2 to the grandparents' and 3 to the grandparents' and so on. The next rule is to denote the father's column number as (A), divided by the mother's column number (B) for the same descendant as A/B to Harry and A/B to Jane. Thus from Column 3; Tom is bred 3/3 to Harry and 3/3 to Jane. The formula for calculating F is :

$$F = (0.5)^P$$

where P = A + B - 1

Hence, F (for Harry) $= 0.5^{(3+3-1)}$

$= 0.5^{(5)}$
$= 0.03125$
Thus, F (for Harry) $= 3.125\ \%$

The procedure is repeated exactly to calculate Tom's breeding to Jane giving a value for F (Jane) of 3.125 per cent also. To calculate Tom's in-breeding we must add the percentages together. Thus, Tom is in-bred a total of 6.25, which is the coefficient expected from a marriage of first cousins.

In many pedigrees of earlier days (and not only these pedigrees!), it is quite common to see the matings of half-brother to half-sister. Although, I would stress that this kind of mating should not be attempted by a novice breeder. It is interesting to see what effect this has on the in-breeding coefficient F.

In this case the above pedigree would denote Ken twice in Column 2, in place of Ron.

Thus, from Column 2; Tom II would be bred 2/2 to Ken and 3/3 to Lou and the same values would apply for Tom II – Ken to Lorna. The formula for calculating F is:

$$F = (0.5)^P$$

where P = A + B - 1

Hence, F (for Ken) $= 0.5^{(2+2-1)}$

$= 0.5^{(3)}$
$= 0.125$
Thus, F (Ken) $= 12.5\%$

From the first calculation we know that Tom II's relationship to Lorna (and Lou) is 3/3 (above).

Therefore, to calculate the degree of Tom II's in-breeding we must add the percentages together (i.e. 12.5% + 6.25%) (Lou) + 6.25% (Lorna).

Thus, Tom II is now in-bred a total of 25. Or to put it another way, 25%, that is one-quarter in-bred.

Colour Inheritance

The colour of a Labrador's coat may be wholly black, yellow or chocolate (liver). Traditionally, a black Labrador may carry a small white spot on his chest or behind either pastern or front paw. On blacks the nose, lips, eye rims, pads and under-belly are generally black. Over the years, a yellow labrador has been called so even though his coat may vary from light cream through merging tones of biscuit, gold, almost coppery, to a reddish-gold colour (termed fox-red). On yellows the nose, lips, eye rims and pads are generally dark, although often not so densely pigmented as in the blacks, and his underparts are pink. A chocolate Labrador can vary in colour from light liver-brown to a dark coffee colour. On chocolates the nose, eye rims and lips may vary from liver-pink through to dark chocolate. Eye colour is frequently lighter and may be yellow, yellow-green or brown.

The reason for the wide variations in colour is the make-up of all the original dog 'contributors' to the retriever type (*see* Chapters 1 and 9). These were all of differing breed and colour. The breeds have modified and strengthened over a very long time so that Labradors tend to breed 'true' or 'pure', that is producing replicates of the same colour generation after generation.

Unfortunately, purity is difficult to maintain in the eyes of Nature and pigmentation from other breeds has been allowed to intrude by outcrossings, sometimes accidentally, and sometimes intentionally by man. Years of pure-breeding has succeeded in correcting some of these intrusions, but they will never be totally eradicated.

Colour Genes

As with all characteristics, colour transmission from one generation of Labradors to the next is governed by hereditary 'units' called genes. The three different colours are produced by interaction between two different pairs of genes. Genes may be of two types, dominant or recessive and they are inherited in pairs. Dominant colour genes pass their characteristics on to the next generation and they can be seen in the individual's appearance. Recessive gene characteristics are only expressed where both parents had that recessive gene to complement each other. The recessive gene is not expressed if its dominant form is present in one of the parents.

A dominant gene is responsible for black pigment and its recessive form is responsible for producing chocolate pigment. On the other hand, yellow colour inheritance is governed by two recessive genes which, when both are present, prevent dark pigmentation (black or chocolate) being formed in the coat. However, it is normal for yellows to have quite dark coloration of the nose and eye rims. Thus when two recessive yellow genes are combined, only yellow pigment appears.

The various shades of cream and gold seen in the coat, and differences in the pigment of the nose and eye rims are probably caused by the action of other colour genes called modifying genes. Yellow Labradors, therefore, may or may not carry a recessive chocolate gene and positive proof of the former chocolate gene is obtained only if a chocolate puppy is produced.

Black Labradors, on the other hand, fall into four genetic kinds (genotypes):

Eng. Sh.Ch. & Am. Ch. Receiver of Cranspire, born 1981, by Dutch Ch. Cranspire Skytrain ex Polly's Pride of Genisval.

1. Dominant black: carrying neither yellow nor chocolate genes. Such a Labrador produces only black puppies regardless of the colour of his mate.
2. Black carrying a yellow gene (a common combination of genes).
3. Black carrying a chocolate gene. (May produce black or chocolate puppies.)
4. Black carrying yellow and chocolate genes. (May produce black, yellow or chocolate puppies.)

In the last three cases, the offspring's colour will be influenced by the genetic make-up of the other parent.

Chocolate Labradors may or may not carry a recessive yellow gene. In the case of the former, only if a yellow puppy is produced will this confirm the inheritance of a yellow gene. If two chocolate dogs, each carrying yellow are bred together, puppies of both colours will be produced. However, the yellow puppies will have yellow coat coloration but with pale liver

Sh.Ch. Bradking Bridgette of Davricard, chocolate bitch, born 1981, by Ch. Fabracken Comedy Star ex Bradking Cassandra.

pigmentation on the nose and lips. Conversely, if only one of the two possesses the yellow gene only chocolate puppies will be produced.

In summary, these are very broad generalizations (which only go to underline the complexity of colour breeding), two black Labradors may produce a typically large litter of only black puppies, or black and yellow puppies, or black and chocolate puppies, or black, chocolate and yellow puppies. Similar combinations are possible in a litter produced by a black mated to a yellow and a black mated to a chocolate. Offspring of a chocolate parent will all carry a chocolate gene whether they are black or chocolate in colour. Two yellow Labradors cannot produce a black or chocolate puppy, because the fact that they are yellow indicates that they have inherited only yellow genes from their parents.

Hereditary Defects and Pitfalls

Problems encountered in the breeding and keeping of dogs may be divided into two categories: first, those that may be an intrinsic part of the animal's make-up from the beginning (inherited) and thus, with the benefit of hindsight, should be known about and guarded against; and second, those that cannot be foreseen and may appear out of the blue. I call the latter, pitfalls.

Hereditary defects, such as hip dysplasia (HD) progressive retinal atrophy (PRA), retinal dysplasia, hereditary cataract, entropian, osteochondrosis and epilepsy broadly fall into the first category. However, current veterinary practice does acknowledge that the causes of several of the above may be due also to each individual dog's environmental conditions or upbringing, such as a difficult whelping or an incorrect exercise regime. Some forms of cataract may be due to injury or accidental exposure to an extra bright light impinging on the eye. Epilepsy has an inherited form and an acquired form, the latter commonly owed to infantile disease, or as a result of injury or its associated trauma.

A description of the more commonly encountered hereditary defects can be found in Chapter 12. It is essential that any breeder is familiar with these and makes every effort to breed from dogs that are unaffected.

A most common pitfall in the breeding of dogs is the acquisition of bad temperament or instability in a formerly well-tempered Labrador. This is nearly always owed to an external source, such as a chance meeting leading to a dog fight, or poor management, or just plain bad luck. The majority of Labradors are born with nice temperaments, but they can easily be 'turned' if they are set a bad example. Hitherto equable bitches may become stressed if they face aggression when they have whelped, or are busy weaning puppies. Young dogs reaching adolescence at about eight or nine months will react in kind if faced with a belligerent sexual competitor. A chance encounter with an aggressor can leave permanent scars, both mental and physical.

Shyness can be inherited either from the bitch or the stud-dog. So it makes sense to check that neither dog nor bitch suffer from this defect before you even consider breeding a litter. Shyness is not typical Labrador temperament. However, it can be passed on to a kennel-mate and once introduced it is almost impossible to eradicate, for all dogs are imitators.

When a Labrador is said to be gun-shy this is a somewhat different condition. In the home or the kennel he may be happy and outgoing and have all the Labrador attributes of a lovely companionable pet. However, his obvious dislike of the noise of gunshot which he may demonstrate by whining will rule him out as a stud-dog. And the same applies to breeding with a gun-shy bitch.

Planning

In planning your first litter you should make a rough estimate of the potential costs. If you should have a serious problem, and sometimes only one puppy is a serious problem, it is better to have an idea before-hand of what the outlay might be. First calculate the costs that you know you will incur. These will include stud fees, veterinary fees (for hip, eye and health certificates, inoculations and check-ups), whelping and puppy-rearing equipment (such as bedding materials, whelping box, puppy pen and so on), the feeding of both bitch and puppies, heating of maternity unit, insurance and the registration fees. In addition you must take into account your time, and possibly any consequent loss of earnings, and make an allowance for unforeseen problems that may require further veterinary attention, such as Caesarean delivery and subsequent convalescence.

This is a necessary exercise because while we all pray that there will be no problem when whelping the bitch it is foolish not to allow for it. Having made your calculation, you will probably find that expense exceeds your expectations. Breeding a litter responsibly is not cheap and serves to underline the importance of securing serious promises of *good* homes before the litter is born. If you decide to keep more than one of the puppies until they are about five months old or so, you must estimate the additional costs that this will involve.

11

Mating, Pregnancy and Whelping

Up to the day your brood-bitch is mated she will have been in season for anything up to fifteen days, during which time she must be guarded from the attentions of other dogs. Bitches can be sneaky and swift so you will have to be on your toes. Most of the time she will be kept indoors. Exercising should be confined to walking around the garden, *not* in the public park!

Following the mating she will require progressively more attention and supervision over the next sixty-three days, but allow three or four days either side of her due date. It stands to reason that you cannot rear a litter of puppies well and socialize them while doing a full-time job, so you must make all the arrangements for leave, family holidays, and so on, well in advance. (Consult the whelping table overleaf).

If you are lucky, after three or four weeks you will be able to start to wean the puppies. Provided the bitch has plenty of milk, this will involve providing meals four times a day; if she does not, you will need to feed the puppies every two hours. Puppies are great time-wasters, so don't expect to keep to a timetable. They will expect you to play with them between feeds after you have cleaned up the nest.

Preparation

Three or four weeks before she is due to come in season, check the health of your bitch with your vet. At the same time, tell him when your bitch is due to be mated, and approximately when she will whelp so that he can be prepared to assist the whelping if necessary. And make sure that you will have transport available when she is due to whelp, because you must be prepared for any emergency.

Make a preliminary appointment with the owner of your chosen stud-dog, and arrange to let him know when your bitch comes in season.

191

MATING, PREGNANCY AND WHELPING

	1	2	3	4	5	6	7	8	9	10	11	12	13	14	15	16	17	18	19	20	21	22	23	24	25	26	27	28	29	30	31
Jan. mating on	1	2	3	4	5	6	7	8	9	10	11	12	13	14	15	16	17	18	19	20	21	22	23	24	25	26	27	28	29	30	31
Whelping March	5	6	7	8	9	10	11	12	13	14	15	16	17	18	19	20	21	22	23	24	25	26	27	28	29	30	31	APR 1	2	3	4
Feb. mating on	1	2	3	4	5	6	7	8	9	10	11	12	13	14	15	16	17	18	19	20	21	22	23	24	25	26	27	28	29		
Whelping April	5	6	7	8	9	10	11	12	13	14	15	16	17	18	19	20	21	22	23	24	25	26	27	28	29	30	MAY 1	2	3		
March mating on	1	2	3	4	5	6	7	8	9	10	11	12	13	14	15	16	17	18	19	20	21	22	23	24	25	26	27	28	29	30	31
Whelping May	3	4	5	6	7	8	9	10	11	12	13	14	15	16	17	18	19	20	21	22	23	24	25	26	27	28	29	30	31	JUNE 1	2
April mating on	1	2	3	4	5	6	7	8	9	10	11	12	13	14	15	16	17	18	19	20	21	22	23	24	25	26	27	28	29	30	
Whelping June	3	4	5	6	7	8	9	10	11	12	13	14	15	16	17	18	19	20	21	22	23	24	25	26	27	28	29	30	JULY 1	2	
May mating on	1	2	3	4	5	6	7	8	9	10	11	12	13	14	15	16	17	18	19	20	21	22	23	24	25	26	27	28	29	30	31
Whelping July	3	4	5	6	7	8	9	10	11	12	13	14	15	16	17	18	19	20	21	22	23	24	25	26	27	28	29	30	31	AUG 1	2
June mating on	1	2	3	4	5	6	7	8	9	10	11	12	13	14	15	16	17	18	19	20	21	22	23	24	25	26	27	28	29	30	
Whelping August	3	4	5	6	7	8	9	10	11	12	13	14	15	16	17	18	19	20	21	22	23	24	25	26	27	28	29	30	31	SEP 1	
July mating on	1	2	3	4	5	6	7	8	9	10	11	12	13	14	15	16	17	18	19	20	21	22	23	24	25	26	27	28	29	30	31
Whelping Sept.	2	3	4	5	6	7	8	9	10	11	12	13	14	15	16	17	18	19	20	21	22	23	24	25	26	27	28	29	30	OCT 1	2
August mating on	1	2	3	4	5	6	7	8	9	10	11	12	13	14	15	16	17	18	19	20	21	22	23	24	25	26	27	28	29	30	31
Whelping Oct.	3	4	5	6	7	8	9	10	11	12	13	14	15	16	17	18	19	20	21	22	23	24	25	26	27	28	29	30	31	NOV 1	2
Sept. mating on	1	2	3	4	5	6	7	8	9	10	11	12	13	14	15	16	17	18	19	20	21	22	23	24	25	26	27	28	29	30	
Whelping Nov.	3	4	5	6	7	8	9	10	11	12	13	14	15	16	17	18	19	20	21	22	23	24	25	26	27	28	29	30	DEC 1	2	
Oct. mating on	1	2	3	4	5	6	7	8	9	10	11	12	13	14	15	16	17	18	19	20	21	22	23	24	25	26	27	28	29	30	31
Whelping Dec.	3	4	5	6	7	8	9	10	11	12	13	14	15	16	17	18	19	20	21	22	23	24	25	26	27	28	29	30	31	JAN 1	2
Nov. mating on	1	2	3	4	5	6	7	8	9	10	11	12	13	14	15	16	17	18	19	20	21	22	23	24	25	26	27	28	29	30	
Whelping Jan.	3	4	5	6	7	8	9	10	11	12	13	14	15	16	17	18	19	20	21	22	23	24	25	26	27	28	29	30	31	FEB 1	
Dec. mating on	1	2	3	4	5	6	7	8	9	10	11	12	13	14	15	16	17	18	19	20	21	22	23	24	25	26	27	28	29	30	31
Whelping Feb.	2	3	4	5	6	7	8	9	10	11	12	13	14	15	16	17	18	19	20	21	22	23	24	25	26	27	28	MAR 1	2	3	4

Table showing dates of whelping.

The Mating

The bitch is taken to the stud-dog on about the eleventh day of her heat. Make sure that you watch her closely when she is due in season so that you know the day when she first shows a red discharge from her vulva. This is day one. When she is due to be mated, the fluid will change colour from red to pinkish/clear (use a piece of paper tissue to check). at this time she will also 'stand' squarely on her legs and arch her tail when you scratch her haunches. Be prepared to take her to the stud-dog for the first time after only nine days of 'show' if she appears to be ready. It is better to use an experienced stud-dog with the aid of helpers for a maiden bitch. If the stud-dog's owner is willing, let them make their own introductions, on or off the lead. Be prepared for the stud owner to cut these proceedings short when the dog shows that he means business.

The stud-dog owner should introduce the dog to the bitch. At first, he will attempt to play, and maybe lick her ears and face. This is a good and natural sign. He will inspect her hindquarters closely. At this point, encourage him to mount her whilst her head is held firmly. (Often it pays to hold her tail with the right hand to prevent it getting in the way.) Allow the dog space to move his hind feet and find the right angle of approach which, surprisingly, is almost vertically upwards. Be prepared for her to protest violently when he achieves his entry. Such protest is brief and no cause for concern. It will cease when the stud-dog has achieved full penetration and penile erection. After a short time, the bulb at at the end of the dog's penis swells, and is then grasped by the bitch's vaginal muscles, preventing either partner from separating. This is what is known as the 'tie'. Sometimes it pays to hold a dog 'piggy-back' fashion on the bitch's back until the tie is secure, after which there is a need to hold both dogs securely as any violent movement could result in a painful injury to the dog.

After two or three minutes the dog will usually raise one back leg and turn, tail to tail with the bitch. They will be more comfortable now with four feet on the ground. If the dog does not turn fairly soon after commencement of the tie, the bitch will probably appreciate your supporting some of his weight until he does. If the tie is good he will remain coupled to her for some time, sometimes for up to forty-five minutes.

Occasionally, she will 'slip' him. If so, walk with him to a quiet part of the ground or garden and allow his penis to retract naturally. He will assist the process by licking. Generally, no harm is done and a subsequent mating twenty minutes later usually proves fruitful and successful. Whilst a tie is not essential to conception, most breeders feel more confident of the mating's success if it has taken place. However, the tie is not dependent only on the dog or the bitch and so neither must be blamed if it does not occur.

Eventually the bitch and dog will release each other, and the mating will be complete; after which the bitch can be quietly returned to the car for a rest. For the next two weeks the bitch must be kept strictly in purdah.

Should the bitch be too early in her cycle for a successful mating, she should be returned to the dog after a day has elapsed. By then he should be fully fertile again and able to complete the union.

It is always better to charge and receive a stud fee if there has been a tie. Alternatively, the prospective breeder may offer a 'pick of the lit-ter' puppy in lieu. This arrangement must be put in writing. Other 'breeding terms' are best left to those with experience. Again, written evidence of the terms is necessary for the future benefit of both parties. The Kennel Club publishes guidelines for this arrangement.

Ten minutes is generally considered to be a minimum time for a suc-cessful mating; anything less than that and a return visit should be arranged for six months hence at the next season. Make sure that you have agreed whether the stud fee includes a free second service in the event that the bitch does not conceive.

Praise the stud-dog himself and make him feel that he is really appreciated, whether he has been successful or not. Give him a hug and a bowl of milk containing two beaten eggs as a reward.

Documentation

Make sure that any necessary documentation is completed on the day. In the UK, the Kennel Club's green document, Form 1: Litter Registra-tion must be to hand. Any documents verifying the date of the mating and other details must be completed without error or alteration. Be sure that the Stud portion is completed, signed and dated by the owner of the stud-dog.

Lack of Libido

Occasionally, you will travel some 160 miles to use a stud-dog, and on introducing the bitch to him, he will look at her as though she was from another planet. He will then stroll over and urinate up the door of his favourite kennel-frau. Your precious lady, in her best courting coat, and on her eleventh day, will take no notice of him whatever.

A stud-dog owner experienced in the vagaries of the arranged marriage, will probably hand the dog's slip-lead to your assistant while you put the bitch on her lead. The owner will then go into the kennel nearby and bring a second, probably younger, dog into an adjacent run. If all goes to plan, the younger dog will look at your bitch, squeak with delight and try to vault over the fence (which is too high even for him). At this point, the wayward stud-dog should remember his reputation and, facing competition, prepare to mount your bitch.

False Pregnancy

Occasionally, older bitches, especially those who have had litters in the past, experience false or phantom pregnancies. In these, the teats swell up and ooze milk and the stomach takes on a 'full' appearance. Sometimes she will become nervous or excited and begin to start nesting. The best treatment is some sympathy and tender loving care from the family in the first instance. If the symptoms persist, your vet will advise you and maybe give her an injection to rectify her condition. It is important to remember that this is a very normal condition for bitches to go through and should not give cause for alarm. If you pay her a little more attention, perhaps change her walking routine or give her an extra car ride to shops or station, she will not repeat the process.

Pregnancy

From the day that you booked to use the stud-dog you should be giving some thought to homes for your puppies. Ideally, you should have a waiting list of three or four potential homes (yourself excluded). Sometimes, the stud owner will receive a few enquiries and is willing to pass them on. If you are a member of the Labrador Retriever Club, it is a good idea to contact the secretary who may also receive enquiries. Personally, I am not in favour of advertising in the press because of the time-wasting, half-hearted nature of many of the respondents. Personal recommendation is by far the best way to place your surplus puppies in good, caring homes.

The Maternity Unit

The whelping box should be located near to the family's comings and goings: a cold draughty shed at the bottom of the garden is not

suitable for you to get to in a snow storm and is in any case too isolat-
ing for the bitch. A heated utility room or workshop is ideal if it is not
too noisy and busy. Your Labrador will tolerate the washing machine
but will not be helped in her labours by noisy high-speed drilling or
similar machinery. The room should be heated to about 65°F (16°C). A
dull-emitter 300W heater lamp should be installed above the box if
there is no other source of heating. Obviously, the bitch will need
access to the garden from time to time and you must watch her to see
that she does not try to make her bed in the old coal bunker or under
the oil tank. A baby safety gate with an opening centre, fitted in the
doorway, is a good way of retaining her in the maternity ward without
removing her from view completely.

Often it is tempting to let her try to find a nice 'natural' spot in the
house. We have tried this, but there was never much room in the air-
ing cupboard normally, so we let her choose a corner of the kitchen.
Our old Sally had her first litter of twelve puppies on the sofa!

It is a good idea to install the mother-to-be in the whelping room
about two weeks before the intended date of whelping. If it is not practical to confine her in a room to herself, you may consider annexing
part of another room that is not a thoroughfare, in which case a wire
mesh puppy pen will come in very useful (*see* Chapter 4). The puppy
pen can be fitted on a waterproof base made of thin plywood sheet,
and the floor protected by a sheet of oilskin tablecloth material.

The whelping box should be big enough for a rotund, pregnant
Labrador bitch to lie out flat in either direction, *plus* about six inches
(15cm) more both ways. I use a design made from plastic (Melamine)
covered boards which are easily cleaned and may be disinfected and re-
used. The side and back boards are ½in (12mm) thick, 18in (46cm) wide
and 40in (1m) long. Two front boards are provided and each has the
same length and thickness as above. The height of these is only 6in
(15cm) and both are removable. I find that the bitch likes to settle into
the box with all the sides completed at first. When she is becoming
uncomfortable with her increased burden I remove the top board
so that it is easier for her to get in. While she is feeding the puppies, it is
a sufficient height to prevent draughts. When the puppies are about
three to four weeks old the bottom board can be removed to allow them
to venture into the remainder of their little run. They will then be trying
to keep the nest clean and to soil the newspaper provided outside
the box.

The base of the box is made from stout 'marine' plywood ½in (12mm)
thick and big enough to fit the external edges of the wall boards. This

wood is fairly waterproof and will stand a lot of wear. The base is screwed to the walls using reinforcing battens of smooth planed wood 1½in (38mm) square, cut to size so that it forms a nice tight fit at the edges to aid good cleaning. The boards are held together using remountable plastic corner fittings (as used in DIY furniture). These are screwed tightly together on assembly but can be taken apart and the whole whelping box, cleaned, disinfected and packed away until the next time.

Some Labrador bitches can become over-enthusiastic with the excitement of puppies and whelping; others are just plain clumsy and prefer to swan around, mostly outside the box. For the safety of the puppies in the box, I fit four new stout broom handles as crash bars around all four sides. They will prevent the bitch from inadvertently trapping and crushing a puppy, and can easily be removed as and when the puppies are big enough. The arrangement of the bars is shown in the illustration below.

In addition to all the preparations discussed above, it is useful to assemble '101' items which you think you might need plus some that you hope you won't need. This checklist is by no means exhaustive but it will serve as a useful reminder of the essentials that you will probably forget in the heat of the moment.

sides: 12mm 'Melamine' board
base: 10mm marine plywood

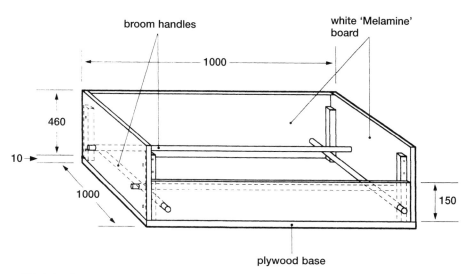

Whelping box.

Whelping Equipment Checklist

- Three clean Vet-beds (the kind with a stiff backing and tight fleece).
- A good supply of newspapers.
- Two or three strong cardboard boxes 2 × 2 × 1ft (61 × 61 × 30cm) for managing puppies in.
- Three or four old towels.
- Roll of dustbin liners.
- Two rolls of kitchen paper wipe.
- Large roll of cotton wool.
- Bottle of mild disinfectant, ready diluted according to the manufacturer's instructions.
- Pair of sterilized surgical scissors.
- Premature baby feeding bottle.
- Large tin of puppy milk powder.
- Box of glucose powder.
- Small bottle of baby gripe water (without dill).
- Small bottle of Milk of Magnesia.
- Bottle (1 litre) of liquid calcium, obtained from your vet.
- Stone hot-water bottle (not the rubber kind).
- Small note book for noting weights, colours and sexes.
- Pencil.
- Spare light bulb.

Pregnancy Signs

From about the fourth week after mating your bitch will probably experience some early morning sickness. This is usually confined to slight retching and sometimes a little food is regurgitated (which she will usually clear up herself). Most certainly she will show a great change in her demeanour and become soulful, clingy and absolutely adorable. Consequently she will be at your side constantly and under your feet. From this time she will appear to 'take care of herself', moving carefully in the garden, picking her way round the furniture and eating somewhat more daintily. (This in itself is unusual in a Labrador.)

Between the fourth and fifth week you may detect a slight swelling just behind the ribs in the loin area. Sometimes this shows as a change in the lie of the coat. From the fifth week onwards she will become heavy behind the ribs and her teats will appear prominent. Check carefully whilst she is resting that the teats are well shaped and healthy looking. It is not unusual for one to be inverted; it will probably correct itself as the pregnancy progresses, but otherwise the puppies will probably do the rest.

In the later stages she will require extra food so it is better to feed her smaller portions more frequently, say three times a day. Let her take her own exercise, as and when she wants it, in the garden. There is no need for her to be exercised in the fields or to collect the children from school. You must avoid overtiring her and protect her from any shocks or encounters of the aggressive kind. Also you must prevent her from meeting any dogs in encounters of the sexual kind!

Pregnancy should last about sixty-three days, but you must prepare for her to whelp up to five days early or even four or five days late. Two weeks before the calculated whelping date, introduce her to the maternity wing. If she has her own bed or blanket let her sleep in that at first. She will inspect the new box out of curiosity and may try it out on her own. Make up the whelping box with old newspapers. Do not use magazines or supplements, which are fastened with metal staples and have poor absorbency. She will have a good scratch and scuff them up to her satisfaction.

Sh.Ch. Novacroft Chorus Girl, born 1978, by Sandylands Charlston ex Novacroft Gay Rhapsody.

Often she will roll on her back with her legs in the air, a rather comical sight. However, this action helps to separate the puppies and prepare them for the journey ahead. Now is the time to prepare your equipment: boxes, towels, and so on, as set out in the list.

The Whelping

In general, bitches are accurate time-keepers, although if she becomes overdue by more than a couple of days contact your vet for advice. When she wants to whelp she will start to look worried and preoccupied. She will begin to pant and whine and refuse her food. She may starve herself for a day. You may even see contractions starting. However excited you feel you must just stay calm and give her encouragement. Allow her to take a little exercise in the garden, but keep a discreet eye on her: one of our bitches produced two puppies in the garden when we thought she was merely spending a penny.

For some reason, most whelpings start between 11 p.m and 2 a.m (so it will be necessary to carry a torch when you accompany your bitch on any excursions to the garden). Clinically, the day before a bitch is due to whelp her temperature will drop by about half a degree Centigrade below her normal temperature of 38.5°C (100.8°F). However, it is not necessary to stress the bitch by taking her temperature with a thermometer. Unless there is a reason to suspect a problem, leave well alone. In any case, your bitch will show far more positive indications that she is about to whelp. When you hear her panting and grunting and nesting violently, she is usually on her way.

There may be some discharge of fluid from her vulva which will cause her to lick herself avidly, the 'waters breaking'. The puppies are born encased in a membrane along with a second, darker-coloured sac, which is the placenta (or afterbirth). Both contain watery fluid. Normally the bitch will open the bag with her teeth and lick each puppy vigorously to dry it. If she does not, ease the bag away from the puppy's nose and mouth with your fingers, and make sure that the airways are clear and that the mouth is open.

Usually the bitch will bite through the umbilical cord herself. However, if the cord has not broken and she seems not to know what to do, nip the cord about 1in (3cm) away from the puppy between your finger and thumb and cut the cord with the sterile scissors.

Let her eat the placenta, because it contains excellent vitamins, hormones and nutrients. Don't be in a great hurry to put the puppy on a teat. If it appears a bit dopey, hold it in your hands, placed together as though in prayer, with the whelp's head towards your fingertips. Gently prise open its mouth with your second fingers and hold it open. Holding it thus, shake it gently, head downwards to expel any fluid from its lungs. After a few shakes, give it a rub with a warm towel.

If there is time, put the first puppy on to a teat. It will assist it if you gently express a little milk from the nearest nipple and aim the puppy's nose towards it. The scent of milk (actually colostrum at this stage), will cause the puppy to seek the teat. Let the puppy suck at the first opportunity. This is important because colostrum is rich in nutrients and antibodies.

Note the time of the first birth in your notebook and the colour and sex, if you can make it out, but do not disturb the bitch to do this as there will be plenty of time for statistics later.

When she can take it, give the bitch a little diluted milk containing a teaspoonful of powdered glucose. After she has whelped two or three puppies offer her a drink of diluted milk and liquid calcium. Check the instructions on the bottle for the correct dose and do not be tempted to overdose (about one dessertspoonful, is a guide).

If you need to handle the babies (and most people do!), follow the example of the shepherd and keep your hands smelling of puppies. Afterbirth fluid from the placenta will stain your fingers green but this fades in a day or two. To have green hands as a breeder is the equivalent of green fingers in a gardener. A sign of privilege and achievement! Do not wash them in antiseptic until after she has finished whelping.

Remove all the uneaten placentae, gunge and wet newspapers but don't try to be too clean until all the puppies have been whelped. Have a good bonfire later. And do *not* be afraid to lose any sickly or malformed puppies. This is a terrible dilemma, but you must allow the bitch to decide whether she is prepared to give them the benefit of the doubt. Sometimes, she will nose a fading puppy into a corner, resisting any attempt you make to revive it by putting it on a teat. Usually, if a whelp is not meant to survive it will have expired within eight hours.

If, either before any puppies have been born or in between whelps, she has contractions and shows signs of straining, but without any results, do not let her continue like this for more than an hour. If the straining stops after a few minutes, and she appears relaxed, take her for a short walk in the garden for two minutes. Often this has a stimulating action and aids the movement of the puppies. If this doesn't work, call the vet.

If all has gone well, daybreak will find a contented bitch feeding a greedy litter of quiet puppies, all safely delivered. Now you can

Letty with a litter of five day-old puppies.

change the newspapers and clean up the box. If you are lucky you can go to bed for an hour or two. Neither my wife nor I ever sleep in the same room with the bitch. She is better left to concentrate and learn her nursing; she will soon establish a routine. But it is sensible to sleep in a room that is not too far away so that you will hear if anything untoward happens. A contented litter with a relaxed mother emits a marvellous sound, somewhere between purring and gurgling. It has a primitive rhythm all of its own.

Postnatal Care

The day after the whelping, arrange for the vet to call to give the bitch an injection that will expel any retained placenta. It is not unusual for a little bloody discharge to appear as the uterus contracts. Also the bitch may have a slight greenish discharge following the whelping. This, too, is quite normal and is related to the removal of the placenta. However, should it be very dark and accompanied by a very nasty smell, ask your vet to check her. (*See* Complications later.)

Do let the bitch look after her own litter and keep handling to a minimum. Feed her a little boiled fish at first, with drinks of milk containing a dose of liquid calcium but get her back on a normal diet within two or three days. Make sure she has plenty of water to drink and that the room is kept at a temperature of about 70°F (21°C) so that the whelping box does not chill.

If after a day or so she becomes very protective of her new family, this is quite normal. To regain her confidence, forbid anyone except yourself to enter the maternity wing for a few days and go about your routine firmly and without fussing her. She will soon be showing them with pride. Bitches hate to be ignored.

On day three you may wish to ask the vet to call to remove the puppies' dew-claws, and also to check the bitch for signs of mastitis. Personally, I do not have the dew-claws removed because I find the dogs use them often as a kind of thumb, especially when scrambling up a grassy riverbank. But this is a matter for you to decide.

By day five your bitch should be on three good-quality meals a day made up from the food she is used to. You must avoid the temptation to change her to a higher protein or 'boosted' diet. So long as she is getting plenty of good-quality meat and biscuit with supplemented vitamins she will do well. Of course, a change of diet of any kind could affect her milk supply, which would mean a lot of work for you. One of our cats brought half a rotten rabbit to our Lottie when she was nursing a litter. She devoured it of course. Mercifully, she only contracted a mild version of food poisoning although, but for the swift action of our vet it could have proved fatal for the litter.

Now is the time to install the new family on a Vet-bed if the weather is cold. In summer, this kind of bedding can prove too insulating and you will find the whelps neatly spread out around the perimeter, cooling down. If so, then bed them on newspaper as before. Also at this time you can trim the puppies' nails. You must use a small pair of good-quality scissors with short blades. Take care to cut off only the hooked tips and no more of the nail (see diagram overleaf). Once you start to trim the nails you will have to keep up the procedure every couple of weeks until the puppies are weaned and up and about.

On or about day twelve the puppies will start to open their eyes. You will be surprised to see how alert they are. Remember, in the wild this and scent would be now their main senses of their mother at a distance, to aid their survival. But now in the litter box the survival of the puppies depends on you. Do not allow them to become a local attraction. By all means allow selected visitors to peep round the door, but do not allow family visits or 'foreign' animals to come near the litter. Even

203

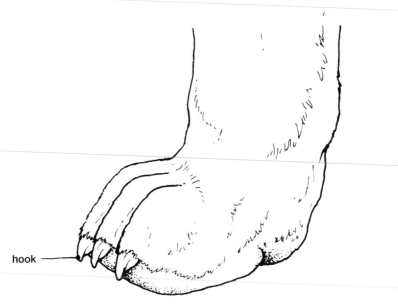

hook

Trim a puppy's nails by removing only the hook at the tip.

though they have a large degree of inborn protection against disease, which is inherited from their mother, there is a chance of infection from unwanted guests and it is not worth the risk. I do not allow anyone outside the family – even potential puppy buyers – to see the puppies until they are at least six weeks old.

Nursing

Sometimes when the milk is in full flow and the puppies seem to be increasingly greedy, the bitch will appear to lose all interest in her food. This may cause panic in the camp but, in fact, it may not be a major cause for concern. The reason for her apparent desire to fast is that she is still clearing up her puppies' faeces when she has the opportunity. Now is the time to get up a little earlier and replace the newspapers in the puppy box so that she does not feel she has to vacuum them. Make sure that she has her daily dose (about a level dessertspoon) of soluble calcium. It is easy to administer this using a plastic syringe. Slip the nozzle between her back teeth and let her swallow the solution slowly without choking.

Try to tempt her with a change of menu. A little boiled fish, such as coley or mackerel (but check for bones before feeding), or some thinly sliced smoked ham. I have found that grilled crispy bacon can also do the trick! She might appreciate a few dog biscuits or other similar treats. When the puppies are about five weeks old, consider restricting her nursing visits to twice daily, morning and evening.

Periodically, you must check the condition of her teats and quarters. The former should not be sore or crusty (check with your vet, if in doubt) and the quarters should be supple even when 'bagged up' and full of milk. If the latter appear hard and feel plate-like under the skin, at the next feed aim one of the larger greedy puppies to the nearest teat and give it preferential treatment. Encourage the bitch to feed the puppies more frequently if you have recently started weaning them. Usually this condition will correct itself naturally within twenty-four hours.

Cleanliness

At all times, cleanliness is important both inside and outside the maternity wing. Set up a parvocide-solution foot dip outside the house. You can use an old plastic washing-up bowl (which will take a large man-sized shoe) and change the fluid every couple of days. No one must be permitted past the dip without using it.

You must change your shoes when you come in from town. If you are a show exhibitor or other competitor, and there are puppies in the house, it is very good practice to strip off all your outer garments including shoes on your return.

As I have said before, the whelping box and puppy run must be kept clean and all the fragrant newspapers burnt at regular intervals. Soon you will have prospective owners visiting. A smart ship leaves a good impression and encourages others to follow her example.

Worming

The puppies *must* be wormed regularly. All puppies have worms: some are visible in the faeces, others are never seen, but they are there all the same. Puppies that have a lot of worms will be pot-bellied and will probably cough. Some people will tell you of perfectly worm-free litters; I do not believe them.

There is a section of the veterinary profession that now advises worming a bitch during pregnancy, while others dispute the wisdom of this. Personally, I take neither side. I follow my own vet's practice and would advise you to do the same. It is very likely that some of your puppies, sold in your area, will eventually receive attention from the same vet. If these have started a fixed worming regime it could be unwise to change it. There are different kinds of worming medicines; tablets, pastes and syrups are among them. I prefer the last kind. Sometimes a puppy will be sick after taking the medicine. If he has kept it down for fifteen to twenty minutes, it will be effective, otherwise that puppy can be wormed again seven days later. Do not be tempted to dose him again the same day!

The worm that most commonly affects puppies, and causes the most concern, is the common roundworm *Toxocana canis*. This is because *T. canis* larvae lie dormant in most adult dogs, but are reactivated in bitches when hormones are released during pregnancy. They then migrate to the puppies *in utero* via the placenta or the milk after she has whelped; in any case it is effectively eradicated by present-day treatments.

It is extremely important to burn all soiled papers and puppy faeces and to wash the bedding frequently. Do *not* bury used puppy papers in the compost heap or in the garden. Any larvae will become active within two or three weeks, capable of infecting any other suitable host, which includes man. Worm eggs are highly resistant to disinfectant, but hot water and scrubbing will remove them physically. However, this in itself is not sufficient. The eggs and larvae are microscopically small and are therefore invisible to the naked eye, so you cannot rely on sight to alert you to their presence. Take care to prevent young children from handling worm-infested waste. Discourage them from letting puppies lick their faces and make sure that they wash their hands frequently. Pregnant women should also avoid handling the waste papers.

Other worms may affect very young puppies, although not so commonly. These include the lungworm *Filaroides osleri* and, in the presence of fleas, the tapeworm *Dipylidium caninum*. (*See* Chapter 12, Diseases, Ailments and First Aid.)

Whelping and Postpartum Complications

In general, and as long as they are fit and healthy, Labradors are easy whelpers. However, while it is unusual for them to require surgical assistance, it is important to be aware of some of the problems that can arise so that you can take the appropriate action.

Inertia

There are two forms of this condition. In the first the bitch fails to produce contractions even though she has demonstrated other signs that she is about to whelp. The second occurs after contractions have begun, and perhaps even half-way through whelping, when contractions and straining fail to produce puppies. The latter may be caused by exhaustion or some obstruction, perhaps created by a puppy exiting backwards or in some other awkward position. If the bitch strains for more than one hour, call your vet, who will either give her an injection to get her going again or clear the obstruction.

Metritis (Pyometra)

This is a serious condition caused by inflammation of the uterus. It may occur as a result of a retained placenta or other foetal material. An affected bitch will have a raised temperature and a greenish-brown discharge (this should not be confused with the normal, greenish post-whelping discharge which is relatively odourless). She will also appear miserable; she may vomit and tense her abdominal muscles. Veterinary attention is vital, as the condition can prove fatal. In chronic cases, pyometra may develop. (*See* Chapter 12.)

Eclampsia

Eclampsia (or milk fever) is a potentially fatal condition that is caused by lack of calcium in the lactating bitch. As the puppies grow and the bitch starts to produce milk, the drain on her calcium resources increases tremendously, which means that bitches with large litters or insufficient calcium in the diet are particularly susceptible. A bitch can reach the verge of collapse surprisingly quickly, so take care to watch your bitch's behaviour when she is feeding a large litter. If she goes off her food, begins to shiver excessively and is feverish or depressed you must contact the vet *immediately*. Eclampsia is a serious emergency. Whilst the vet is on his way, you can encourage the bitch to drink a mixture of diluted puppy milk (or cow's milk) and liquid calcium, but this is not sufficient on its own: calcium (and vitamins) administered intravenously is the only sure remedy. The injection will have her on her feet again quite quickly, but give her a day off from feeding the litter so that she has time to regain her body's calcium balance. Follow the vet's advice in improving the calcium content of the bitch's diet while she is lactating.

Mastitis

If the milk glands appear to contain hard lumps or become very swollen and inflamed, mastitis should be suspected. This is very painful for the bitch and you must be very gentle. If there is a discharge from the nipple which is not milk and may be dark in colour, get help immediately. However, if the glands are swollen with milk and some nipples are hard with a crust-like texture, they may have been neglected by the puppies and ceased to give an easy drink. In which case, bathe them with warm water and gently express a little milk and encourage the puppies to suck from them. With a little luck they will soon be being used normally.

Hand-rearing a Litter

It can happen, although infrequently with Labradors, that the nursing bitch loses her milk. Then you will have to hand-rear the puppies yourself. If you have never done this before it is essential to get someone experienced in breeding to help you. He may even have a bitch in milk who could help out. The type of breed is not very important and it might mean splitting up the litter between mothers, although obviously you must take care that the nursing bitches do not meet at feeding times.

Hand-rearing means giving each individual puppy a feed every three hours round the clock followed by 'topping and tailing' using cotton wool wads soaked in warm water. This is very important, especially in a case where the natural mother is not taking part in any of the litter's care. It is necessary to use the cotton wool to simulate the bitch's licking, which stimulates the puppy's bowel and bladder after every feed. If you are lucky enough to get someone reliable to help you, a system of four-hour shifts will work quite well for the three week period. When you are hand-rearing, work closely with your vet and keep him in the picture.

Weaning

Weaning the puppies should start when they are between two and three weeks old. This depends on the size of the litter: a large litter will need weaning earlier and more help for the mother. It will help the mother if you can start them with a little cereal baby food after she has fed them last thing at night. This will allow her to get some respite from their demands. Do not forget to wipe them clean with a damp cloth or else they will chew each other's coats when they try to lick the food off. The same applies as the puppies get older. If you do not keep them clean, they could get into the habit of chewing ears and necks, especially if there are tasty morsels embedded there.

Gradually, after a day or two, you will get them to eat good-quality minced red meat but do not use pet mince at this stage as it is too fatty; buy the type intended for human consumption. Add, just a little puppy-size biscuit meal that has been soaked for ten minutes in hot water. When the puppies are about four weeks old, you can give a puppy milk powder or goats-milk powder mixed with water (4oz per pint/100ml per litre) after each of their four meals per day. The puppies should be fed at 8 a.m., 12 noon, 4 p.m. and 8 p.m. each day. Do not feed raw eggs as they can affect the vitamin uptake of the puppies.

Weaning is a very gradual process; you are trying to balance the bitch's milk production against the rising demands of the litter. When the litter is four or five weeks old, you can start gradually to reduce the quantities of your bitch's food. Do not let the puppies monopolize her completely. By the time they are six weeks old she should be on a normal diet with the puppies weaned off her.

Regurgitation

When the litter is between four and five weeks old a maternal Labrador bitch may consider it necessary to begin her own weaning

Two Abbeystead puppies at three weeks old.

regime in earnest. About a quarter of an hour after she has eaten her own meal she will enter the puppy pen, assume the lazy feeding position (that is standing over them with legs astride) and commence nursing. Before they have had time to settle to their task, she will regurgitate her last meal which has been part digested and thus finely prepared. The puppies will eat it up in double quick time. This is a perfectly normal and natural occurrence and you must not criticise her. It will do no harm to the puppies, or to the mother, in the short term.

However, if you allow her to continue this weaning unchecked, the bitch's condition will suffer because she might become deprived of the essential vitamins and minerals which are necessary for her coat and condition. By the time the puppies are five weeks old, she should be *prevented* from regurgitating her food for them: now you will have upped the quantities of food given to the litter as described above. During the next few days you should endeavour to manage her comings and goings with the litter and continue with your weaning programme as described. Make sure that she has plenty of fresh water available and give a drink of milk occasionally. At the same time you must restrict her visits to the puppies to a token few minutes each evening, although many mothers are not slow to take the hint and pass the rearing over to the housemaid (you). With a six-week-old litter many bitches are content just to watch the proceedings from afar.

Pedigrees and Registration

All the puppies in a litter should be registered by name at the English Kennel Club at about three weeks old. All the puppies must be entered on the same form otherwise any omissions may not subsequently be considered for registration. The appropriate payment must accompany the registration. The rules covering the names that can be given to the puppies are stated on the back of the document. These rules also show you how to apply for a kennel name (or affix). An affix may be used solely by its owner as part of the names of any dogs owned or bred by him.

The registration certificate will state the relevant dates of whelping and registration, the name of the dog, colour and the names of his sire and dam, together with their hip scores and eye status if these are known.

Optionally, a registration certificate may be endorsed by you as owner of the puppies, with the following provisos. The object of these endorsements is to safeguard the puppy's future:

210

- Progeny not eligible for registration.
- Not eligible for issue of an export pedigree.

It is worth noting at this stage that the English Kennel Club will not register a litter where a dam has already had six litters or when she is over eight years old, except by special permission.

You will need to write out a pedigree for each puppy. Standard pedigree forms designed for the purpose are available. When you do this, it is useful to make up a plastic pocket file or wallet in which you can keep all the information about the litter. This makes for easy reference and reduces the chances of important documents becoming mislaid. Such a file might include:

- The pedigrees of the sire and dam, with photographs.
- Copies of Hip and Eye Certificates of sire and dam.
- Kennel Club Registration forms.
- Pedigrees of the puppies.
- Vaccination certificates.
- A book of receipts with counterfoils.
- Feeding and care instructions.
- Simple puppy sale agreement.
- Insurance leaflets.

New Homes

As a responsible breeder you will think very hard about the kind of homes your puppies will find. Try to imagine it from the puppies' point of view. It is not the same as adopting a human child: the puppy will not ask the reasons for choosing him, neither will he accuse his mother of deserting him, nor will he apportion any blame if the home is not as comfortable as his birthplace. What he desires, above all, is security, for which his forebears risked the flames of the hunter's campfire in order to trade the freedom of the wilderness for a full tummy and a warm bed. As a bonus he also gained care and affection.

The quality that we should primarily be looking for in a purchaser then, is the ability to provide security, correct feeding, a dry bed, constant care, and plenty of affection. The security requirement rules out those who are being posted abroad, those who are in the process of divorce and those who are moving house in the near future. It is possible that you may have enquiries from abroad. Here the degree of

Life is one long… yawn, when you are three weeks old.

security will depend upon the trust you can build up between you and the buyer. By far the best way is to have a mutual friend who will vouch for the puppy's new home and perhaps visit it there before you commit yourself to the sale.

I will never sell puppies via a third party. You must beware of dealers and traders in this respect. They can be very plausible. However, should you mention that as a rule all your puppies have their Kennel Club Registrations endorsed 'Not eligible for Export Pedigree', this may cause them to be a little less persistent. And could save you much potential heartbreak. (*See* Registration earlier in this chapter.)

The price you charge will largely depend on two factors: the current puppy price for Labradors in your part of the world, because it is a buyer's market, and the ability of the purchaser to meet that price. Correct feeding requires a good supply of quality food which, even at bulk prices, will cost annually the equivalent of a week's holiday for one person. So you must be confident that the potential purchaser can afford a Labrador.

Along with a quality diet and a bed – somewhere to call his own territory and to feel safe – a puppy will require company and a great deal of attention if he is to become a sociable, amiable and useful companion. While he is untrained and unsure, if he is left alone for more than half an hour he will pine, then he will become bored, probably noisy, and eventually he could become incredibly destructive. This will rule out another category of purchaser: the part-time owner, who always has a friend, neighbour or great-aunt who will look after the puppy while they are at work. Do they really want a weekend dog? Wouldn't a library book be less trouble? Personally, I will not sell a puppy to people who are out at work during the day, no matter what arrangements they intend to make to take care of it. Anyone who would spend on a puppy an amount equivalent to the cost of an expensive outfit of clothes, saying that they were for weekend wear only, would be better off buying the clothes. And the puppy is better off with a full-time owner.

It should also be borne in mind that newborn babies and little puppies do not mix, so I will not sell to a prospective purchaser who is pregnant, and is best advised to wait a couple of years before committing herself to the demanding care of a young puppy.

Finally, I very rarely let a puppy go to its new home under eight weeks of age, and certainly not under seven weeks, I think that a puppy can suffer psychologically (some may become traumatized, which implies that any damage might be permanent) if it is stripped from the litter before it is ready. Such dogs can become very submissive and insecure, which I am sure does not help them when you try to train them later on. Certainly, a puppy of less than eight weeks old is very immature physically and therefore at a disadvantage when he tries to make a new start in a new home.

The moral is, ask as many relevant questions as are necessary to find out how the puppy will be kept, who will look after it, who will pay for its feeding and clean up after it, and who will exercise it and take it for walks. Ask whether the prospective owner has an enclosed garden or lives close to a busy road. Does he live near a river? Do not be afraid to ask personal questions: How many children? What are their ages? Or, are they getting married? If so, when? Or divorced? Are they living in the same house? Is it a good idea to have a dog before a family? Why? And so on, and so on. It is important to build up a good picture of the potential owners of your stock. You will be amazed at some of the answers. As long as you are polite, a potential owner who is genuinely responsible and caring will not object to your questions. Anyone who does object should be viewed with suspicion.

Be a little wary of overconfident would-be buyers who appear to have had a long succession of dogs. You should enquire closely as to

Playtime at Brigburn.

what has happened to them and be suspicious of their explanations. Perhaps they become quickly disillusioned when their dogs reach maturity, none of which have lived up to their high expectations in the show ring or achieved the requisite level of obedience training. Family expectations of the ideal dog should not be obtained merely by trial and error.

When you are satisfied that the puppy buyers are the people who they say they are, that they seem to be conscientious and caring, and that their circumstances meet your high standards, you should ask for a deposit of between one-third and one-half of the purchase price to be posted to you; in return you will provisionally pencil them in an appointment to see the litter. When you receive the deposit you can confirm the appointment and fix a time. Meanwhile, if you still have any nagging doubts arrange for their cheque to be 'specially' presented as a further security.

Choice of Puppy

Do not fall into the trap of allowing prospective buyers to choose the puppy of their choice. You may already have decided on the ones that you want to keep, but keep this information to yourself, otherwise you can be sure that your preference will be their preference! Obviously, all members of the litter are of equal quality. Usually dogs will be slightly heavier, but the bitches will be prettier. Often the smallest bitch is the prettiest of them all. When you have made your mind up at about six weeks old and you have not seen fit to change it even when they are eight weeks old, you may agree to allow the purchaser to choose between two of the remainder, especially if you are going to 'run on' two bitches and they have ordered a dog.

If you have trouble deciding which is the nicest of, perhaps, three puppies when they are four or five weeks old, put a little dab of pink nail varnish on the inside of the ear flap as a marker. Then you will be able to spot 'left ear', 'right ear or 'no ears' quite easily. However, you must be very careful not to get any varnish in the ear or on the skin.

Sale Agreement

A simple puppy sale agreement is a safeguard for the responsible breeder in these most litigious days. It is a good idea to set out in simple terms the degree to which you have tried to produce a puppy which will live a happy, healthy and useful life. Conversely, the onus is on the purchaser to accept that there is a great deal of responsibility on his or her part for the continuing health and upbringing of their new Labrador. How one wishes that the conditions of human lives could be so ordered!

A sale agreement should be signed by both seller and purchaser. (When drafting out your first sale agreement, it is well worth consulting your legal adviser to be sure that the agreement is binding.) A copy of the signed agreement should be given to the purchaser along with the feeding instructions and general care information.

After-sales

Send your puppies to their new homes with a survival pack containing two or three days' supply of their usual food. This will help them to settle in. At the same time it will enable the new owner to concentrate on acquainting the baby with its new surroundings, without having to bother preparing his food during the first days. However, you will be surprised with many owners just how well prepared they are. They will arrive to collect the puppy with beds, blankets and toys. I have even seen a set of collars arrive 'to allow him to grow into them' and a canvas dummy for retriever training accompanying a puppy who is just eight weeks and two days old.

The new owner should be given some simple instruction on feeding and general care. These should indicate how many times and with what treatment the puppy has been wormed, when the next one is due, and an instruction to contact the vet for worming supervision and general advice. They should also remind the owner that inoculation against distemper, hepatitis, leptospirosis and parvovirus (DHLP) must be carried out by the vet, who will advise the best time, and a warning to take care with whom and to what the puppy is introduced in its first six months. These instructions will also, of course, include a diet sheet, which might look like this:

Diet Sheet

Eight weeks: four meals per day

8.00 a.m. One Weetabix, cup of milk, sweeten with glucose.

Noon One small cup of puppy meal or 'mixer' plus a cup of beef mince and cooked veg. Soak the meal for at least ten minutes in hot water. Cut up food finely and *don't* feed it too hot.

4.00 p.m. Milk feed. Rice pudding or puppy milk thickened with Farex. Sweeten as above. You may add one mashed, lightly boiled egg to above occasionally.

6.30 p.m. As for noon plus good-quality proprietary vitamin supplement (do not overdose). Occasionally give two or three dog biscuits or shapes, but nothing after 7 p.m. or he may not be clean in the night.

The diet sheet should include some important dos and don'ts. While these may seem obvious to you, it is surprising how many new owners do not take them into account:

1. Never feed poultry bones, potatoes, white bread, sweets or cakes.
2. Use conditioning tablets as sweets not tit-bits, and feed according to manufacturer's instructions.
3. **Always have clean water available**.

Follow this with dietary instructions for the puppy at four months, six months and twelve months of age.

Routine Care

Along with the diet sheet and information on vaccination and worming programmes, you should provide the purchaser with some general instructions for routine care and management. These should include advice on house-training, bedding and grooming, along with some general tips, such as recommendations to rub down a wet dog with a chamois leather rather than a towel, and suggestions on how to go about joining a training class. You will also need to provide a list of safety precautions, such as checking fences and gates are secure and ceasing all use of garden chemicals and poisons, such as slug bait. Once again, although it may seem obvious, remind the owner *never* to leave the dog in a car on a warm day.

Breeding Worldwide

Generally, in Australia, it is a requirement that the whole of a litter is registered with the State Canine Council (SCC) unless the dog is not to be bred from. The SCC code of ethics states that puppies must be vaccinated at six weeks and must not be sold before they are eight weeks old, during which time the vaccine becomes effective. In addition, puppies should not be exported under twelve weeks old. All new owners get a health certificate with their puppy. Vaccination is carried out against distemper (hardpad) and parvovirus; kennel cough is optional. All puppies should be wormed for round-, hook-, whip-, tape- and heartworms in Australia.

Health insurance for breeders' dogs is not generally employed in Australia because complications arising from mating, whelping and hereditary problems would be excluded from the cover. More breeders are now using hip X-ray and eye-testing schemes than before so the situation is improving, thanks to SCC and the breed clubs' code of ethics which recommends this practice. Also, legal action is more likely now in the event of a problem occurring. Most club members who breed follow the hip and eye test guidelines and some are X-raying elbows for osteochondrosis as well. (*See* Chapter 12.)

The SCC or local Canine Association regulates the breeding, trialling and showing world in all its aspects. All State Canine Associations or Councils are members of the Australian Kennel Council. However, the keeping of domestic dogs is controlled by each state's Municipal Council who stipulate usually only two dogs per household in urban

Zenchel Darius Jedburgh, chocolate. (Owner: Mrs Power, Australia.)

areas, so breeders and boarding establishment proprietors tend to live in the rural areas. A permit is required to keep more than two dogs but not for breeding as such. Most breeders line-breed to selected bloodlines and import stock or semen as needed, because the gene pool in Australia is not very great.

In Denmark Rules for Breeding are set out by the Danish Canine Council (DKK). In order to get permission from the DKK to breed a litter you must have shown your Labrador and won third prize or above. From 1994 onwards, breeding bitches must be over twelve months of age, tattooed with an individual registration number and hold clear hip and eye certificates.

When the puppies are three weeks old the breeder may obtain their pedigrees from the DKK. In the seventh week they are tattooed by an approved technician, but the puppies may not be sold until they are eight weeks old. Chocolate puppies are a little more expensive owing to their relative rarity. Interestingly, third-party insurance is compulsory for dog owners in Denmark, although relatively few dogs are insured for veterinary fees. When breeding a litter, most Danish breeders commonly outcross their lines and then linebreed when it appears safe to do so with future litters. Breeding bitches and stud-dogs must have good hips graded A (normal) or B (transitional). The grades below B are C (mild HD), D (medium) and E (severe) hip dysplasia.

In Finland the Labrador is the fifth most popular breed, lying just behind the Elkhound and the Golden Retriever in the list of registrations at the Finnish Kennel Club (FKC). In order that puppies may be registered, both parents must have X-rayed hips and be graded highly. Also both parents must hold clear eye certificates for HC, PRA and RD. These certificates are issued annually. For official eye tests and hip-scoring, including X-raying, the dog must be tattooed with a registration number. In France, dogs and bitches need good hips and eyes as shown on the test certificates. Line-breeding and out-crossing of pedigrees are fairly common practices among breeders. In France, it is common for the purchase cost of a puppy to be refunded if subsequently it fails hip or eye tests or if a dog is not entire at maturity.

In Germany, both the sire and the dam must have good hips, a current 'PRA clear' eye certificate and also be able to pass a basic temperament test to show that they are not bad-tempered, nervous or gun-shy. Hip condition is quantified by scoring the hip X-rays, which are graded A to E. At the present time there is no requirement to score elbows but some breeders do it all the same. For breeding, both the dog's hips must score a total of C (equivalent to 15 in the UK) or better. When a puppy is sold it must have the same injections (HDLP) as for the UK, and it must also be tattooed with a registration number. Breeders commonly line-breed to dogs with known virtues hoping to get good even puppies of similar type and good temperament.

In South Africa, line-breeding is the norm for the majority of breeders and most avoid in-breeding altogether. Outcrossing, sometimes with imported blood, is desirable periodically to bring in some hybrid vigour.

All puppies are vaccinated at six weeks and then again at fourteen weeks for the most common canine diseases plus rabies and annual boosters are given. Most breeders belonging to the South African Labrador Club have their dogs X-rayed and the hips scored and eyes tested for PRA. Eye-testing of stock, while not widespread, is becoming more common among the more established enthusiasts. Hip dysplasia is graded 0–4 on either side: 0 being free and 4 being severe dysplasia.

In the USA, puppies must have full registration with the American Kennel Club (AKC). For this they can compete in shows and their progeny can be registered. All puppies must be registered before they attain six months of age. The AKC also operates a

Am. Ch. Braemar Anchor Boy marking a water retrieve. (Owner: Mrs Borders, USA.)

system of limited registration which precludes show competition, but allows the dogs to compete in obedience competitions and field events. Progeny cannot be registered but the breeder can change to full registration at any time.

All puppies must be inoculated against the same common canine diseases that are inoculated against in the UK (HDLP). The inoculation is known as a '5ml'. In some states it is the practice to buy a vaccine kit off the shelf and administer it oneself. The Canine Orthopaedic Foundation (USA) grant permanent certificates from scored X-rays for dogs of two years of age. However, some breeders begin to scan X-rays of stock as young as six months of age for an indication of their status. Hip (HD) and elbow (OCD) conditions are considered very serious problems, as are eye defects such as progressive retinal atrophy PRA). Severely suffering stock are not prolifically bred from. Generally breeders require hip and elbow 'free' certificates when the dog is two years of age before a Limited Registration may be upgraded to Full. Texas State law requires that all dogs over twelve months old must be vaccinated annually against rabies.

12

Diseases, Ailments and First Aid

When you are the owner of a beautiful pedigree Labrador, you owe it to him to give him a secure, interesting and, above all, healthy life. For your peace of mind and his you must develop a good mutual partnership with your vet and you must not be afraid of spending a little (and, occasionally, quite a lot) of money in order to protect your Labrador from common canine diseases and to help him recover if he is unfortunately injured. Often, an early visit to the surgery will save you money: a condition left unattended could eventually lead to a bill in excess of the cost of an early diagnosis and treatment. Develop a mutual trust between you, your vet and your Labrador and you will all benefit in the long run.

It will also help if you get into the habit of giving your Labrador a general health check as part of the grooming routine. Check that the ears are nice and clean and that the eyes are clear and free of any discharge. For example, the appearance of even a little coloured discharge in the eye corners is often a sign of infection of the ears or eyes (and sometimes even of a bad tooth) and should be checked out by the vet if it persists for more than a few days. Check his feet for any small injuries and under the tail for any swellings. In a bitch, especially an older one, check regularly for signs of pyometra. Check in the mouth for any loose teeth, swelling of the gums or heavy deposits of tartar, all of which should be examined by your vet.

However well you care for your Labrador though, no one is immune from the occasional accident, injury or infection. In this chapter, I shall outline some of the conditions and symptoms that you should be aware of so that you can take early action or administer first aid where appropriate. In any event, it bears repeating that you should always seek your vet's advice as soon as possible.

221

Accidents and Emergencies

Put together a first-aid kit and keep it in a safe but accessible place. It is well worth making up a second kit to keep in the car. It should include:

- Plastic bottle of antiseptic.
- Bandage roll 2in (5cm) wide.
- Pair of blunt-ended scissors.
- Nylon lead with slip-ring.
- Old pair of tights for emergency muzzle.
- Roll of cotton wool.
- Roll of plaster.
- Roll of kitchen towel.
- Anti-histamine.
- Small plastic container each of sodium bicarbonate and vinegar.
- Blanket.

Artificial Respiration

If a dog is lying motionless and is not breathing (and provided you are sure that he has not suffered an epileptic fit or is so severely wounded that to move or manipulate him might cause further injury) you can attempt artificial respiration: lie him on his side; make sure the mouth is clear; place both hands round his jaw and blow up his nose quite hard, as you would blow a trumpet. With any luck, he will gasp and splutter. If this fails after two or three attempts, alternate the blowing by applying gentle pressure on the chest wall. Count to five as the pressure is applied, then blow again. Keep on with this routine until he begins to gasp. As this process entails a lot of stress for the dog, keep him warm, dry and as quiet as possible.

Shock

After any major accident or trauma, and even in some minor cases, a dog will be suffering from some degree of shock. Shock is a clinical condition caused by collapse of the circulatory system and characterized by paleness of the lips, gums and eye rims, a drop in body temperature and rapid shallow breathing. Shock can in itself be fatal and is therefore an emergency. Cover the dog loosely with a blanket to keep him warm, but do not attempt to give liquid or food. Take the dog to the vet immediately.

Bites and Stings

In the case of an adder bite, an angry, very painful swelling of the affected area around the location of the bite will occur; it is often indicated by two small wounds about ½in (15mm) apart. Do not try to walk him as this will encourage the poison to circulate. Get him to a car (flag one down if necessary!) and take him to a vet immediately so that he can administer the correct antidote. It helps to apply a tourniquet between the wound and the body to prevent the poison spreading. To do this, tie a handkerchief or a lady's stocking or tights to form a binding around the limb and twist it with a pencil or small stick so that the veins can be seen to swell. However, you must stay with the dog whilst this is being done and loosen the binding every ten minutes or so. A tourniquet left in position for more than twenty minutes may result in gangrene of the lower part. Avoid the temptation to wedge the binding tightly. You must control the blood flow to the limb until a vet can take over.

Bee stings may be relieved with sodium bicarbonate, wasp stings with vinegar. Stings to the mouth and throat need veterinary attention.

Bloat (Gastric Dilation and Torsion)

Bloat is one of the *most serious* emergencies to afflict an animal and veterinary help must be obtained immediately. Fortunately, it is not often seen in Labradors. The condition is characterized by a gross swelling of the abdomen as a result of gas being trapped in the intestines; it is further complicated if – as sometimes occurs – twisting (torsion) of the gut takes place. Bloat can be fatal within a very short time, and since no first aid may be attempted, it is essential to get the dog to a vet by the quickest means possible.

Drowning

The first thing to do with a dog that appears to have drowned is to clear his mouth and ease his tongue into its natural position. Second, pick him up around the middle and hold his legs skywards with his head near the ground. The combination of pressure on the body and gravity will encourage some water to drain from his lungs and throat. Then artificial respiration (*see* above) can be given. Once he has recovered, treat him for shock and keep him warm.

Owners of swimming pools should remember that dogs cannot jump out of them, so access should be prevented by fencing.

223

Eye Injury

An injury to the eye will usually need prompt veterinary attention. If you can, wrap a coat or small blanket around the dog's neck to form an 'Elizabethan collar'; hold it there to prevent his scratching his eye with his paws and making things worse. If the dog appears to be in great pain, a cold, wet, sterile pad may be applied gently to relieve it until the vet can attend to it. Stay with him, if it is practicable, while someone contacts the vet, and stay with him if he is taken by car.

Heatstroke

Like all dogs, Labradors are provided with sweat glands, but these are not so efficient as ours. The dog loses heat primarily via the mouth and tongue (facilitated by panting), and via the pads. With their thick, heat-retaining coats, Labradors are prone to heat stroke and great care must be taken when they travel by car in *any* sun-drenched place. Black Labradors are especially at risk because their coat colour is heat-absorbent.

Heatstroke is fatal. If you suspect that a dog is affected, you must act very quickly. It is essential to reduce the body temperature, so he should be immersed in cold water immediately. Use a nearby river or pond, or the sea, or a bathtub. Get his head wet also, and the back of his neck. Encourage him to drink if he can. After first aid, veterinary assistance is essential. The dog will probably also need to be treated for shock.

Heatstroke most commonly occurs in dogs left in a car on a warm day (it does not have to be hot). The car's interior will rise in temperature, and heatstroke, followed by death, can occur surprisingly quickly. *Never* leave a dog in a car if the sun is shining. And never be tempted to relax the rule in the case of an air-conditioned car: if the engine stalls or the air-conditioning breaks down, the dog will die.

Impalement

Impalement is most likely to occur in the countryside when you are walking or shooting with your dog. Broken fencing, iron debris, wooden spikes may all pose this danger. In the event of impalement, the first thing to do is to reach him if you can and restrain him from moving or struggling. (Take care not to get bitten: if he is in great pain this is a normal reaction.) Support him so that the pressure is off the wounded area. Help should be sent for immediately; although if you are alone

224

with your dog, you will have to shout loudly for help and hope that you will be heard. If it becomes necessary to attempt to disengage him yourself, it is worth remembering that often the best way is to feed the spike forwards through the wound if it is protruding sufficiently and is detached. It may be necessary to apply a bandage and tourniquet to control loss of blood until veterinary attention is obtained. Treat for shock.

Poisoning

The obvious signs of poisoning are diarrhoea, violent sickness and retching; the dog may also stagger, collapse and, in serious cases, will become comatose. It is important to get immediate veterinary help. Make sure that you have a detailed check of anything that he may have eaten. If there is a package or bottle, or a half-eaten carcass of a bird or animal , which you suspect may be responsible, put on some rubber gloves and put it in a plastic bag to take to the vet. *Never* be tempted to make a poisoned dog sick unless you are absolutely certain that the poison is not a corrosive. The safest immediate first aid is to encourage water intake.

Many common household and garden chemicals are potentially poisonous to dogs. Medicines, detergents, disinfectants, paint, creosote, anti-freeze, slug-bait, weedkiller, sodium chlorate or paraquat, and rat poison are all toxic. Many houseplants and seeds (such as daffodil bulbs and laburnum seeds) are poisonous to dogs and must be stored out of reach.

Parasites

At different times throughout your dog's life, he will come into contact with various parasites, both external and internal. The most common external parasites are fleas, ticks and lice (mange mites are discussed under Skin conditions.) The internal parasites with which owners need to be most concerned are roundworm, tapeworm and, in some countries particularly, heartworm, whipworm and lungworm.

Fleas

Apart from the obvious irritation to your dog (and possibly yourself) fleas can cause skin problems in some dogs which have an allergic reaction to their bites. Contact your vet immediately and use a modern anti-flea treatment which is easily administered directly to the surface of the skin. Flea treatments from your vet are usually far more effective and longer-lasting than those obtained from pet shops. In all cases, it will be necessary to obtain a different preparation to treat his bed, his blanket, and any areas of carpet or soft furnishings with which your dog has frequent or prolonged contact. This is because most of the flea's life-cycle occurs away from the host in the surrounding environment, where eggs are laid. Your vet can advise you on the most appropriate programme for eradicating fleas.

Lice

Lice spend their entire lives on the host and are passed from dog to dog by direct contact. Again, the vet will provide an effective treatment.

Ticks

Ticks are most commonly picked up in rural areas. They usually select a site near the head or around the chest or shoulders, where they pierce the skin with mouthparts that, once embedded, are very difficult to remove intact. In most cases, a tick will not be detected until it has been there long enough to become engorged, when it may reach the size of a pea. Do not attempt to remove a tick without first loosening its grip by soaking it with surgical spirit or ether. If the mouthparts are left in the skin, they may cause infection. If in doubt consult your vet.

Roundworm

The roundworm that most commonly occurs in dogs, *Toxocara canis*, has already been mentioned in Chapter 11 because it is passed to puppies via the placenta or the milk of the dam. In adult dogs, it can be picked up from contact with infective ground or faeces. The adult worm is round, white and fine, and 3–6in (75–150mm) long. Although worms may occasionally be noticed in faeces, the eggs are invisible to the naked eye. The eggs are passed into the environment with the faeces and the larvae become infective within about two or three weeks.

T. canis can affect man. However, control is straightforward: a suitable worming programme will be provided by your vet. It is important to realize that *all* dogs must be wormed regularly throughout their adult lives, not just in puppyhood, if control is to be effective.

T. leonina, another roundworm that is similar to *T. canis* with the exception that it is not passed from dam to puppies *in utero*, is controlled by the same preparation used to treat *T. canis*.

Tapeworms

The most common tapeworm, *Diplydium caninum*, is shaped like a ribbon and can grow to a length of up to 20 inches (500mm). The worm is made up of segments, each of which contains eggs. The segments break off from the rear of the adult worm and are released into the environment with the faeces. They are easily seen, appearing like grains of rice on the ground, in the faeces or in the dog's coat. These are then eaten by the flea larvae, in which they form cysts containing immature worms. When the adult flea carrying the cyst bites the dog, the dog nibbles at the irritation caused by the bite and in doing so swallows the flea and cyst together. Once in the gut the worm larvae mature into adult worms

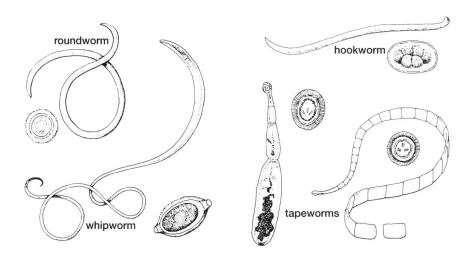

Some parasitic worms and their eggs (not to scale).

within three to four weeks. It can be seen, therefore, that the life cycle of this worm depends upon its intermediate host – the flea – being present, which is one of the reasons that flea eradication and routine control is so important. *Diplydium* cannot be passed directly from dog to dog.

Two other tapeworms, *Taenia hydatigina* and *Echinococcus granulones*, may occur in dogs, though less commonly. Both are ingested by eating the raw or partly cooked, contaminated offal of sheep or other farm animals. *Echinococcus* segments are microscopically small, but pose a serious threat to man in whom they develop into life-threatening cysts.

As with the roundworm, regular worming treatment will keep your dog free from tapeworm infestation.

Toxoplasma gondii

This parasite is most commonly present in cats. However, dogs can be infected through ingesting the cysts present in cat faeces or contaminated meat. Infection with this parasite is known as toxoplasmosis. It can be transmitted to man and is of particular concern for pregnant women in whom it can cause miscarriage, stillbirth or foetal abnormalities. Therefore, it is important that puppies (and all dogs) are prevented from eating cat faeces and thus aiding the transmission of worm eggs to humans. Cat trays should be kept away from dogs and puppies, and cleaned out regularly. (But not by women who are pregnant.)

Heartworm, Hookworm, Lungworm and Whipworm

These parasites are fairly uncommon in the UK but are sometimes found in large commercial kennels. All mature dogs and puppies are wormed for heartworm, hookworm and whipworm in Australia, South Africa and the United States.

Heartworm, *Dirofilasia immitis* is a common cause of heart disease in warm climates. It is not passed directly from dog to dog, but via the mosquito, the worm's intermediate host.

Hookworm (*Uncinaria*) larvae infect dogs either by being swallowed or by penetrating the skin. Larvae migrate to gut where the mature hookworm attaches itself to the intestine wall.

The lungworm *Filaroides osleri* is commonest in breeding kennels. It inhabits the windpipe near the lungs. The larvae are coughed up into the mouth and either swallowed into the gut or passed from dam to puppy during licking. The larvae cause partial blockage of the airway and a resultant dry cough.

The whipworm *Trichoris vulpic* has a fairly simple life cycle. Dogs ingest the larvae from contaminated ground. The adult worm inhabits the blind gut where it lays eggs which are passed in the faeces.

Dermatitis

Inflammation of the skin can occur on many parts of the dog's body; sometimes it is transient and sometimes it can be a constant problem. This is because its causes are many and varied. Fungi (usually ringworm), bacterial infections, parasites, irritants and temperamental condition can all be involved, and it is often difficult to isolate a specific cause in each individual case. In some cases, hypersensitivity to house dust-mites can cause an allergic skin complaint.

Often the symptoms are excessive paw chewing, abdomen licking and itching ears. These may appear in the first two years of the dog's life. Things to look for are: a brownish saliva staining of the groin, armpits and between the toes; also a change of skin colour from pink to mottled black. It is essential to involve your vet as soon as possible. Treatment will include (in ascending order of importance), flea control, treatment with essential fatty acids (often a neglected part of the Labrador's diet), antihistamines, steroids. In the limit, vaccines may be needed for long-term control. It is worth noting that many skin problems are thought to be hereditary.

Mange

There are two main types of mange, each caused by a different mite. However, both will cause hair loss and, in the case of sarcoptic mange, intense irritation. The mites are not visible and veterinary diagnosis of the condition is necessary. Demodectic mange, which is hereditary, is notoriously difficult to treat and in extreme cases causes such loss of condition and illness in the animal that euthanasia may be indicated. Sarcoptic mange is extremely contagious and, in man, is known as scabies.

Infectious Diseases

All puppies should be vaccinated against the four main infectious diseases – distemper, hepatitis, leptospirosis and parvovirus – and given annual boosters thereafter to ensure continued protection. The standard vaccine is known in the UK is known as HDLP. In the USA, rabies vaccine is given at the same time. It is also possible to vaccinate against kennel cough although this is not usually done unless the dog either lives in, or will be boarded in, kennels.

Distemper

Canine distemper is fortunately relatively rare nowadays owing to the widespread use of modern vaccine. However, the virus manifests itself with severe flu-like symptoms and the dog is lethargic and often prostrate. If you suspect that a dog has distemper, *do not* take him to the vet. Get veterinary assistance at once. Hard-pad is a highly infectious form of canine distemper, and so called because it causes hardening of the foot pads.

Hepatitis

This is a viral disease, which in dogs is commonly known as Infectious Canine Hepatitis. It is transmitted from one dog to another via the urine. Symptoms of infection may include a high temperature, wasting, anaemia, lethargy, and convulsions. Vomiting and diarrhoea may persist for a week. However, in some acute cases, a dog may show no apparent symptoms at all and will die within a very short time. There are two forms of the disease, one being associated with respiratory disease, the other with the liver, eye and kidney. Cirrhosis of the liver may result from hepatitis infection.

Leptospirosis

This disease is caused by a bacteria called *Leptospires*. It can be transmitted to children and adults, in whom it manifests itself as Weil's disease. Transmission occurs via rats' urine, so strict vermin control must be carried out in kennels and attention paid to good food hygiene. Dogs should be prevented from drinking from any water source that could be contaminated. Labrador owners who live near farms and livestock where quantities of animal feed are stored in bulk should be especially vigilant.

The signs of the disease are severe fever, depression and vomiting. There may also be a marked thirst, loss of weight and foul breath. Jaundice usually follows, and then collapse, coma and death. In the early stages it can be treated, so veterinary assistance should be sought immediately if the condition is suspected.

Parvovirus

This persistent virus, known in dogs as canine parvovirus (CPV), has been controlled by vaccination since the late 1970s but if contact with an infected dog is made the disease is often fatal because it destroys the lining of the intestines. The virus may be caught from infected faeces, clothing and footwear, hence the need for a strict change of clothes routine when attending shows or 'unknown' kennels.

If a breeding dam has not been vaccinated she will not pass on any protection to the puppies and the whole litter may not survive longer than four weeks, dying quite suddenly. The virus will also attack young offspring up to one year and sometimes older. The symptoms are characterized by severe gastro-enteritis, and bloody diarrhoea. Vomiting and severe depression may also occur.

Parvovirus is almost totally resistant to disinfectant. Kennels of infected stock should be burnt and rebuilt on fresh ground.

Kennel Cough

This is caused by a group of viruses and bacteria that are transmitted in the same way as human influenza, via coughs and sneezes. It is most prevalent during the winter months and results in a severe bronchitis which can prove fatal to small puppies and elderly dogs. As there are several strains of the disease, it is possible to catch more than one in succession. Hence the choice of vaccines offered may not always prove effective and you should take the vet's advice if an epidemic occurs in your area. The disease is very infectious so you must stay away from shows and training classes for at least three weeks after the coughing has stopped.

Rabies

Rabies is a horrific and usually fatal disease which is carried by bats, wild foxes, small rodents, uncontrolled dogs and sometimes cats. Affected animals transmit the infection via their saliva, so the danger posed by a bite is obvious. The virus creates a severe inflammation of the brain that causes changes in the animal's personality, which progresses from dullness to indifference to ferocious aggression. Later, the appetite becomes deranged, the face has a vacant stare and the pupils dilate. In the later stage, paralysis of the lower jaw and hindquarters occurs; the dog is silent, staggers and death ensues. In some cases the dog will omit the aggressive or excitable stage and progress immediately to paralysis.

Prolonged vaccination programmes have controlled the disease in most countries. In the UK, rabies vaccines are available only to dogs that are being exported. Any UK breeder requiring more information must contact the Ministry of Agriculture, Fisheries and Food.

In all Continental and Scandinavian countries vaccination against rabies is carried out before the dog attains the age of sixteen weeks. In Finland and Denmark vaccinations against all the common canine diseases including rabies are given at twelve and sixteen weeks old. Rabies vaccination is also carried out in the USA. Texas State law requires that all dogs over four months old are vaccinated against rabies and a booster shot given annually.

Hereditary Defects and Diseases

Hereditary defects such as hip dysplasia (HD), progressive retinal atrophy (PRA), retinal dysplasia (RD), hereditary cataract, entropian, osteochondrosis (OCD) and epilepsy broadly fall into this category. However, current veterinary practice does acknowledge that the causes of several of the above defects may be brought about by an individual dog's environmental conditions and upbringing. A difficult whelping or an incorrect exercise regime could be contributory factors in HD, RD and OCD.

Some forms of cataract may be caused by injury or accidental exposure to an extra bright light impinging on the eye. Epilepsy has an inherited form and an acquired form, the latter resulting from infantile disease, injuries or trauma.

Ectropian and Entropian

Entropian is an hereditary malformation of the eyelids. The eyelashes are brought into constant contact with with the eyeball causing pain and irritation. With ectropion, the eyelid and lashes are permanently turned outward giving a loose, open appearance. Treatment in both cases requires a corrective operation which is aimed at reducing the amount of discomfort caused to the dog. However, because the condition is hereditary, afflicted dogs should not be used for breeding. As a result of modern, responsible breeding programmes entropian in Labradors has been greatly reduced of late.

Epilepsy

Epilepsy or 'fitting' is a condition which causes the dog to collapse and start to shake violently with all muscles twitching. However, epilepsy should not be confused with 'active dreaming' which occurs in all dogs. It is quite normal for a dog, deeply asleep and usually lying on his side, to go through the motions of running excitedly with twitching paws and yelps of delight. After a short time, usually less than a minute, he will resume his slumbers.

A feature of epilepsy is that it occurs when the dog is awake and active. The onset of the epileptic fit is a total collapse followed by violent convulsions and muscular spasms. These can last for several minutes and are distressing to observe. As the dog recovers, albeit rather shakily at first, he may appear to be unable to see properly. Epilepsy can occur in nearly all dog breeds, but nowadays is not commonly found in Labradors.

The fits usually follow a pattern, which varies between different dogs. Some dogs will have several short occurrences followed by nothing for two years; others will exhibit the symptoms more frequently. In the interim, the dog will appear perfectly normal.

In the event of your dog's succumbing to a fit, roll up some old blankets or gardening clothes and wedge him so that any violent movement will not cause him to injure himself. Turn off the lights if you can because darkness will help him to recover. For the vet's benefit, try to keep a note of the duration of the fit.

Epilepsy can be of the inherited kind or it can be caused by a variety of means, such as injury, tumour or illness during puppyhood. Some fitting can be linked to the onset of a bitch coming in season, thus spaying can be beneficial. Otherwise, drugs are available that moderate the symptoms and frequency of occurrence, but the dog will continue to need these for the rest of his life.

Hereditary Cataract

A cataract is an opaque blemish found in the cornea (front 'window') of the eye. The most serious form obliterates most of the window and becomes progressively worse, usually culminating in total blindness. A polar cataract is a very tiny blemish which does not interfere with the overall sight.

Both kinds of cataract may be inherited, although the polar version can result from injury or illness and may have no hereditary basis. The progressively opaque cataract is hereditary, but since the responsible gene is recessive, and its means of inheritance complex, not all offspring will carry the means of producing it and thus it may skip several generations before reappearing.

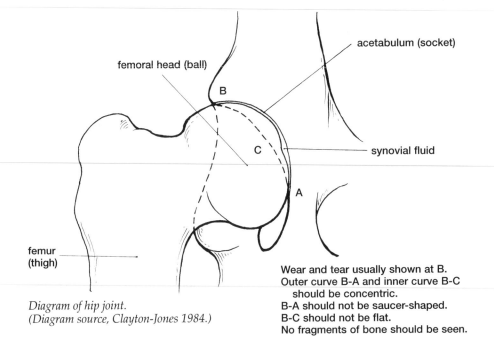

Diagram of hip joint.
(Diagram source, Clayton-Jones 1984.)

femoral head (ball)

acetabulum (socket)

B

C

synovial fluid

A

femur
(thigh)

Wear and tear usually shown at B.
Outer curve B-A and inner curve B-C
 should be concentric.
B-A should not be saucer-shaped.
B-C should not be flat.
No fragments of bone should be seen.

Hip Dysplasia

Hip dysplasia (HD) can occur in nearly all dog breeds, but it is most prevalent in the medium to large fast-growing breeds, such as Newfoundlands, Labradors, GSDs and Bullmastiffs. It is caused by a malformation of the hip joint. This joint is a kind of ball and socket arrangement where the 'ball' is a roughly spherical knob on the upper end of the thigh bone or femur. The knob fits into a cup-shaped socket called the acetabulum which is part of the pelvis. Any inherited tendency for the ball and socket to fit together incorrectly will cause a dog to limp and in severe cases the joint can become dislocated. Some small degree of imperfection in the joint can be tolerated because the controlling muscles become stronger to cope with the extra stresses. However, in many cases he will develop arthritis after the age of four or five.

To check a Labrador's hips for evidence of HD the dog is anaesthetized and placed on his back. Then the whole pelvic area is X-rayed.

Photographs of the Labrador's hip joints are scored by measuring the degree of variation of the two edges of the ball and socket from an ideal conformation. In contrast to sports and games where high scoring is a sign of excellence, exactly the reverse is true for hips. Thus, the lower the number of deviations and malformations, the lower the score and the better the hip joint.

In the UK, a panel of experts is authorized to score hips under the KC/BVA scheme. In general, you should breed from dogs and bitches that have below average scores and use a dog with a lower score than the bitch. However, HD is not just hereditary; in fact some suggest that it is responsible for between 30 and 40 per cent of all cases. Many an affected dog can have very low-scoring forebears.

Present data shows that most pure breeds of dog have total hip scores (the number of detrimental points measured for each hip, right and left, added together) lying in the range of 12–20 out of a possible 106. The average total score for retrievers is about 17. So, Labradors having total hip scores of less than 16 are better than average.

Osteochondrosis

This condition may occur in any dogs of medium to large size, when they are in the process of growing up but usually between the ages of two and six months. Such dogs grow very quickly, and for reasons that are not wholly clear, the bone surfaces at the main joints may not form correctly, and small particles may develop and lodge in the surrounding cartilage. As the joints usually affected are the elbow, the stifle or the hock, it is not surprising that the condition gives rise to inflammation (osteochondritis) and limping. (Incidentally, the condition is not unknown in horses and humans.)

The degree of OCD is about as variable as HD and even after treatment to remove the bony particles has been undertaken the animal can experience stiffness and a tendency to arthritis in later life. Hereditary factors and adverse environmental conditions (including under- and over-supplementing his food with additives) are all thought to be to blame. In my view, a sensible, balanced diet and controlled exercise are the only means of prevention. Breeding from affected dogs or bitches should not be undertaken as it will only lead to more problems and heartbreak for future generations.

Progressive Retinal Atrophy

Progressive Retinal Atrophy (PRA) is a condition in which the retina, the back surface of the eyeball which converts the seen image into brain impulses, starts to degenerate. This results in a progressive loss of vision and, ultimately, in the worst of cases, blindness. Some thirty years ago, a centralized form of the disease (CPRA), caused by pigment accumulation beneath groups of retinal cells in the centre part of the eye, was diagnosed in Irish Setters, and subsequently in retrievers, including the Labrador. A system of careful selective breeding, encouraged by J.A. Rasbridge, revealed the method of hereditary transmission and consequently CPRA has been virtually eliminated by selective breeding over a period of about twenty years.

Unfortunately, in recent years a more generalized form of PRA (GPRA) has been identified. GPRA results in a gradual deterioration of the whole of the retinal tissue (referred to as 'rods and cones') but it may only become evident at a much later stage. Labrador breeders must be vigilant and try to limit the continuance of this type of PRA by annual testing and avoiding breeding with affected dogs and proven GPRA carriers. GPRA can be detected at an early age (two years) but it is more likely to be detected after the dog is five years old.

All breeding Labradors should be examined annually by veterinary members of the KC/BVA/ISS panel using an ophthalmoscope. In some cases, eye drops are used to dilate the pupils. Currently, the Animal Health Trust is developing a gene mapping test for GPRA in Labradors. It is hoped that a test will soon be developed to diagnose potential sufferers based on blood samples from related dogs.

Retinal Dysplasia

This condition may occur when a dog sustains injury to his retina as a result of violent physical action. Their susceptibility to the injury is thought to be hereditary via a simple recessive link, and as the disease can be detected at as early as eight weeks of age, owners can avoid its occurrence by breeding with care. It is fairly uncommon in Labradors.

Pyometra

Older and maiden bitches are most susceptible to this condition, in which the uterus becomes infected and fills with pus (although it may also develop as a later symptom of metritis). In 'open' pyometra, there is unusual vaginal discharge. In the 'closed' form, the pus is unable to escape and causes swelling in the abdomen, which is usually the first sign. It is an extremely serious condition, and in acute cases, hysterectomy may be necessary. Advanced pyometra will cause toxaemia and if left untreated can be fatal. At the first signs contact the vet without delay.

13

The Labrador Around the World

The pure bred Labrador is arguably the most popular dog in the world: statistically, there are more Labradors currently registered annually by the Kennel Club (UK) than any other breed of dog. Over 29,000 Labrador registrations were processed in 1994. Because of its great population, there should be a large number of good, typical Labradors available for breeding, showing and working duties as well as family pets. In order to illustrate this, I have cited a good number of dogs and bitches from a wide variety of kennels as representatives of the depth of quality in Labradors which is to be found in different parts of the world. However, significant kennels in the UK have been discussed in an earlier chapter, so the kennels here are from other parts of Europe, Australia, South Africa and the USA. However, space does not permit me to include them all.

Australia

Labradors are extremely popular in the whole of Australia. Of the pedigree breeds registered in New South Wales and Victoria, the Labrador's popularity is second only to the German Shepherd Dog: in 1994, about 1,300 Labradors were registered in Victoria alone. Yellow bitches are by far the most requested puppies, followed by black bitches and yellow dogs. The price of an eight-week-old puppy, registered with the New South Wales State Canine Council (SCC), includes the cost of the first vaccination (usually carried out when the puppy is six weeks old), and is usually equivalent to the stud fee charged by the average breeder. The SCC regulates the breeding, trialling and showing world in all its aspects and therefore all dogs must be registered with them.

The State Canine Associations and Councils are members of the Australian National Kennel Council (ANKC).

Most breeders line-breed to selected bloodlines and import stock and semen as needed to supplement the gene pool in Australia is not very great. The breed reached a peak in the period from 1960 to the late 1970s. Most kennels have been based on Ch. Sandylands Tan, a lovely-headed yellow dog bred by Mrs Gwen Broadley in 1959 and imported by Mr and Mrs Sutch. Other important imports at that time were Wendover Jonah and Rookwood Nutcracker. Mr Sutch later imported two more yellow dogs, Ch. Diant Jaysgreen Jasper, sired by Tandy out of Diant Whisper, and Ch. Sandylands Master Mind, a son of Ch. Sandylands Mark.

Other important Australian imports were E. Aust. and NZ Ch. Ballyduff Marshall, Ch. Balrion Knight Errant, Ch. Lawnwoods Peppercorn and Ch. Rookwood Blond Boy. The last two figured strongly in the breeding of Ch. Waintree Talking Boy, a yellow dog bred by Messrs Keys and Prior.

The Strangways Labradors, owned by Mrs Dunstan, includes Ch. Timspring Comfrey, who was imported from England and sired Ch. Gunnislake Peppercorn, out of Ch. Gunnislake Charade. Mrs Dunstan bred Dual Ch. Strangways Top Hat, Aust. NZ Ch. Strangways Sorrel, NZ Obed. Ch. Strangways Stardust and Aust. Ch. Strangways All Black (the latter sired by Aust. and NZ Ch. Image Maker Veralea). Also from her breeding, Strangways Statesman put to Ch. Kadnook the Silhouette produced the winning yellow triple Ch. Kadnook the Prophet.

Also in New South Wales is Mrs Spanswick, a senior breeder of Labradors, and the owner of Aust. Ch. Cambewarra Fife'n'Drum, sired by Aust. Ch. Strangways Sorrel out of Aust. Ch. Driftway Fine'n'-Dandy and Aust. Ch. Cambewarra Ripple by Driftway Sandpiper out of Aust. Ch. Cambewarra A Bounty.

In 1982, Mr Spagnolo bred Aust. Ch. Driftway Statesman using the imported English Ch. Longley Speak Easy, put to the bitch Driftway Dusky Dreamer (who had Ballyduff lines). Later, Statesman sired Aust. Ch. Driftway Capt. My Captain.

Mrs Hutcheson's Aust. Ch. Southbank Piano Man (by Ch. Trenow Music Man out of Aust Ch. Trenow Prelude) was produced by artificial insemination. Mrs Hutcheson also imported Aust. Ch. Trenow Megan (by Sh.Ch. Sandylands My Guy out of Ch. Trenow Briar Rose).

Another later import, Blondella Spring Shades (by Ch. Keysun Crispin of Blondella out of Shades of Blondella) was obtained by Mrs Powers Zenchel kennel in 1986. More recently, she imported Aust. and NZ Ch. Black Shadow of Veralea 'Drift' (by Cambremer Thatcher out of NZ Ch. Mascot Rayners Game) from New Zealand. Drift was top show Labrador in 1986.

Dee-Fair Star Original Olga. (Owner: Mrs Johansen, Denmark.)

Denmark

The Labrador is the second most popular breed in Denmark, the top breed being the German Shepherd Dog. In the last few years, 4,000 Labradors were registered by the Danish Kennel Club (DKK).

Some dogs that have exerted a strong influence in Denmark in the last ten years are Mr Jonassen's Ch. Timspring Sultan, born 1973 and exported by the late Mrs Macan from England; Ch. Passingbridge Black Prince; Ch. Ballyduff Flint bred by Mrs Docking; Ch. Sandylands Strinesdale O'Malley bred by the late F Belshaw; and Ch. Sandylands Night Flight bred by Mrs Broadley.

The Deefair kennel of Mr and Mrs Johansen started with the importation of Sandylands Repartee (by Sh.Ch. Sandylands My Rainbeau out of Sandylands Sparkle). Later Ch. Sandylands Night Flight sired by Sh.Ch. Sandylands Newinn Columbus out of Sh.Ch. Sandylands Longley Come Rain was owned in partnership with Gunilla Anderssen of Sweden. Later home breeding produced Dee-Fair Star Original Olga, while Dee-Fair Jayncourt the Captain was imported from the UK.

From 1994 onwards, breeding bitches must be over twelve months of age, tattooed with an individual registration number and hold clear hip and eye certificates.

Finland

In Finland the Labrador is the fifth most popular breed, lying just behind the Elkhound and the Golden Retriever in the list of registrations at the Finnish Kennel Club (FKC). In order that puppies may be registered by the FKC, both parents must have X-rayed hips and be graded. Also parents must hold clear eye certificates for HC, PRA and RD. These certificates are issued annually. Black puppies are the most sought after. Most Labradors in Finland are kept indoors for quite long periods during the cold winter months, and adore the short but warm summer when they can exercise in the open wetlands.

An important dog imported by Mrs Nurmi was Int., Swed. and Fin. Ch. Balrion Knight's Quest, a yellow male (born 1982 and by the English Sh.Ch. Bradking Cassidy out of Eng. Sh.Ch. Balrion Wicked Lady). Quest won many Best of Breeds at the Labrador Club of Finland shows. By the same breeding was Mrs Kaitila's Fin. Ch. Balrion Witching Hour, another lovely dog.

The well-known Mellows kennel of Mrs Johanssen bred Fin. Ch. Mellows Lilac Time, using the imported Swedish dog, Nor. Ch. Baronor Phoenix (a Mark son), out of Fin. and Nor. Ch. Roseacre Madcap (a bitch sired by Eng. Sh.Ch. Ardmargha Mad Hatter).

A more recent winning bitch is Int., Fin. & Ger. Ch. Caveris Ellen, born in 1986 (by Hirsipirtin Q'Makoira out of Mellows Pop Primavera). Int., Fin., Dan. & Sp. Ch. Aprilmist Apricot Flower was also born in 1986 (sired by Int. & Nor. Ch. Mallards Clay Basker out of Fin. Ch. Tsarodej April Flower).

Other important winners after this era were Fin. Ch. M'Lady's Snow-ball, born 1990; Fin. Ch. Rosanan Mardi Gras (a black male born 1991); Fin. Sh.Ch. Wetten Uisko; Fin. Sh.Ch. Hirsipirtin Cicari-Cacari; the home-bred bitch Follies Viscountess; and three imported bitches, Heatherbourne Party Piece, Fin. Ch. Balrion Witching Hour and Balnova Blushing Bride.

Currently on the scene is Fin. Ch. Kokkokallion Oliwer, a dog sired by Sandylands Brig (by Trenow Brigadier out of Sandylands Rae) and Fin. Ch. Half a Sixpence de St. Urbain (by Mardas Maritime Man out of Int. Ch. Lejie Goody Two Shoes).

France

Approximately 8,000 Labradors are registered with the Kennel Club of France (Societé Centrale Canine). The most popular colour is yellow, and the price of puppies is the same regardless of sex or colour.

The Gladlab kennel is owned by Marc Gad is currently represented by the Swiss. Ch. Gladlab Chase Me Charley and the Ger. VDH and Euro. Ch. Gladlab Gone with the Wind (by Charley out of Gladlab China Rose). In the late 1980s, the important English and American stud-dog Sh.Ch. and Am. Ch. Receiver of Cranspire was obtained and has been used to good effect on many Continental bloodlines. Subsequently the Eng. Sh.Ch. Rocheby Royal Oak was added to the stock.

Ch. Carromers Charlie Chalk, obtained by Mme Leith-Ross of Tintagel Winds kennel, has proved to be a consistent field-trial winner and Best of Breed at Championnat de France 1990. He was sired by Sh.Ch. Rocheby Royal Oak out of Carromer Glamour Girl. Also being campaigned is Ch.Dusky du Parc de Bois Renard (by Ch. Lejie Master of Arts out of Belstame Pot Pourri).

Germany

The popularity of the Labrador in Germany is increasing all the time, although the German Shepherd Dog remains the most popular dog. In 1994, 660 puppies were registered by the Labrador Retriever Club of Germany (LDC). The LCD, together with the DRC (German Retriever Club), are members of the Kennel Club of Germany (VDH), which is affiliated to the Féderation Cynologique Internationale (FCI) and which authorizes the issuing of pedigrees.

Some important dogs are Dr Kraft's black Ger. Ch. Charway Sea Beaver (born 1985 and by Ch. Kupros Master Mariner out of Charway Sally Brown, a Merrybrook Black Stormer daughter); Ger. & Lux. Ch. Lawnwoods Town Talk, a black bitch sired in 1986 by Wetherlam Storm of Lawnwood out of the bitch Lawnwoods Crepe Susette; and Ger. and Lux.Ch. Charway Blackjack, a black dog sired by Ch. Charway Ballywillwill.

Two useful imported dogs of the same period were Ch. Sandylands Night Flight and Int. Ch. Cambremer Jazz Singer. The black dog VDH Ger. & Int. Ch. Dee-Fair Amazing Fame bred by Lene and Henrik Johansen in Denmark, has also proved a useful sire and also a steady showman, winning Best of Breed at the World Show. Owned by Frau

Int. Ch. Dee-Fair Amazing Fame, by Ch. Sandylands Night Flight ex Aroscas Amazing Miss. (Owner: Mrs Gabriel, Germany.)

Gabriel, Fame is a son of Night Flight out of the Swedish bitch Aroscas Amazing Miss, who was bred by Mrs Andersson to the lines of Ch. Sandylands Blaze. Fame's progeny include Fame-Flair Amazing Mister (out of Dee-Fair Sweet Sensation Queen) and Fame-Flair Clinton So Far (out of Ger. Ch. Donacre High Promises), herself a Jugenchampion (German Junior Champion). Later breeding has produced Fame-Flair Busy Belinda of Jazz (by Cambremer Jazz Singer out of Sweet Sensation Queen).

Presently, two winning Labradors are Ger. & Lux. Ch. Kimvalley Legend, a son of Ch. Lasgarn Laudrup out of Kimvalley Pearly Queen and Ger. Ch. Dolwen Ocean Child, a granddaughter of Sh.Ch. Tibblestone the Chorister.

Holland

In common with many parts of Europe, the popularity of Labradors in Holland is spreading. Dutch Ch. Sandylands Kingfisher, owned by Mrs. L. van Peursem, has proved to be an important sire. He was bred in England, sired by Ch. Bradking Cassidy out of Sandylands Baba. Two other champions of note are Dutch & Ger. Ch. Balnova Sultan (by Boothgates Headliner out of Wetherlam Willow, a Ballywillwill daughter) and Dutch Ch. Friarsgarth Kingfisher (by Ch. Balrion King Frost).

Dutch Ch. Sandylands Kingfisher, by Sh.Ch. Bradking Cassidy ex Sandylands Rum Baba. (Owner: Mrs L. van Peursem, Holland.)

Ireland

Irish Ch. Castlemore Zachary (by Ir. Ch. Rebel of Abelstown out of Cornlands Lady Daphne) won Best in Show at the Labrador Retriever Club of Ireland Shows in 1992 and 1994. Some other important stock are Mrs O'Donaghue's Ch. Philipstown Juno (by Oakhouse Melodramatic out of Ch. Philipstown Lady Dee), Sh.Ch. Philipstown Kandy (by Poolstead Pocket Knife), Sh.Ch. Rocheby Huntsman at Philipstown, a..d Mrs Ryan's Ir. Ch. Ryanhurst Johnny O'Day (by Poolstead Pocket Knife out of Ryanhurst Glengrant). Also produced by Pocket Knife is Leonard's Sh.Ch. Lendora Oak.

South Africa

South Africa has an extremely mild climate, and there the Labrador is regarded as a dog of the outdoors, so he can be kennelled without heating as temperatures seldom drop below freezing. All dogs are

243

SA Ch. Sandylands Masterpiece of Breckondale by Ch. Sandylands Mark ex Sh.Ch. Longley Come Rain and SA Ch. Lord of the Manor of Breckondale by Ch. Squire of Ballyduff ex Ch. Balrion Wicked Lady. (Owner: Mr Copestake, SA.)

registered by the Kennel Union of South Africa (KUSA). For most breeders, line-breeding is the norm and most people avoid in-breeding to any degree. However, outcrossing, sometimes with imported blood, is regularly done to bring in some hybrid vigour.

Some influential Labradors to be bred or imported to South Africa are Ch. Follytower Old Oak of Sleepy Hollow, owned by Mrs Cabion; Ch. Charway Craftsman of Sleepy Hollow; Ch. Sandylands Master Piece of Breckondale (by Ch. Sandylands Mark out of Sh.Ch. Sandylands Longley Come Rain), owned by Mr Copestake; Ch. Balrion Lord of the Manor of Breckondale (by Ch. Squire of Ballyduff), who during the period 1979–1993 was the winner of forty-eight Best of Breed awards, five groups and Best in Show at the KUSA Eastern District Championship Show; Ch. Breckondale True Love; and Ch. and KUSA Nat. Ch. Balrion Bowled a Bouncer of Breckondale (born 1989, and sired by Sh.Ch. Sandylands Royal Escort out of Balrion Bowled Over), who has won thirty-eight Best of Breed awards including Best in Show in 1992.

Sweden

In 1991 there were over 2,000 Labradors registered in Sweden. Early kennels like Mrs Gunilla Andersson's Aroscas kennel (based on Sandylands April Madness, Nor. Ch. Aroscas Country Song, Ch. Aroscas I'm Queens Blaze, and Aroscas Blaze Glory), Country Song's kennel (based on Wishwood Shuttle), and Ducklings kennel (based on Mallards, Minnows, Minvans, Rocksteady, Smart Fellows, Surprisings

Swed. Ch. Aroscas I'm Queens Blaze. (Owner: Mrs Andersson, Sweden.)

and Willows), were established before 1980. Nor. Ch. Baronor Phoenix (by Mark out of Baronor Vesta, who was a Ch. Ramah Benedictus daughter) was imported. Phoenix sired Int. Nor. Ch. Licithas Blizzard who himself was the sire of Ch. Aditis Becky of Foxrush.

Whelped in 1979, Swed. Ch. Attikonak Khatrine was bred by Mrs Ek, using the imported sire Grock of Mansergh on her bitch Ch. Poolstead Premonition. Khatrine won six CCs and was the dam of Ch. Attikonak Margreth O'Kelly (born 1982) and winner of Best in Show Veteran at the Malmö International Championship Show in 1991.

Later kennels include Applejack's (Applejack's Sweet Kokomo; Applejacks Try to Trick Me and Applejack's Sempre Sempre, a triple CC winner at Stockholm International Show 1992, 1993 and 1994) and the In Borns kennel with Swed. Ch. In Borns' Rip Roaring.

Switzerland

The number of Labradors entered at the Swiss Retriever Club Show in 1990 was 130. Some important kennels are Fairfield, owned by Mrs Banbury, who bred Int. Ch. Fairfield Hot News (by Ch. Lejie Master of Arts out of Int. Ch. Heatherbourne Brown Sugar); the Hochgrut Labradors, owned by Mrs Wolfensberger, with Pinia von Hochgrut, by Dutch Ch. Sandylands Kingfisher ex Tibblestone Rising Water and Swiss. Ch. Radscher von Hochgrut, owned by Mr Kneubuhler; and Mrs Wild's Toopines kennel with Ch. Toopines Penny (by Toopines

Swiss Ch. Radscher Von Hochgrut. (Owner: Mr Kneubuhler, Switz.)

Leonardo ex Toopines Moonflower). Penny won the Best Brood-Bitch Trophy at SWRC 1994. Other top stud-dogs are Swed. Ch. Beltarn Black Prince, Ch. Glenmore Carnaby and Ch. Kerry of Crooked House.

United States of America

Labradors have been the most popular registered gundog in the USA over the last three years. They have overtaken the next most popular breeds, American Cocker Spaniels and German Shepherd Dogs.

The most popularly requested puppies in California are yellow females, and this seems to be fairly general in most States. Very few chocolates are being bred at the present time. The cost of a puppy in the USA varies from State to State but the price does not take account of sex or colour, although some chocolate puppies can command a premium price.

The important dogs in the last few years include Mrs Wiest's Beechcroft Labradors, Am. Ch. Beechcroft Clover of O'Henry, for

246

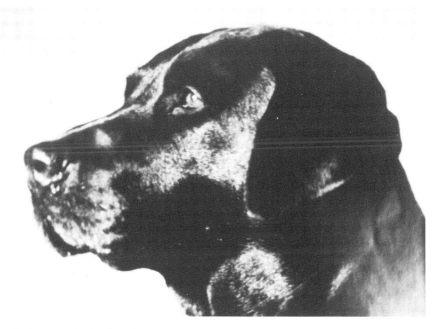

Am. Ch. Braemar Drake CD WC. (Owner: Mrs Borders, USA.)

example. Ch. Dickendall Moorwood Token; Ch. Killingworth Cinderella; Am. Ch. Jayncourt the Professor; the chocolate Eng. & Am. Ch. Lawnwoods Hot Chocolate; and Am. Ch. Ballyduff Lark, who was the dam of seven American champions and two Canadian champions. Another important sire in his few years of residence in the USA was Eng. Sh.Ch. & Am. Ch. Receiver of Cranspire who was imported by Mr Herr.

In California, the Braemar kennel owned by Mrs Borders has sound retrieving stock in Ch. Braemar Heather CDX WC, born in 1977; Ch. Braemar Anchor Boy WC; and Ch. Braemar Duggan (who won Best of Breed at the National Speciality Show 1979). The Rev. Parsons bred Bluffdale Eider, incidentally a granddaughter of Sh.Ch. Melfin Half Guinea, well known in the UK.

Another successful import was Eng. Sh.Ch. Lindall Mastercraft, who was later campaigned to American and Canadian Champion status in joint ownership with Mrs Pfeifle (USA) and Mrs Porter (UK). Other important kennels in the USA are Hennings Mill (Mrs Galvin), Hawksmoor (Mrs Perry), Kellygreen (Mrs Kelly) and Ayr (Mrs Martin of Pennsylvania).

Appendix

Pedigrees of Some Important Dogs

Sh.Ch. Croftspa Hazelnut of Foxrush
Yellow bitch

Show Champion record holder   born 20.11.1983

Sh.Ch. Ardmargha Mad Hatter (yellow)	Ch. Sandylands Mark	Ch. Reanacre Mallardhurn Thunder
		Ch. Sandylands Truth
	Hope of Ardmargha	Ch. Sandylands Tandy
		Ch. Kilree of Ardmargha
Foxrush Caprice of Croftspa (yellow)	Sh.Ch. Crawcrook Cavalier	Lawnwoods Fandango
		Crawcrook Countess
	Ch. Croftspa Charlotte of Foxrush	Sandylands Charlie Boy
		Ch. Sandylands Geannie

Sh.Ch. Ransom of Sandylands
Yellow dog

Show Champion   born 16.9.1983

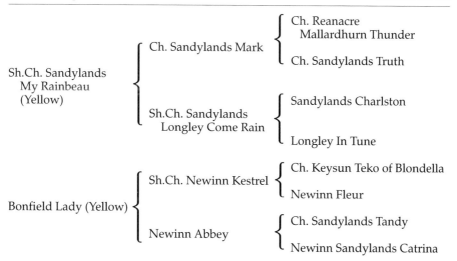

- Sh.Ch. Sandylands My Rainbeau (Yellow)
  - Ch. Sandylands Mark
    - Ch. Reanacre Mallardhurn Thunder
    - Ch. Sandylands Truth
  - Sh.Ch. Sandylands Longley Come Rain
    - Sandylands Charlston
    - Longley In Tune
- Bonfield Lady (Yellow)
  - Sh.Ch. Newinn Kestrel
    - Ch. Keysun Teko of Blondella
    - Newinn Fleur
  - Newinn Abbey
    - Ch. Sandylands Tandy
    - Newinn Sandylands Catrina

Ch. Mansergh Ships-Belle
Black Bitch

Full Champion   born 22.8.76

- Sh.Ch. Sandylands Storm-Along (Black)
  - Ch. Follytower Merrybrook Black Stormer
    - Ch. Sandylands Tandy
    - Follytower Old Black Magic
  - Sh.Ch. Sandylands Girl Friday
    - Sh.Ch. Sandylands Garry
    - Trewinnard Sandylands Tanita
- Ch. Mansergh Ooh-La-La (Black)
  - Am. Ch. Mansergh Merry Gentleman
    - Ch. Groucho of Mansergh
    - Ch. Damson of Mansergh
  - Ch. Mansergh Antonia
    - Ch. Sandylands Mark
    - Ch. Damson of Mansergh

Sh.Ch. Poolstead Pipe Smoker
Black dog

Show Champion   born 7.3.1987

- Sh.Ch. Poolstead Preferential (Yellow)
  - Sh.Ch. Poolstead Problem
    - Eng. Sh.Ch. Aust. Ch. Sandylands My Lad
    - Poolstead Pussy Willow
  - Sh.Ch. Poolstead Preface
    - Sh.Ch. Sandylands Storm Along
    - Poolstead Prelude
- Poolstead Positive Mystery (Black)
  - Ch. Charway Ballywillwill
    - Ballyduff Spruce
    - Charway Simona
  - Poolstead Package Holiday
    - Sh.Ch. Poolstead Problem
    - Poolstead Prelude

Ch. Lawnwood's Hot Chocolate
Chocolate dog

Full Champion   30.10.1973

- Ch. Follytower Merrybrook Black Stormer (black)
  - Ch. Sandylands Tandy
    - Aust. Ch. Sandylands Tan
    - Sandylands Shadow
  - Follytower Old Black Magic
    - Ch. Ballyduff Hollybranch of Keithray
    - Ch. Follytower Silsdale Old Chelsea
- Lawnwood's Tapestry (yellow)
  - Ch. Lawnwood's Fame and Fortune
    - Rockabee Tobin
    - Spinneyhill Lilac of Lawnwood
  - Ch. Poolstead Personality of Lawnwood
    - Ch. Reanacre Mallardhurn Thunder
    - Braduke Julia of Poolstead

FT Ch. Glencoin Dean of Drakeshead
Black dog
Field Trial Champion and trial winner   22.11.1983

F.T.Ch. Breeze of
Drakeshead
- F.T.Ch. Drakeshead
  Tinker
  - F.T.Ch. Swinbrook Tan
  - Dipper of Drakeshead
- Carrington Fay
  - Anglesey Swift
  - Teal of White Fen Drove

Glencoin Daffodil
- F.T.Ch. Westhead
  Shot of Drakeshead
  - F.T.Ch. Swinbrook Tan
  - Angelstown Calcedory
    Donna
- Glencoin Rosemary
  - Ch. Reanacre Twister
  - Glencoin Braeroy Rue

Silver Larch of Nazeing
Yellow dog
Novice Trial winner   5.10.1989

Priorise Bespoke
- F.T.Ch. Nazeing Bruin
  - Nazeing Brewin
  - F.T.Ch. Nazeing Zelstone
    Lively Lady
- Little Barrow Dandelion
  - Ch. Kimbo of Ardmargha
  - Nazeing Bee

Pusey Pippin
- Threepears Follywood
  - Ch. Lawnwoods Midnight
    Folly
  - Threepears Woodpie
- Lincoln Inn Lupin
  - Coombe Hill Tracker
  - Langdale Garland

251

Bibliography

Books

Clayton, H.W. *Books of Labrador Pedigrees 1972–1992* (Published privately, available only from the author.)

Clutton-Brock, J. *Domesticated Animals from Early Times* (Heinemann, 1981)

Croxton-Smith, A. *About Our Dogs* (Ward Lock, 1947)

Evans, J.M. & White, K. *The Doglopaedia* (Henston, 1985)

Frankling, E. *Practical Dog Breeding and Genetics* (Popular Dogs, 1987)

Howe, Countess Lorna *The Popular Labrador Retriever* (Popular Dogs, 1957)

Hutchinson, Gen. W.N. *Dog Breaking* (John Murray, 1898)

Labrador Retriever Club *A Celebration of 75 Years* (Private publication, 1991)

Lee, R.B. *Modern Dogs* (Horace Cox, 1897)

Leedham, C. *Care of the Dog* (Constable, 1962)

Leighton, R. *The Complete Book of the Dog* (Cassell, 1922)

Morris, Jan *A Venetian Bestiary* (Thames & Hudson, 1982)

Roslin Williams, M. *The Dual-Purpose Labrador* (Michael Joseph, 1969)

Roslin Williams, M. *Advanced Labrador Breeding* (H.F. & G. Witherby, 1988)

Scales, S. *Retriever Training* (Swan Hill Press, 1992)

Stonehenge (Walsh, J.H.) *The Dog in Health and Disease* (Longmans, Green & Co., 1879)

Vesey-Fitzgerald, B. *About Dogs* (Faber & Faber, 1963)

Wilson, Leo C. *The Kennel Encyclopaedia* (Virtue & Co., 1956)

Journals

Canine Journal, Royal New South Wales Canine Council, PO Box 632, St Marys, NSW 2760, Australia. Tel. (02) 834 3022; fax (02) 834 3872

Country Sports, British Field Sports Society, 59 Kennington Road, London SE1 7PZ, UK. Tel. 0171 928 4742; fax 0171 620 1401

Dog World, 9 Tufton Street, Ashford, Kent, TN23 1QN, UK. Tel. 01233 621 877; fax 01233 645 669

International Labrador Newsletter, 2 Blake Road, Croydon CR0 6UH, UK. Tel/fax 0181 681 8323

Kennel Gazette, Kennel Club, 1–5 Clarges Street, Piccadilly, London WIY 8AB, UK. Tel. 0171 493 6651

Labrador Digest, Water Dog Publishing, Box 17158, Fayetteville, NC 28314 USA. Tel. 513 773 6691; fax 910 487 9625

Our Dogs, 5 Oxford Road, Station Approach, Manchester M60 1SX, UK. Tel. 0161 228 1984; fax 0161 236 0892

Pure Bred Dogs/American Kennel Gazette, 51 Madison Avenue, New York, NY10010, USA. Tel. (212) 696–8200

Useful Addresses

Kennel Clubs

American Kennel Club Inc.
51 Madison Avenue
New York
NY10010
USA
Tel. 212/696 8329

Australian National Kennel Council
PO Box 285
Red Hill South
Victoria 3937
Australia
Tel. 00-61/015 304 338

Danish Kennel Club (DKK)
Parkvej 1
2680 Solrod Strand
Copenhagen
Tel. 0045 56 14 74 00

Finska Kennelclubben
Kamreerintie 8
SF 02770
Espoo
Finland
Tel. 00358/0 805 722

Irish Kennel Club
Fotterell House
Greenmount Office Park
Dublin 6
Tel. 00 353 533 300

The Kennel Club (UK)
1–5 Clarges Street
Piccadilly
London
W1Y 8AB
UK
Tel. 0171 493 6651

Kennel Union of Southern Africa (KUSA)
PO Box 2659
Cape Town 8000
South Africa
Tel. (21) 23-9027

FCI, Federation Cynologique Internationale
12 Rue Leopold II
B-6530 Thuin
Belgium

Schweizerische Kynologische Gesellschaft SKG
Postfach 8217
CH-3001
Bern
Switzerland
Tel. 0041 3130 15819

Société Centrale Canine
155 Avenue Jean Jaures
93535 Aubervilliers
CEDEX
France
Tel. 00 33 1 49 37 54 00

Swedish Kennel Club
S-16385 Spånga
Sweden
Tel. +46-8-795 30 00
Fax +46-8-795 30 40

Verband fur das Deutsche Hundeween e.V.
Westfalendamm 174
D-4600
Dortmund
Germany
Tel. 00 49 231 56500-0

Index

ears 43
eclampsia (milk fever)
    207
elbows
entropian 232
epilepsy 44, 189, 232–3
eye wipe 114, 116
eyes 87
    colour 33, 38
    problems 221, 224, 232

Fabracken kennel 105
Fame-Flair kennel 242
FCI (Federation
    Cynologique
    Internationale)
    143–6, 152
feeding 55, 72–6, 208, 216
feet 34, 40, 77–8, 78, 169,
    204
field trials 113–19
first-aid 222–5
fits (see epilepsy)
fleas 60, 226
flyball 110
Follies kennel 142, 240
Follytower kennel 19, 26,
    28, 126, 131
Foxrush kennel 26, 130,
    140, 248

Gallybob kennel 58
genetics 186–9
Gladlab kennel 144, 241
Glencoin Dean of
    Drakeshead FT Ch.
    251
grooming 63, 77, 135
Guide Dogs for the Blind
    Association 120, 121
gun shy 190, 219
gundog working tests 111

hand signals 104
handling: obedience
    91–3, 108
    show 133, 138
    working and trials
    112–15
hard mouth 114
hard-pad 230

heartworm 228
heat stroke 224
hepatitis 230
hip dysplasia 43, 189, 234
Hochgrut kennel 246
hocks 31, 35
Holton kennel 19, 21
hook worm 228
house training 62–3
Howe, Lorna, Countess
    15, 18, 28, 31, 177

in 'season' 79
infectious diseases 229
Ingleston Ben, Ch. 17
inoculations (see vaccina-
    tions)
insurance 50, 219,

Jayncourt kennel 174,
    239, 247
jealousy 74

Keithray kennel 20
kennel club: America 36,
    118, 146, 219–20, 253
    Australia 237, 253
    England 16, 50, 253
    Europe 253
    South Africa 146, 253
kennel cough 231
kennel type 155, 161
Kimvalley kennel 24, 242
Kinley kennel 22, 25
Knaith kennel 22
Kupros kennel 140

Labrador Retriever Club
    16, 22, 29, 31
Landyke kennel 23–5,
    177
Lasgarn kennel 108
Lawnwood's Hot
    Chocolate, Ch. 165,
    250
Lawnwoods kennel 26,
    28, 102, 147, 162, 165,
    241, 250
Lenches kennel 134
leptospirosis 230
lice 225–6

Liddly kennel 20
line-breeding 182–5
liver (colour) (see choco-
    late)
lungworm 228

Malmesbury, The Earl of,
    11, 15, 17
Mansergh kennel 19, 25,
    114–5, 162, 249
Mansergh Ships-Belle,
    Ch. 26, 249
mastitis 203, 208
mating 193
mating and whelping
    dates, table of 192
metritis (see pyometra)
milk fever (see mastitis)
movement 170, 171

nail care 77, 78, 203, 204
Nazeing kennel 113,
    251
neutering 80
Novacroft kennel 199

Oakhouse kennel 28, 81,
    131
obedience 89, 107
osteochondrosis 44, 189,
    235
otter tail 13, 22, 34–9
out-crossing 123

parasites 60, 205–6, 225
Parsons, The Reverend
    247
parvovirus 231
pasterns 35, 39, 169
patrol dog certificate 111
pedigrees 50, 210, 248–50
pets as therapy (PAT)
    dogs 123
Philipstown kennel 243
placenta 201
points of labrador 157
poisoning 225
Poolstead kennel 25, 27,
    162, 243, 250
Poolstead Pipe Smoker,
    Sh.Ch. 164, 250

Poppleton kennel 23
pregnancy 191–2
Priorise kennel *99*
progressive retinal atrophy 43, 189, 232
puppy purchase 43, 51–3, 215
puppy sale agreement 47, 215
pyometra 207, 221, 236

rabies 231
Ramah kennel 28
Ransom of Sandylands, Sh.Ch. *163*, 249
Raybooth kennel *121, 179*
registration of litter 194, 210–12, 217–20
retinal dysplasia 235–6
retrieving 94–106
ringcraft 125
Rocheby kennel *126*
Roslin Williams, Mary 12, 14, 27, 155 (*see also* Mansergh kennel)
Rossbank kennel 19
rough shooting 119–20
roundworm 227
Roydwood kennel 24
rules: FCI (Europe) 232
field trials: 116, 118
showing 127–9, 132, 141–7
working trials 112, 114

Ruselton kennel *181*

Sandringham kennel 10–11, 17–18
Sandylands kennel *9*, 18, 20, 25, 28, *140, 162–3, 243, 244*, 249
Sandylands Mark, Ch. *20*
Search and Rescue Dog 123–4, *124*
shock 222
short coupling 33, *35*, 166
show dogs *134, 140, 142, 147*
show gundog working certificate 111
show quality 139
Silver Larch of Nazeing *113*, 251
snake bite 223
sniffer dog 123, *124*
Southbank kennel 238
spaying 80
Staindrop Saighdear, Dual Ch. 21–2
stiff tail 67
stings 223
Strangways kennel *117*, 238
stud book 131
stud dog 16, 180, 194

tapeworm 226–7
tattooing 219, 240
teeth 58–9, *167*

temperament 29, 41, 154
temperature 200
Thrumsdorn kennel *66*
Tibblestone kennel 4, 28, *44, 137, 140*
ticks 227
tracking dog certificate 111
Trenow kennel *132*

utility dog certificate 111

vaccinations 50, 59, 76, 219–20, 229–32

weaning 208
Wetten kennel 240
Whatstandwell kennel 21
whelping 200–2
whelping and mating dates, table of 192
whipworm 228
working dog certificate 111
working: stake 115
test 112
trial 110–11
worms 205–6, 216, 226–8

Yellow Labrador Club 17, 22, 30

Zelstone kennel 22, *30*
Zenchel kennel *218*, 238